THE ADVENTURES AND SUFFERINGS

of

John R. Jewitt

CAPTIVE OF MAQUINNA

THE ADVENTURES AND SUFFERINGS

of

John R. Jewitt

CAPTIVE OF MAQUINNA

ANNOTATED AND ILLUSTRATED BY

HILARY STEWART

University of Washington Press
Seattle

University of Washington Press
PO Box 50096, Seattle, Washington 98145-5096

Published simultaneously in Canada by Douglas & McIntyre Ltd.,
1615 Venables Street, Vancouver, B.C. V5L 2H1

Library of Congress Cataloging-in-Publication Data

Jewitt, John Rodgers, 1783–1821
    The adventures and sufferings of John R. Jewitt.
    A new edition with over 200 annotations and quotations
from Jewitt's journal first published in 1815 and titled:
Narrative of the adventures and sufferings of John R. Jewitt.

    Bibliography: p.
    Includes index.

    1. Jewitt, John Rodgers, 1783–1821   2. Nootka
Indians—Captivities.   3. Indians of North America—
British Columbia—Captivities.   I. Stewart, Hilary.
II. Jewitt, John Rodgers, 1783–1821. Narrative of the adventures
and sufferings of John R. Jewitt.
III. Title.
E99.N85J47   1987   971.1'00497   87-16071
ISBN 0-295-96547-9

Design by Barbara Hodgson
Typeset by The Typeworks
Printed and bound in Canada

Financially assisted by the Government of British Columbia
through the British Columbia Heritage Trust.

CONTENTS

PREFACE

I first came across a book titled *The Adventures and Sufferings of John R. Jewitt* while researching material for my book *Indian Fishing: Early Methods on the Northwest Coast,* published in 1976. Jewitt was a ship's armourer held as a slave by Maquinna, the chief of Yuquot, a village on Nootka Sound on the west coast of Vancouver Island. During his captivity from 1803 to 1805, Jewitt kept a journal, writing a few lines or a paragraph daily to record his observations and activities.

Within a few months of his rescue ship arriving back at Boston, Massachusetts, he published a slim, forty-eight-page volume entitled *A Journal Kept at Nootka Sound,* thought to be an exact copy of his journal. Among many mundane entries, there are a good number pertaining to native village life at the time.

Copies of the *Journal* are now valued collectors' items, with probably less than a dozen still in existence. Even the only reprint from the original, published in 1931 by Charles E. Goodspeed & Company of Boston, Massachusetts, is a rare find, since it was a limited edition of one hundred copies.

About seven years after Jewitt published his *Journal,* it caught the attention of Richard Alsop, an accomplished writer who was one of the Connecticut Wits, a group of well-known authors of the day. Because of his love of adventure and the exotic, he saw the potential for creating a full book from Jewitt's simple but intriguing volume. Alsop worked closely with Jewitt, questioning him intensely to bring out all the details behind the journal entries, and to add further anecdotes, episodes and descriptions of the culture of which Jewitt had been an observant participant.

In 1815, in Middletown, Connecticut, Jewitt's story was published with the lengthy title *A Narrative of the Adventures and Sufferings of John R. Jewitt; Only Survivor of the Crew of the Ship Boston, During a Captivity of Nearly 3 Years Among the Savages of Nootka Sound, with an Account of the Manners, Mode of Living, and Religious Opinions of the Natives.* The book is now referred to simply as the *Narrative.*

Narratives of capture and adventurous hardship were popular at a time when people were exploring new lands and broadening their horizons, and interest in discoveries and developments on the northwest coast of North America was widespread. So popular was the *Narrative* that 1815, the first year of publication, saw three editions printed; and by 1817, 9000 copies had been sold. It has continued to be reprinted for over 170 years, in some twenty editions, including a German translation. There have been, in addition, a fictional account written in the third person, children's editions and a novel loosely based on the subject.

My interest in Jewitt deepened with visits to Yuquot on my way to camp on the outer coast of Vancouver Island. Still inhabited, Yuquot had been Maquinna's summer village. Eventually, I acquired a leather-bound, gold-embossed 1851 copy of Jewitt's *Narrative* through Bill Ellis, an antiquarian book dealer and a long-time friend and supporter. When I decided to make the *Narrative* the subject of my next book, he graciously parted with his only copy of the rare *Journal,* and I began two years of research, writing and illustrating that were to prove endlessly fascinating.

As it always does, research brought delights and the unexpected. I visited with Ambrose Maquinna, who claims descendancy from Jewitt's captor and the hereditary title of chief, and though Maquinna knew his people's history and traditions, as a contemporary figure he was more concerned with present-day problems than with the distant past. I also met with Andy Callicum, fifth-generation descendant of Callicum, who was the second-highest ranking chief at Yuquot. He talked at length about family histories, ceremonies, bad medicine, beliefs, shamans and more, answering specific questions I asked. Talking with both these men enhanced my sense of continuity with the past.

The real surprise of the research came not only with the discovery of a living sixth-generation descendant of Maquinna's young slave, but in finding that he carried the same name—John Rodgers Jewitt. With great anticipation, I met with John Rodgers Jewitt VI, a young man in his early thirties, and discovered that he bore a strong resemblance to the young Jewitt in the early watercolour portrait of him that my research had turned up. "I do look quite a lot like my grandfather," he admitted. Born in Cleveland, Ohio, Jewitt VI had long been aware of his connection to his famed ancestor. His mother, Patricia, had given him in Grade 2 a children's edition of the *Narrative,* and he felt a sense of pride at having the same name and being related to the hero in the book. In Grade 8 he was given an 1815 copy of the *Narrative,* "But I really had no idea at all where Nootka or Vancouver Island was—it was just way off, far away somewhere," he said, waving a hand vaguely northward, "and my interest wasn't all that strong. But now that I'm living on the Northwest Coast (and you have rekindled my interest), I want to go to Nootka Sound, take my canoe and go to some of the places mentioned in the *Narrative.*"

He allowed me to handle the hefty, leather-bound Bible given to the first John Jewitt and his wife at their wedding in 1809. I also read old, faded letters written with a quill pen on fragile paper. One letter had sealing wax still attached. As I read this correspondence, including several letters from Jewitt to his wife and two letters to him from his stepmother, the past took a leap across time, bringing the now legendary saga of the ship's armourer into the present.

Jewitt's *Narrative* has remained in print due in part to its astounding story told with simplicity and candour. Equally important is its contribution to our knowledge of the Indian culture of the area. Although explorers and traders brought many changes to the native people's way of life, much of the traditions, technologies and beliefs were still intact at the time of Jewitt's sojourn. His keen observation and attention to detail, his ability to master some of the language, and his genuine interest in the people, their activities and their surroundings are evident throughout his story. He took note of the physical differences between certain tribes, recorded who came from where and what they wore, and described various technologies and food. He counted things: the number of canoes and people arriving, how many boxes or baskets were unloaded, and the quantities and kinds of food and other goods brought ashore. And he measured things: the length of canoes, the size of beams, the dimensions of boxes and the width of planks.

Jewitt also noticed the etiquette practised by villagers in such things as eating, gift giving and the order of seating in canoes; he understood the ranking system, and he witnessed dancing and certain ceremonial practices, paying attention to the masks and other regalia used. To a small degree, he even had a grasp of such abstract concepts as native religion and mythology.

He asked many questions and experienced or heard first-hand accounts of the activities he describes, and his words carry a simple ring of sincerity. Nevertheless, in reading the *Narrative,* it is important to keep in mind that Jewitt brought with him all the moral codes and conventions of his own English and Christian background, and that these often coloured his comments and judgements of a people whom his culture, with all its insular concepts and prejudices, considered savage.

Subsequent ethnographic and archaeological studies

have confirmed a great many of Jewitt's observations and understandings, and there seems little reason to doubt the authenticity of those subjects about which we have little or no other information. Jewitt does make errors in judging distances or naming species of trees and mollusks, and occasionally he fails to understand (or perhaps fails to record) the significance of certain ceremonials, but these and a few other inconsistencies need not detract from the importance and enjoyment of the record he left for posterity.

This new edition includes a full range of explanatory material, including annotations, numerous illustrations and maps, as well as a comprehensive index. The text of the *Narrative* is taken from the 1851 Ithaca, New York, edition, and retains the original spelling and grammatical forms (including mistakes and typographical errors), as well as the nine rather quaint engravings.

My pen-and-ink illustrations of native people are drawn from archival photos of varying dates, with all the people being, as far as is known, Nuu-chah-nulth, except as noted. I have taken certain liberties with some photos, removing or substituting clothing or backgrounds not in keeping for the period in question. Illustrations of actual ethnographical and archaeological specimens, as well as the drawings of people, carry a reference number identifying their source or location, but natural history subjects, drawn from several sources or specimens, do not. The reference key to sources is located at the back of this book.

Most non-native people of early times had little respect for native people and had a stereotyped image of the Indian as a savage bedecked in warpaint and feathers. They regarded the native people either as quaint or as obstacles to the colonization of the new lands. Eventually, over the years, native people had to adapt to the continual changes brought about by the new and dominant society. Now, many of them suc-cessfully interact with that society, taking their place in politics, law, education, business and the arts, while remaining prideful of their distinctive heritage.

I hope this edition of the *Narrative* by John R. Jewitt will give readers a new and thoughtful insight into the history of British Columbia and its indigenous people, and that they will view this early nineteenth-century saga with a humanistic understanding and sensitivity so often lacking in the populace of the past.

It was archaeologist Jim Haggarty, grinning broadly after hearing of my latest research find, who declared: "Research is such a hoot!"

The surprises and delights in discovering archaeological, ethnological, historical, maritime, botanical, genealogical and other information pertinent to the many aspects of this book have, indeed, often been a hoot. I am indebted to many people with specialized knowledge and skills who gave generously of their time.

Steve and Andrea Lunsford, the former an antiquarian book dealer, gave me a limited facsimile edition of John R. Jewitt's *Narrative,* saving much wear and tear on my 1851 leather-bound edition. Anne Yandle, head of Special Collecions at the University of British Columbia Library, allowed me the delight of examining its collection of eighteen editions of Jewitt's *Journal* and *Narrative.*

Valuable research assistance came from: Sister Thelma Boutin, Archives of the Sisters of St. Ann; David Dodge, supervisor, Gordon MacMillan-Southam Observatory; David Griffiths, Underwater Archaeological Society of British Columbia; Jim Haggarty, head of archaeology, British Columbia Provincial Museum; Stephanie Hewlett, staff biologist, Vancouver Public Aquarium; Bill Holm, former curator of Northwest Coast Indian Art, Burke Memorial Museum; Ruby Hunt, board of directors, Donington School; Joy Inglis, anthropologist; Peggy Martin, volunteer, Vancouver Museum; Nora McLaren, librarian, Vancouver Museum; Alan McMillan, archaeologist, Douglas College; Jay Powell and Dale Kincaid, professors of linguistics, University of British Columbia; June Power, master graphoanalyst; Michael Robinson, president, Arctic Institute of America; librarians at the Vancouver Public Library, and Alan Whitney, captain of the *Darwin Sound*. Heather Stewart valiantly assisted with my research at the British Museum Library and other institutions.

I received courtesies from the Historical Society of Pennsylvania; the British Columbia Provincial Archives; the Oregon Historical Society; the National Archives in Washington, D.C.; the National Maritime Museum, London, and especially the Ethnology Division of the British Columbia Provincial Museum.

Hupquatchew (Ron Hamilton), a Nuu-chah-nulth artist, gave me helpful insights into his culture; Ray Williams, resident of Yuquot, provided historical and cultural information, as did Andy Callicum, formerly of Yuquot; Chief Ambrose Maquinna of the Moachat Band allowed me the privilege of meeting a descendant of the legandary Maquinna of Jewitt's time.

Linguist Barbara Efrat, Manager of Special Projects in the Special Cultural Programmes Branch, B.C. Government, and W. J. Langlois, former head of the Aural History Division of the B.C. Provincial Archives, gave me permission to quote from their interviews with Nuu-chah-nulth elders Winnifred David of Port Alberni and Peter Webster of Ahousat, as published in *Sound Heritage,* Vol. VII, No. 1. Richard Inglis, Curator of Ethnology, British Columbia Provincial Museum, gave generously of his time, advising me on a variety of subjects and reviewing the manuscript.

Neil Henderson was instrumental in locating John R. Jewitt V, who put me in touch with several other family members, all of whom have been most responsive to my requests. John R. Jewitt IV, who is in his nineties, wrote me with family information; Edith Williams, great-great-granddaughter of John R. Jewitt I, loaned me her photograph of his portrait with permission to use it, and provided me with a family genealogy; Patricia Jewitt, mother of John R. Jewitt VI, sent me details of their ancestor's 1809 Bible; Sally Jewitt Street Remage, another great-great-granddaughter of the famed armourer, enthusiastically pursued Jewitt memorabilia.

My meeting with John Rodgers Jewitt VI, great-great-great-grandson of the captive Jewitt, and examining his collection of family memorabilia, was the highpoint of three years of engrossing research.

To all of the aforementioned, and those not listed who have been a part of this book, my deep appreciation and very warm thanks, for without your generous help, abundant energy and continued interest, my contribution to this volume would be meagre indeed.

Hilary Stewart

PART I
BEGINNINGS

BEGINNINGS

Walking along the beach of Friendly Cove gave me a strange feeling. I was conscious of my footsteps sinking into the wet sand and gravel, leaving imprints that the incoming tide would erase. There would be no mark of my having passed that way, just as the village fronting the beach held no visible mark of the drama played out between Jewitt and Maquinna, though my sense of it was strong. At the south end of the beach I walked up the sloping pathway, flanked by high banks of black earth, noting the finely crushed clamshell and fire-cracked rocks embedded in it. This was midden soil, the compacted accumulation of soil and household trash that told of lengthy human habitation. Standing on the deep midden deposit was the almost deserted village of Yuquot.

A man came to the door of the first house of the single row of houses. It was Ray Williams, whom I had met on previous visits to the cove. Exchanging greetings, I said I was glad to see that he was still living in the village: his was the last remaining family there. "It's my home," he said, "I don't ever intend to leave," and there was a ring of permanence to his words. We talked a while, and I asked for and received his permission to walk through the village.

I walked along the pathway edging the bluff, aware that I was in the same village where, early in the nineteenth century, John R. Jewitt and Maquinna had lived as slave and master for three summers. On the beach below me, a mature bald eagle left the fish carcass it had been devouring and flew over the village, across the neck of land to the beach on the other side, and disappeared. This fertile land had once been a low gravel spit connecting the rocky islands at one end of the village, where a lighthouse stood, to the land mass on the

John Rodgers Jewitt the first, holding his book; from an original watercolour portrait, artist unknown. Note scar on his forehead. Courtesy Edith Williams.

other. The buildup of midden was 5.5 m (18′) deep. In 1966 an archaeological excavation uncovered the remnants of human activities, resources and skills in a time sequence unbroken for about 4500 years. The hunting and fishing gear, the tools, and the implements of bone, stone and shell reflected the cultural continuity of a people well adapted to coastal living. Near the surface, archaeologists found evidence of the recent intrusion of a new and very different culture: fragments of a glass tumbler, earthenware mugs, a rusted gunlock and glass beads were among items identified as being of English, Spanish and French origin.

I looked beyond the tangled blackberry bushes at the bluff edge and across the sound that opened to the Pacific Ocean. Bands of wispy clouds wrapped some of

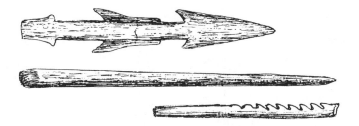

Some of 5000 artifacts unearthed during 1966 excavation of Yuquot, archaeological site number DjSp 1. Artifacts dating between 1000 B.C. and A.D. 800. Top: Shouldered harpoon head, bone or antler, may have been used for hunting sea mammals. Centre: Probably salmon harpoon foreshaft, whalebone Bottom: Barbed arrow point, bone, tip missing.

Copper cooking pot, capacity 6.8 L (1½ gal.), found by Rod Palm in Friendly Cove at location where, according to native history, the Boston *was beached. The trade value of such pots lay in their material rather than their function. Drawn from photograph by Edmond Hayes, courtesy David Griffiths.*

the distant mountains, and the ocean swell was gentle. My mind slipped back to 1778, and I envisioned Capt. James Cook's sailing ships "standing up the sound," as he put it. He named that body of water King George Sound, then later wrote, "but I afterwards found, that it is called Nootka by the natives." Thus did the village at the entrance to the sound become known as "Nootka," as did the island on whose shore it sat. But in 1792 the Spanish seafarer Esteban José Martínez wrote in his journal: "I do not know through what error this island has been given the name of Nootka, since these natives do not know the word and assure me that they had never heard it until the English began to trade on the island."

It is not difficult to see how the mistake was made, and various versions of the story explaining how the error came about are repeated along the coast. Winnifred David, recalling aural history in the 1970s, told linguist Barbara Efrat and W. J. Langlois that two canoes with paddlers, sent to take a closer look at Cook's ships, had tried to direct the white strangers to their villages: "They started making signs and they were talking Indian and they were saying: nu·tka·ʔ icim, nu·tka·ʔ icim, they were saying. That means, you go around [to] the harbour. So Captain Cook said, 'Oh, they're telling us the name of this place is Nootka.' . . . So ever since that it's been called Nootka. . . . But the Indian name is altogether different. It's Yuquot that Indian village."

No one knows when the village was first called Yuquot, since the hectic fur-trading era caused enormous upheaval and jockeying for position among the different villages and their chiefs, but many seafarers of history knew it by that name. A variety of spellings over the years tell of their attempts to transcribe it into English, and these include: Yokwat, Yogwat, Yucuat, Youkwat, Eughuot, Uquat, Yuquatl and Ycoatle. The name is derived from *yukwitte,* meaning "to blow with the wind." The cove that sheltered the village became known to the visitors as Friendly Cove, named thus by trader James Charles Stuart Strange in 1786 because the native people had been friendly to both himself and Cook. Today the name Friendly Cove is often used to refer to the village also.

In later times linguists gave the name Nootka to a language comprising several separate dialects spoken along the coast of Vancouver Island from the Brooks Peninsula to Bamfield. As a result, people who spoke these dialects were called Nootka Indians, or Nootkans, and the error lived on. When Efrat and Langlois interviewed elder Peter Webster of Ahousat in the 1970s, he declared: "I don't agree with that word, because, you know, it's not right. And we're called Nootkans from Port Renfrew to Kyuquot."

Modern-day artists and others from this area who had long resented the meaningless label wanted to be known as the West Coast people, and this term took on limited use through the 1970s. But being an English-language term (and one that was easily confused with the general term Northwest Coast people), it did not sit comfortably with the Indian people who wanted a new, and this time native, name. The Tribal Council representing the thirteen bands on the west coast of Vancouver Island discussed the matter, and in 1980 chose the name Nuu-chah-nulth, meaning "all along the mountains." The name refers to the long range of mountains that runs down the island and that all the groups have in geographic communality. Redress had finally come to a long-standing historical misnomer.

From around the rocky island at the south end of the beach appeared a fishboat that sliced the still water, leaving a V-shaped trail as it headed up the sound. Fishing the sea, the inlets and the rivers that poured into them had supplied the subsistence vital to the ancient culture. The people had also once hunted land and sea

Habitations in Nootka Sound, *redrawn from watercolour sketch by John Webber, official artist with Capt. James Cook's expedition of 1778. Although not named, the village depicted is most likely Yuquot.* 23

mammals—even the great humpback whales—and gathered the rich resources of the intertidal zone, the river estuaries, the meadows and the forest. By swift canoe they had journeyed for harvesting, visiting, raiding, trading and making seasonal rounds, often travelling long distances.

One of the animals they hunted was the sea otter. During Cook's month-long stay in the sound, some of his crew bought skins for pewter ware and what they considered mere trinkets, with six of the finest furs being exchanged for a dozen large green beads. When Cook's ships reached China, the crew found that the pelts sold for up to $120 each, a large sum at that time, to provide high-ranking Chinese people with long, shimmering capes of extraordinarily thick, dark fur. Thus was launched the great fur trade of the Northwest Coast. A few years later, in 1785, Capt. James Hanna outfitted a small ship in Macao (a Portuguese settlement in China) and, naming the vessel *Sea Otter,* headed for the Pacific Northwest Coast to reap a fortune in furs. Word was out, and the following year eight trading vessels plied the coastal waters; six years later there

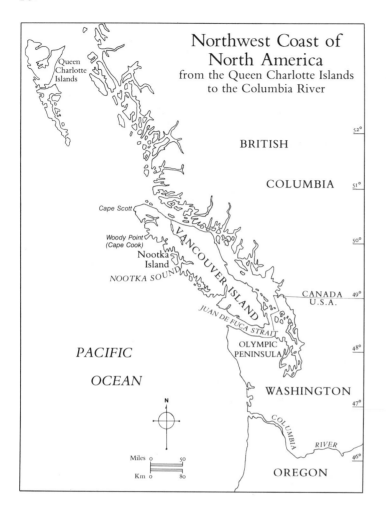

Northwest Coast of
North America
from the Queen Charlotte Islands
to the Columbia River

were twenty-one. Ships from France, England, Spain and the eastern seaboard of America made the long journey across the Atlantic Ocean, around Cape Horn and up the Pacific coast. Initially, they regularly stopped in at the sheltered waters of Nootka Sound to trade for furs, buy fresh fish from the native people, replenish supplies of wood and water, and make necessary repairs, often cutting down the tall trees to replace masts and spars. Then they continued on up the coast to further trade. In 1792, Capt. George Vancouver listed the vessels trading on the coast: 11 British, 7 American, 2 Portuguese and 1 French. Yuquot became the hub of the fur trade. On 22 September 1793, no less than ten vessels were riding at anchor in the small cove, with two more being built on shore.

As shipping increased, the number of furs changing hands soared: between 1799 and 1802, around 48 000 skins had sold for nearly $1,500,000, with one trader, William Sturgis, collecting 6000 pelts on a single voyage.

Meanwhile, back at the stately palaces of England and Spain, a dispute arose over who had the right to claim ownership of the Pacific Northwest Coast, which included the seafarers' haven of Nootka Sound. The Spanish, great explorers that they were, had already established settlements in California and laid claim to the Pacific coast all the way north to the Russian outposts in Alaska. A Spanish ship had indeed been on the coast near Nootka Sound four years prior to Cook's arrival, but due to threatening weather it had weighed anchor and departed without anyone landing. Cook, exploring in search of the elusive Northwest Passage for England, had landed and spent a month making observations of the people, plants and animals. He also set up "proper Marks and Inscriptions to take possession of the land for England." It seems not to have occurred to anyone that all the land was, in fact, already owned and occupied—as it had been for an exceedingly long time.

I left the bluff and wandered down onto the beach. The wispy clouds had taken leave of the mountains, revealing huge areas of clear-cut logging. The havoc of stumps, slash and brown earth reminded me that the ownership of the land is, ironically, still in question, with the conflict now between the "Crown" and descendants of the original inhabitants.

The conflict between the Spanish and English at Yuquot went on for several years. In 1788 an Englishman, Capt. John Meares, constructed a building at the north end of the cove to house the men building a forty-ton (41-t) schooner. Called the *North West America,* it was the first ship to be built in what later became British Columbia. The following year the Spanish took over Yuquot, demolished the natives' houses, and built a temporary garrison to back up their country's claim to sovereignty in the area. Next year they built a permanent settlement. The rocky island at the end of the cove bristled with cannon and seventy soldiers, while the Spanish flag fluttered defiantly in the Pacific breeze.

In 1792, José Francisco de la Bodega y Quadra of Spain met with Capt. George Vancouver at Yuquot to try to resolve their nations' differences, but came to no agreement. The historic meeting is, nevertheless, commemorated in one of two stained-glass windows in the Church of Pope Pius V at Yuquot—a gift of the Spanish government in 1957. Three years later, the two countries settled their differences, and the Spanish pulled out. Within a year the native people had returned, torn down the European-style buildings and rebuilt their own traditional homes.

Throughout all this there was the legendary Maquinna, a man remarkable for his appearance and character, a man pivotal to the Nootka Sound fur trade, and

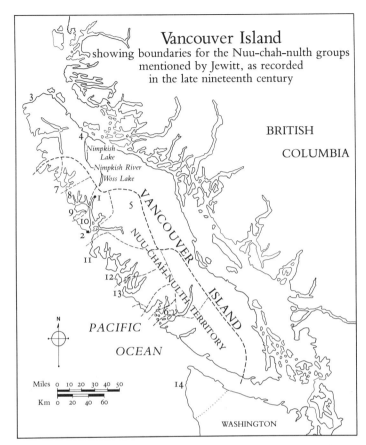

Vancouver Island
showing boundaries for the Nuu-chah-nulth groups
mentioned by Jewitt, as recorded
in the late nineteenth century

BRITISH COLUMBIA

Nimpkish Lake
Nimpkish River
Woss Lake

VANCOUVER ISLAND

NUU-CHAH-NULTH TERRITORY

PACIFIC OCEAN

WASHINGTON

Miles 0 10 20 30 40 50
Km 0 20 40 60

1 Tashees (Tahsis)	9 Neu-chad-lits (Nuchatlaht)
2 Yuquot ("Nootka")	10 Mo-watch-its (Mowachaht)
3 Neu-wit-ties (Nawitti)	11 Esquiates (Hesquiaht)
4 Newchemass (Nimpkish)	12 Ah-owz-arts (Ahousaht)
5 Mich-la-its (Muchatlaht)	13 Kla-oo-quates (Clayoquot)
6 Aytch-arts (Haachaht)	14 Kla-iz-zarts (Makah)
7 Cay-u-quets (Kyuquot)	
8 Ai-tiz-zarts (Ehattesaht)	

Charcoal portrait by Spanish artist Suría, circa. 1791, shows Maquinna wearing whaler's hat and fur-trimmed cedar bark garment, both symbols of high rank. MNM, Neg. 70636.

a man who left an indelible mark on the history of the coast. As with Yuquot, the name Maquinna also has a wide variety of spellings: Moqwina, Makouina, Mocuina, Muquinnah, Mokquilla and Maquilla are examples. The latter two spellings are interesting because, in some Nootka dialects (and not a great deal is known about them), words having the "l" sound changed to the "n" sound. This accounts for Maquinna's name being spelled with ls by some early scribes having contact with speakers who had not made the sound change.

At the time of Captain Cook's arrival in 1778, Maquinna was a young man of high rank, possible twenty years old, and his father, Yallower, held the position of chief of the household. On Yallower's death, Maquinna became chief. Each family had a head, or chief, of the household, each of whom had a place in an established order of social rank. The chief with the strongest leadership, greatest wealth and most influence, shrewdness in trading and leadership ability, quickly rose to a position of power, making decisions of importance to the whole village.

A decade after Cook's visit, Meares described Maquinna as being "about thirty years, of a middle size, but extremely well made and possessing a countenance that was formed to interest all who saw him." This probably referred to his roman nose, rather unusual for a coastal Indian, as Jewitt himself remarked. The Spanish artist José Cardero found Maquinna to be "endowed with remarkable ability and quickness of intelligence." Alexander Walker, travelling the coast in 1785, saw him as "a stout handsome young Man, with a fine manly countenance," and said that "He was the most intelligent Person we met with, and sufficiently shrewd." Maquinna handled white society with an easy grace. Often invited aboard ships to dine with their captains, he observed their table manners and sipped a glass of wine with self-assurance and dignity. Warm and generous at times, the capricious chief could also be callous, morose, moody and flare up in sudden anger.

Shrewd Maquinna certainly was, particularly in trading. Through conquest, marriage alliances and other means, he gained control of many groups in his region, and had hunters from all the villages of his confederacy bringing in a variety of skins. He paid them with food and gifts from his storehouse of trade goods and supplies. This ensured Maquinna a constant flow of wealth goods to allow him to enhance his rank and social status through feasting and potlatching.

Clambering over a rocky outcrop, I came to the north end of the beach where the *Boston* is said to have been run aground. Three white gulls fighting over some food scraps were all that disturbed the tranquil scene.

I walked back through the village, paused at the church with stained-glass windows, then followed the path to the fenced-in Christian cemetery. Wooden crosses and marble headstones bearing names and dates stood amid a profusion of coastal vegetation. One headstone, topped by a cross, was in memory of Stanislans Maquinna, son of Napoleon Maquinna. He died in 1915, at four years of age. A turbulent history lay between the time when Jewitt and Maquinna lived and the cemetery came into being; in those years many changes had been wrought.

The well-worn path continued on past the graveyard, and I followed it for some distance. The trees on the left eventually gave way to an open vista of the Pacific, edged by a steep beach of black pebbles. On the opposite side, backed by mountains, was a lake, Jewitt Lake. I sat on the bank watching a pair of ducks preening themselves, and thought about the nineteen-year-old Jewitt who had so often come here to wash his and Maquinna's garments and "to pray to God to send a ship to release us," as he noted in his journal.

Deeply religious, Jewitt had abiding faith in eventual

Headstone in Yuquot Christian cemetery is for Stanislans Maquinna, Napoleon Maquinna's four-year-old son who died in 1915. 23

Jessie Maquinna, wife of Napoleon Maquinna (grandnephew of Maquinna, Jewitt's captor). *

rescue, which no doubt contributed to his survival, but there certainly were more important factors. The most notable were his personality and his attitude to life during his enslavement; he was resigned to making the best of a bad situation. Gilbert Sproat, a pioneer business-man in Alberni on the west coast of Vancouver Island, heard about an Indian elder who had known Jewitt personally, and wrote in his 1868 publication, *Scenes and Studies of Savage Life:* "Jewitt, it seems, was a general favourite, owing to his good humour and general light-heartedness, and he often sang and recited in his own language for the amusement of the Savages." Sproat added: "He was described as being a tall, well-made youth, with a mirthful countenance." Jewitt was also congenial, diplomatic and eager to please, qualities that proved to be an asset in helping him to survive the years of captivity.

Other characteristics of Jewitt's personality surface through his handwriting, analysed by graphoanalyst June Power of Vancouver, B.C. She saw that he was "blessed with both courage and an above-average intellect." His intelligence was probably the reason why his father sent him to an academy for a good education and had plans for him to take up medicine. Choosing to be a blacksmith instead led to his tragic plight and yet, ironically, his skill at the forge was the reason his life was spared. Jewitt's ability to write (at a time when a great many were illiterate), combined with his genuine curiosity about other lands and peoples, assured him a place in posterity beyond anything he could have imagined. June Power continues: "He was not one to admit defeat and though he lacked a certain practical sense, had a strong instinct for survival. His mind ensured that his journey through life would never be dull or boring." It wasn't.

Little is known about Jewitt's companion in slavery, John Thompson. An American from Philadelphia, he was the sail-maker on the *Boston,* with many years experience at sea behind him. This old sea dog (he turned forty on 25 August 1804) was uneducated, strong and rugged, with a nature quite opposite to that of Jewitt. Irascible, insensitive, selfish, defiant and vengeful, he harboured a deep hatred of the native people, took no interest in their culture and often provoked trouble for himself.

Jewitt and Thompson were two of twenty men on board the brigantine *Boston,* in addition to the captain, first mate and second mate. Originally built in Salisbury, Massachusetts, in 1799, the three-masted vessel measured 27.4 m (90 feet), drew 3.3 m (11 feet), was square-sterned, had one deck and a figurehead. After the *Boston* made two voyages between the East Indies and Europe for the tea trade, her owners, Boston merchants Thomas and Francis Amory, decided that greater profits were to be had in the lucrative fur trade on the North American coast, and had her refitted. A deck was added to accommodate a larger crew and more cargo space, increasing her tonnage from 222 t (218 tons) to 250 t (246 tons). The new master was Capt. John Salter. Early in the summer of 1802, the *Boston* sailed to Hull, on the east coast of England, to complete the outfitting and to load up with the largest, most valuable cargo ever assembled for the fur trade. A few months later she set sail for the Northwest Coast.

With her went John Jewitt, full of lofty hopes and eager anticipation, on his first sea voyage. Ten days after arriving at Nootka Sound, disaster struck. The *Boston*'s captain and crew were slaughtered by Maquinna and his warriors, who left everyone dead except Jewitt. Thompson was later flushed from hiding.

What happened to cause such an unexpected and bloody massacre? Certainly it was triggered by an insult to the high-ranking Maquinna, as Jewitt relates, but behind the deed also lay a buildup of injustices and mistreatment of the native people by intolerant and greedy white traders. Jewitt tells of one such incident when the commander of a schooner, well treated while wintering in the cove, took advantage of Maquinna's absence from the village to steal forty of his best sea otter furs.

Maquinna later told Jewitt that at about the same time, four native chiefs "were barbarously killed" by Martinez, commander of the Spanish settlement, although history records a single death. One was Callicum, the second-highest ranking chief at Yuquot; his death was a deep tragedy for the inhabitants.

Not long after, a native aboard the *Sea Otter* stole a chisel from the carpenter. In anger, Captain Hanna fired the cannon into canoeloads of people alongside, killing over twenty men, women and children, including several chiefs. There were other instances of brutal and

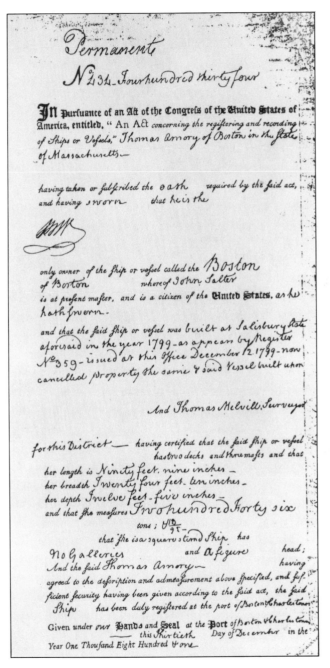

Registration of the Boston *after her refit for the North American fur trade, dated 1801. NA*

unnecessary violence on the coast, including the burning down of Opitsat village, of which Wickanninish, Maquinna's brother-in-law, was chief.

As the number of trading ships increased and furs became less plentiful, competition became keener. Natives played one trader against another, holding out for higher prices, and captains' tempers ran short. Skins were taken from natives by force, or they were compelled to sell for unfairly low prices. Eventually, the trust and goodwill that had built up between white traders and coast inhabitants gave way to suspicion, mistrust and insecurity, which often led to tragedy on both sides.

Ever present in the minds of Maquinna and his people was the traditional code of seeking revenge—not necessarily on the guilty party. With the sting of Salter's verbal insult still hurting deeply, Maquinna held council with the other chiefs. The official speaker reiterated past indignities and mistreatments, inflicted by various traders, that had never been avenged, and the list was long. Another consideration in taking revenge on the *Boston* may well have been the prospect of having the ship's enormous cargo intact. With the Spanish trading post gone, fewer ships calling in to Nootka Sound, and fewer furs to offer in trade, Maquinna no longer had the steady flow of goods needed to maintain his new social and political position. With the decision made, and the plan of attack cleverly conceived, the *Boston* became the first ship on that part of the coast to be successfully taken, and all of Yuquot was ecstatic.

Trader William Sturgis, in considering the reason for native attacks on ships, wrote: "I . . . with opportunities for investigating and ascertaining the truth, find the causes in the lawless and brutal violence of white men; and it would be easy to show that these fatal disasters might have been averted by a different treatment of the natives, and by prudent and proper precaution." Unlike the conservative English traders, who conducted business only over the ship's railing, the easy-going Americans allowed the native people to board freely, a factor strongly contributing to the success of the seizure of the *Boston*.

Although the victim of such an attack himself, Jewitt, too, was sensitive to the underlying causes of the conflicts. He wrote:

> I have no doubt that many of the melancholy disasters have principally arisen from the imprudent conduct of some of the captains and crews of the ships employed in this trade, in exasperating them by insulting, plundering and even killing them on slight grounds. This, as nothing is more sacred with a savage than the principle of revenge, and no people are so impatient under insult, induces them to wreak their vengeance upon the first vessel or boat's crew that offers, making the innocent too frequently suffer for the wrongs of the guilty.

The sun broke through the separating clouds as I walked away from Jewitt Lake, down the sandy slope onto the steep, pebbled beach and looked out over the open Pacific Ocean. A single sailboat, mainsail taut to the wind, cut through the heaving swells. Each incoming wave flung waterworn pebbles up the beach; and receding, drew them back down again with a resounding clatter. The sound, like a great supernatural shaman's rattle, accompanied me as I walked back to Maquinna's village.

PART II
NARRATIVE

THE SHIP BOSTON TAKEN BY THE SAVAGES AT NOOTKA SOUND.

NARRATIVE

OF THE

ADVENTURES AND SUFFERINGS

OF

JOHN R. JEWITT,   1

ONLY SURVIVOR OF THE CREW OF THE   **2**

SHIP BOSTON,

DURING A CAPTIVITY OF NEARLY 3 YEARS AMONG THE   **3**

SAVAGES OF NOOTKA SOUND:

WITH AN ACCOUNT OF THE

MANNERS, MODE OF LIVING, AND RELIGIOUS

OPINIONS OF THE

NATIVES.

ITHACA, N.Y.

ANDRUS, GAUNTLETT & CO.

1851.

1 *R.* The initial stands for Rodgers, which was the maiden name of Jewitt's mother.

2 *only survivor.* Jewitt was not the sole survivor. John Thompson, the ship's sail-maker, also survived both the massacre and the captivity.

3 *3 Years.* The length of captivity was, in fact, two years and four months. Distortion of the time and of the fact that there were two survivors were no doubt intended to enhance the drama of the title page.

Names of the Crew of the Ship Boston, belonging to Boston in Massachusetts, owned by Messrs. F. & T. Amory, Merchants of that place—All of whom excepting two, were on the 22d of March, 1803, barbarously murdered by the Savages at Nootka.

John Salter,	of Boston,	Captain.
B. Delouissa,	Do.	Chief-Mate.
William Ingraham,	of New-York,	Second-Mate.
Edward Thompson,	of Blyth, (England,)	Boatswain.
Adam Siddle,	of Hull, Do.	Carpenter.
Philip Brown,	of Cambridge, (Mass.)	Joiner.
John Dorthy,	of Scituate, Do.	Blacksmith.
Abraham Waters,	of Philadelphia,	Steward.
Francis Duffield,	of Penton, (England,)	Tailor.
John Wilson, (blackman)	of Virginia,	Cook.
William Caldwell,	of Boston,	Seaman.
Joseph Miner,	of Newburyport,	Do.
William Robinson,	of Leigh, (Scotland,)	Do.
Thomas Wilson,	of Air, Do.	Do.
Andrew Kelly,	Do. Do.	Do.
Robert Burton,	of the Isle of Man,	Do.
James M'Clay,	of Dublin,	Do.
Thomas Platten,	of Blakeney, Norfolk, Eng.	Do.
Thomas Newton,	of Hull, Do.	Do
Charles Bates,	of St. James Deeping, Do.	Do.
John Hall,	of New-Castle, Do.	Do.
Samuel Wood,	of Glasgow,(Scotland,)	Do.
Peter Alstrom,	Norwegian,	Do.
Francis Marten,	Portuguese,	Do.
Jupiter Senegal,(blackman)		Do.
John Thompson,	Philadelphia,	Sail-Maker, who escaped—since dead.
John R. Jewitt,	of Boston, in England,	Armourer,

the writer of the Journal from whence this Narrative is taken, and who at present, July, 1815, resides in Middletown, in the State of Connecticut.

A LIST OF WORDS IN THE NOOTKIAN LANGUAGE, THE MOST IN USE.

Check-up,	Man.	Toop-helth,	Cloth.
Klootz-mah,	Woman.	Cham-mass,	Fruit.
Noowexa,	Father.	Cham-mass-ish,	Sweet or pleasant to the taste.
Hooma-hexa,	Mother.		
Tanassis,	Child.	Moot-sus,	Powder.
Katlahtik,	Brother.	Chee-pokes,	Copper.
Kloot-chem-up,	Sister.	Hah-welks,	Hungry.
Tanassis-check-up,	Son.	Nee-sim-mer-hise,	Enough.
Tanassis-kloots-mah,	Daughter.	Chit-ta-yek,	Knife or dagger.
Tau-hat-se-tee,	Head.	Klick-er-yek,	Rings.
Kassee,	Eyes.	Quish-ar,	Smoke.
Hap-se-up,	Hair.	Mar-met-ta,	Goose or duck.
Naetsa,	Nose.	Pook-shit-tle,	To blow.
Parpee,	Ears.	Een-a-qui-shit-tle,	To kindle a fire.
Chee-chee,	Teeth.		
Choop,	Tongue.	Ar-teese,	To bathe.
Kook-a-nik-sa,	Hands.	Ma-mook-su-mah,	To go to fish.
Klish-klin,	Feet.	Ar-smootish-check-up,	A warrior.
Oophelth,	Sun or Moon.		
Tar-toose,	Stars.	Cha-alt-see-klat-tur-wah,	Go off, or go away.
Sie-yah,	Sky.		
Toop-elth,	Sea.	Ma-kook,	To sell.
Cha-hak,	Fresh water.	Kah-ah-pah-chilt,	Give me something.
Meetla,	Rain.		
Queece,	Snow.	Oo-nah,	How many.
Noot-chee,	Mountain or hill.	I-yah-ish,	Much.
Klat-tur-miss,	Earth.	Kom-me-tak,	I understand.
Een-nuk-see,	Fire or fuel.	I-yee-ma-hak,	I do not understand.
Mook-see,	Rock.		
Muk-ka-tee,	House.	Em-me-chap,	To play.
Wik,	No.	Kle-whar,	To laugh.
He-ho,	Yes.	Mac-kam-mah-sish,	Do you want to buy.
Kak-koelth,	Slave.		
Mah-hack,	Whale.	Kah-ah-coh,	Bring it.
Klack-e-miss,	Oil.	Sah-wauk,	One.
Quart-lak,	Sea-otter.	Att-la,	Two.
Coo-coo-ho-sa,	Seal.	Kat-sa,	Three.
Moo-watch,	Bear.	Mooh,	Four.
So-har,	Salmon.	Soo-chah,	Five.
Toosch-qua,	Cod.	Noo-poo,	Six.
Pow-ee,	Halibut.	At-tle-poo,	Seven.
Kloos-a-mit,	Herring.	At-lah-quelth,	Eight.
Chap-atz,	Canoe.	Saw-wauk-quelth,	Nine.
Oo-wha-pa,	Paddle.	Hy-o,	Ten.
Chee-me-na,	A fish-hook.	Sak-aitz,	Twenty.
Chee-men,	Fish-hooks.	Soo-jewk,	One hundred.
Sick-a-minny,	Iron.	Hy-e-oak,	One thousand.

NARRATIVE OF JOHN R. JEWITT.

I was born in Boston, a considerable borough town in Lincolnshire, in Great-Britain, on the 21st of May, 1783. My father, Edward Jewitt, was by trade a blacksmith, and esteemed among the first in his line of business in that place. At the age of three years I had the misfortune to lose my mother, a most excellent woman, who died in child-bed, leaving an infant daughter, who, with myself, and an elder brother by a former marriage of my father, constituted the whole of our family. My father who considered a good education as the greatest blessing he could bestow on his children, was very particular in paying every attention to us in that respect, always exhorting us to behave well, and endeavouring to impress on our minds the principles of virtue and morality, and no expense in his power was spared to have us instructed in whatever might render us useful and respectable in society. My brother, who was four years older than myself, and of a more hardy constitution, he destined for his own trade, but to me he had resolved to give an education superior to that which is to be obtained in a common school, it being his intention that I should adopt one of the learned professions. Accordingly at the age of twelve he took me from the school in which I had been taught the first rudiments of learning, and placed me under the care of Mr. Moses, a celebrated teacher of an academy at Donnington, about twenty miles from Boston, in order to be instructed in the Latin language, and in some of the higher branches of the Mathematics. I there made considerable proficiency in writing, reading, and arithmetic, and obtained a pretty good knowledge of navigation and of surveying; but my progress in Latin was slow, not only owing to the little inclination I felt for learning that language, but to a natural impediment in my speech, which ren-

1

2

3

4

5

6

School in Donington, Lincolnshire, attended by Jewitt; now called Cowley's School after its founder. Bell tower is original, sundial over portico dated 1719. Drawn from photograph, courtesy Ruby Hunt, MBE, chairman of school's governing body.

1 *I was born.* The baby was baptized at St. Botolph's Church in Boston, Lincolnshire.

2 *my mother.* Catherin Jewitt (née Rodgers) was Edward Jewitt's second wife. He married her about 1780.

3 *infant daughter.* The daughter's name was Eleanor.

4 *elder brother.* The half brother's name was Frank.

5 *Mr. Moses.* William Moses, and later his son, also William Moses, were headmasters (principals) of the school from 1793 to 1853—sixty years—giving rise to the nickname "Moses Academy."

6 *academy at Donnington.* The school at Donington (now spelled with one "n") was founded in 1710 by Charles Cowley to teach twenty children to read and write. Rebuilt in 1812, today it is a modern secondary school.

dered it extremely difficult for me to pronounce it, so that in a short time, with my father's consent, I wholly relinquished the study.

The period of my stay at this place was the most happy of my life. My preceptor, Mr. Moses, was not only a learned, but a virtuous, benevolent, and amiable man, universally beloved by his pupils, who took delight in his instruction, and to whom he allowed every proper amusement, that consisted with attention to their studies.

One of the principal pleasures I enjoyed was in at **1** tending the fair, which is regularly held twice a year at Donnington, in the spring and in the fall; the second day being wholly devoted to selling horses, a prodigious number of which are brought thither for that purpose. As the scholars on these occasions were always indulged with a holiday, I cannot express with what eargerness of youthful expectation I used to anticipate these fairs, nor what delight I felt at the various shows, exhibitions of wild beasts, and other entertainments that they presented. I was frequently visited by my father, who always discovered much joy on seeing me, praised me for my acquirements, and usually left me a small sum for my pocket expenses.

Among the scholars at this academy, there was one named Charles Rice, with whom I formed a particular intimacy, which continued during the whole of my stay. He was my class and room mate, and as the town he came from, Ashby, was more than sixty miles off, instead of returning home, he used frequently during the vacation, to go with me to Boston, where he always met with a cordial welcome from my father, who received me on these occasions with the greatest affection, apparently taking much pride in me. My friend in return used to take me with him to an uncle of his in Donnington, a very wealthy man, who, having no children of his own, was very fond of his nephew, and on his ac-

1 *the fair*. Held in May and October, the Donington fair continued on into the twentieth century, closing only after the Second World War.

count I was always a welcome visitor at the house. I had a good voice, and an ear for music, to which I was always passionately attached, though my father endeavoured to discourage this propensity, considering it, (as is too frequently the case) but an introduction to a life of idleness and dissipation, and having been remarked for my singing at church, which was regularly attended on Sundays and Festival days by the scholars, Mr. Morthrop, my friend Rice's uncle, used frequently to request me to sing; he was always pleased with my exhibitions of this kind, and it was no doubt one of the means that secured me so gracious a reception at his house. A number of other gentlemen in the place would sometimes send for me to sing at their houses, and as I was not a little vain of my vocal powers, I was much gratified on receiving these invitations, and accepted them with the greatest pleasure.

Thus passed away the two happiest years of my life, when my father, thinking that I had received a sufficient education for the profession he intended me for, took me from school at Donnington in order to apprentice me to Doctor Mason, a surgeon of eminence at Reasby, in the neighbourhood of the celebrated Sir Joseph **1** Banks. With regret did I part from my school acquaintance, particularly my friend Rice, and returned home with my father, on a short visit to my family, preparatory to my intended apprenticeship. The disinclination I ever had felt for the profession my father wished me to pursue, was still further increased on my return. When a child I was always fond of being in the shop, among the workmen, endeavouring to imitate what I saw them do; this disposition so far increased after my leaving the academy, that I could not bear to hear the least mention made of my being apprenticed to a surgeon, and I used so many entreaties with my father to persuade him to give up this plan and learn me his own trade, that he at last consented. More fortunate would it probably have

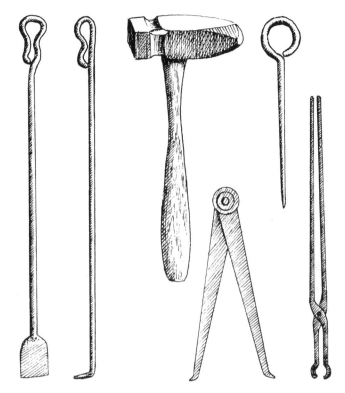

Blacksmith's tools include, left to right: fire shovel, fire hook, set hammer, calipers, scriber, tongs. 25

1 *Sir Joseph Banks.* Banks, who lived at Reasby, was a botanist on the *Endeavour* (which sailed with Captain Cook's expedition to the South Pacific) and was also president of the Royal Society of London for Improving Natural Knowledge, a scientific institution founded in 1660.

Hull, Lincolnshire, 1796. NMM

been for me, had I gratified the wishes of this affectionate parent, in adopting the profession he had chosen for me, than thus induced him to sacrifice them to mine. However it might have been, I was at length introduced into the shop, and my natural turn of mind corresponding with the employment, I became in a short time uncommonly expert at the work to which I was set. I now felt myself well contented, pleased with my occupation, and treated with much affection by my father and kindness by my step-mother, my father and kindness by my step-mother, my father having once more entered the state of matrimony, with a widow much younger than himself, who had been brought up in a superior manner, and was an amiable and sensible woman.

About a year after I had commenced this apprenticeship, my father finding that he could carry on his business to more advantage in Hull, removed thither with his family. An event of no little importance to me, as it in a great measure influenced my future destiny. Hull being one of the best ports in England, and a place of great trade, my father had there full employment for his numerous workmen, particularly in vessel work. This naturally leading me to an acquaintance with the sailors on board some of the ships, the many remarkable stories they told me of their voyages and adventures, and of the manners and customs of the nations they had seen, excited a strong wish in me to visit foreign countries, which was increased by my reading the voyages of Capt. Cook, and some other celebrated navigators.

Thus passed the four years that I lived at Hull, where my father was esteemed by all who knew him, as a worthy, industrious, and thriving man. At this period a circumstance occurred which afforded me the opportunity I had for some time wished, of gratifying my inclination of going abroad.

Among our principal customers at Hull, were the Americans who frequented that port, and from whose

1 *matrimony*. Edward Jewitt's third wife was named Anne. There were no children of this union.

2 *Hull*. Located at the junction of the Humber and Hull rivers and at the head of a long inlet on England's east coast, Hull is one of the most important ports of entry on the North Sea.

3 *reading the voyages of Capt. Cook*. The journals of Capt. James Cook's journey to the Pacific Ocean were published some seventeen years prior to Jewitt's decision to seek adventure in other lands. This hefty volume contains maps and engraved illustrations of new lands and their peoples. Ironically, it includes a portrait of Maquinna (Jewitt's captor), as well as a view of his summer village and another of the interior of a large house (most probably Maquinna's), both places destined to become central to Jewitt's life.

conversation, my father as well as myself formed the most favourable opinion of that country, as affording an excellent field for the exertions of industry, and a flattering prospect for the establishment of a young man in life. In the summer of the year 1802, during the peace between England and France, the ship Boston, belonging to Boston, in Massachusetts, and commanded by Capt. John Salter, arrived at Hull, whither she came to take on board a cargo of such goods as were wanted for the trade, with the Indians on the North-West coast of America, from whence, after having taken in a lading of furs and skins, she was to proceed to China, and from thence home to America. The ship, having occasion for many repairs and alterations, necessary for so long a voyage, the captain applied to my father to do the smith work, which was very considerable. That gentleman, who was of a social turn, used often to call at my father's house, where he passed many of his evenings, with his chief and second mates, Mr. B. Delouisa, and Mr. William Ingraham, the latter a fine young man of about twenty, of a most amiable temper, and of such affable manners, as gained him the love and attachment of our whole crew. These gentlemen used occasionally to take me with them to the theatre, an amusement which I was very fond of, and which my father rather encouraged than objected to, as he thought it a good means of preventing young men who are naturally inclined to seek for something to amuse them, from frequenting taverns, ale houses, and places of bad resort, equally destructive of the health and morals, while the stage frequently furnishes excellent lessons of morality and good conduct.

In the evenings that he passed at my father's, Captain Salter, who had for a great number of years been at sea, and seen almost all parts of the world, used sometimes to speak of his voyages, and observing me listen with much attention to his relations, he one day when I had

1

1 *the ship Boston*. Built in 1799, the brigantine *Boston* was registered in Boston, Massachusetts, on 12 December of the same year and was owned by Francis and Thomas Amory of that port. Her registration papers state that she "has two decks and three masts" and that:

    her length is Ninety feet—nine inches [28 m]
    her depth Twelve feet—five inches [3.8 m]
    and that she measures Two hundred Forty tons [244 t]:
    that she is a square stern'd ship has No Galleries and [has] a
    figure head.

A gallery was a platform or balcony, sometimes enclosed and with windows, that projected from the stern of a sailing ship.

Top: Small pot, circa 1789, of the type used for trading on the coast. Diameter 19 cm (7½″). PC

Bottom: Skinning knife, popular trade item. 26.7 cm (10½″). PC

Right: Cutlass, approximately 106 cm (42″), used in hand-to-hand fighting. 23

1 *the one I have shipped.* The *Boston's* crew list shows a John Dorthy as blacksmith, probably the one with whom Captain Salter was dissatisfied.

brought him some work, said to me in rather a jocose manner, John, how should you like to go with me? I answered that it would give me great pleasure, that I had for a long time wished to visit foreign countries, particularly America, which I had been told so many fine stories of, and that if my father would give his consent and he was willing to take me with him, I would go. I shall be very glad to do it, said he, if your father can be prevailed on to let you go, and as I want an expert smith for an armourer, the one I have shipped for that purpose not being sufficiently master of his trade, I have no doubt that you will answer my turn well, as I perceive you are both active and ingenious; and on my return to America, I shall probably be able to do something much better for you in Boston. I will take the first opportunity of speaking to your father about it, and try to persuade him to consent. He accordingly the next evening that he called at our house introduced the subject: my father at first would not listen to the proposal. That best of parents, though anxious for my advantageous establishment in life, could not bear to think of parting with me, but on Capt. Salter's telling him of what benefit it would be to me to go the voyage with him, and that it was a pity to keep a promising and ingenious young fellow, like myself, confined to a small shop in England, when if I had tolerable success, I might do so much better in America, where wages were much higher and living cheaper, he at length gave up his objections and consented that I should ship on board the Boston as an armourer, at the rate of thirty dollars per month; with an agreement that the amount due me, together with a certain sum of money which my father gave Capt. Salter for that purpose, should be laid out by him on the North-West Coast in the purchase of furs on my account, to be disposed of in China for such goods as would yield a profit on the return of the ship; my father being solicitous to give me every advantage in his power, of well establishing myself in my trade in Boston or some other maritime town of America. Such were the flattering expectations which this good man indulged respecting me. Alas! the fatal disaster that befel us, not only blasted all these hopes, but involved me in extreme distress and wretchedness for a long period after.

The ship having undergone a thorough repair and been well coppered, proceeded to take on board her **1** cargo, which consisted of English cloths, Dutch **2** blankets, looking glasses, beads, knives, razors, &c. **3** which were received from Holland, some sugar and molasses, about twenty hogsheads of rum, including **4** stores for the ship, a great quantity of ammunition, cutlasses, pistols, and three thousand muskets and fowling **5** pieces. The ship being loaded and ready for sea, as I was preparing for my departure, my father came to me, and taking me aside, said to me with much emotion, John, I am now going to part with you, and heaven only knows if we shall ever again meet. But in whatever part of the world you are, always bear it in mind, that on your own conduct will depend your success in life. Be honest, industrious, frugal, and temperate, and you will not fail, in whatsoever country it may be your lot to be placed, to gain yourself friends. Let the Bible be your guide, and your reliance in any fortune that may befall you, that Almighty Being, who knows how to bring forth good from evil, and who never deserts those who put their trust in him. He repeated his exhortations to me to lead an honest and a christian life, and to recollect that I had a father, a mother, a brother, and sister, who could not but feel a strong interest in my welfare, enjoining me to write him by the first opportunity that should offer to England, from whatever part of the world I might be in, more particularly on my arrival in Boston. This I promised to do, but long unhappily was it before I was able to fulfill this promise. I then took an

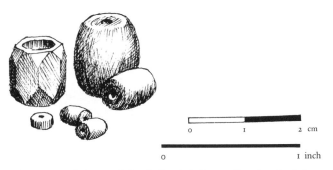

Left: Variety of glass trade beads found during 1968 archaeological excavation at Coopte (Cooptee). Drawn from photo, courtesy Alan McMillan. PC

1 *well coppered.* To protect their wooden hulls from damage by shipworm (teredo) and other marine infestations, sailing vessels were sheathed in copper. Depending on its size, a ship required between 700 and 4000 sheets of copper. A standard sheet of copper measured 61 cm × 45.7 cm (24″ × 18″).

2 *Dutch blankets.* Soft woollen blankets made by the Dutch in New York came to be known as Dutch blankets and were much favoured by native people, who wore them as clothing in place of cedar bark garments. Blankets also became a standard trade item along the entire coast.

3 *beads.* A common item of early trade, glass beads were useful to exchange for small articles such as a fish. The beads, generally deep blue and often multifaceted, came in several sizes; early Russian traders also used them in trading.

4 *hogsheads.* The word hogshead (which translates to "oxhead" in European languages) was first described in an English statute of 1423 as being "63 old wine gallons." Later, a hogshead of spirits equalled a little over 74 imperial gallons; thus, the *Boston* had aboard over 1480 gallons (6730 L) of rum, a trading item with the potential of death and devastation among a people unaccustomed to the effects of liquor.

5 *fowling pieces.* A fowling piece was a light gun for shooting wild fowl.

affectionate leave of my worthy parent, whose feelings would hardly permit him to speak, and bidding an affectionate farewell to my brother, sister, and stepmother, who expressed the greatest solicitude for my future fortune, went on board the ship, which proceeded to the Downs to be ready for the first favourable wind. I found myself well accommodated on board as regarded my work, an iron forge having been erected on deck; this my father had made for the ship on a new plan, for which he afterwards obtained a patent; while a corner of the steerage was appropriated to my vice bench, so that in bad weather I could work below.

On the third day of September, 1802, we sailed from the Downs with a fair wind, in company with twenty-four sail of American vessels, most of which were bound home.

I was sea-sick for a few of the first days, but it was of short continuance, and on my recovery I found myself in uncommonly fine health and spirits, and went to work with alacrity at my forge, in putting in order some of the muskets, and making daggers, knives, and small hatchets for the Indian trade, while in wet and stormy weather I was occupied below in filing and polishing them. This was my employment, having but little to do with sailing the vessel, though I used occasionally to lend a hand in assisting the seamen in taking in and making sail. As I had never before been out of sight of land, I cannot describe my sensations, after I had recovered from the distressing effects of sea-sickness, on viewing the mighty ocean by which I was surrounded, bounded only by the sky; while its waves rising in mountains, seemed every moment to threaten our ruin. Manifest as is the hand of Providence in preserving its creatures from destruction, in no instance is it more so than on the great deep; for whether we consider in its tumultuary motions the watery deluge that each moment menaces to overwhelm us, the immense

1 *the Downs.* The Western Downs and South Downs are the rolling, chalky hills along England's south coast, the north side of the English Channel. Ships from the east and south coast often rendezvoused in the channel and set sail together to start crossing the Atlantic Ocean.

2 *obtained a patent.* Jewitt's father may have intended to patent his forge, but never actually did; a search of the Patent Office in London, England, failed to reveal any trace of such a patent.

violence of its shocks, the little that interposes between us and death, a single plank forming our only security, which, should it unfortunately be loosened would plunge us at once into the abyss, our gratitude ought strongly to be excited towards that superintending Deity who in so wonderful a manner sustains our lives amid the waves.

We had a pleasant and favourable passage of twenty-nine days to the Island of St. Catharine on the coast of **1** Brazils, where the Captain had determined to stop for a few days to wood and water. This place belongs to the Portuguese. On entering the harbour we were saluted by the fort, which we returned. The next day the Governor of the Island came on board of us with his suite; Captain Salter received him with much respect and invited him to dine with him, which, he accepted. The ship remained at St. Catharine's four days, during which time, we were busily employed in taking in wood, water, and fresh provisions, Captain Salter thinking it best to furnish himself here with a full supply for his voyage to the North-West coast, so as not to be obliged to stop at the Sandwich Islands. St. **2** Catharine is a very commodious place for vessels to stop at that are bound round Cape Horn, as it abounds with springs of fine water, with excellent oranges, plantains, and bananas.

Having completed our stores we put to sea, and on the twenty-fifth of December at length passed Cape Horn, which we had made no less than thirty-six days before, but were repeatedly forced back by contrary winds, experiencing very rough and tempestuous weather in doubling it.

Immediately after passing Cape Horn, all our dangers and difficulties seemed to be at an end; the weather became fine and so little labour was necessary on board the ship that the men soon recovered from their fatigue and were in excellent spirits. A few days after we fell in

1 *Island of St. Catharine.* This is the island of Santa Catarina, just off the coast of Brazil, about 725 km (450 miles) southwest of Rio de Janeiro.

2 *the Sandwich Islands.* Captain Cook in 1778 named the Sandwich Islands after the Earl of Sandwich, First Lord of the British Admiralty. Their present name, the Hawaiian islands, is derived from Hawaiki, the name given by early Polynesians, after their legendary homeland to the west. Making a stop at Hawaii, instead of Santa Catarina, would have added considerable distance to the voyage.

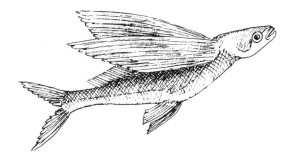

*Flying fish (*Exocoetus volitans*), most commonly found in Atlantic Ocean. Length 18 to 25.5 cm (7" to 10"). 23*

*Dall's porpoise (*Phocoenoides dalli*), the species of porpoise most likely to have been encountered by the* Boston. *Up to 1.8m (6'). 20*

1 *reeve a topsail.* To reeve or reef a topsail is to reduce the area of sail presented to the wind by tying up (reefing) the lower portion. This may be necessary in very strong winds.

2 *to make a tack.* To change a ship's course, to port or starboard, by moving the position of its sails. With a head wind, frequent tacking was necessary to maintain a set course—a lot of work on a three-masted brig.

3 *tomahawks.* Light axes used by the native people of eastern North America as a weapon and a tool. The word "tomahawk," brought into common usage by early traders, is derived from *tomahakan,* a word meaning "that which is used for cutting" in the Virginia dialect of the Algonquin language.

4 *whales.* Whales are not fish, but sea mammals.

5 *porpoises.* Porpoise are also sea mammals, not fish. The name has its roots in the French for herring hog: i.e., *porc* (pig) and *poisson* (fish), a fish that tasted like pig.

with an English South Sea Whaling Ship, homeward bound, which was the only vessel we spoke with on our voyage. We now took the trade wind or monsoon, during which we enjoyed the finest weather possible, so that for the space of a fortnight we were not obliged to reeve a topsail or to make a tack, and so light was the duty and easy the life of the sailors during this time, that they appeared the happiest of any people in the world.

Captain Salter, who had been for many years in the East-India trade, was a most excellent seaman, and preserved the strictest order and discipline on board his ship, though he was a man of mild temper and conciliating manners, and disposed to allow every indulgence to his men, not inconsistent with their duty. We had on board a fine band of music, with which on Saturday nights, when the weather was pleasant, we were accustomed to be regaled, the Captain ordering them to play for several hours for the amusement of the crew. This to me was most delightful, especially during the serene evenings we experienced in traversing the Southern Ocean. As for myself, during the day I was constantly occupied at my forge, in re-fitting or repairing some of the iron work of the vessel, but principally in making tomahawks, daggers, &c. for the North West coast.

During the first part of our voyage we saw scarcely any fish, excepting some whales, a few sharks, and flying fish; but after weathering Cape Horn we met with numerous shoals of sea porpoises, several of whom we caught, and as we had been for some time without fresh provisions, I found it not only a palatable but really a very excellent food. To one who has never before seen them, a shoal of these fish presents a very striking and singular appearance; beheld at a distance coming towards a vessel they look not unlike a great number of small black waves rolling over one another in a confused manner and approaching with great swiftness. As soon as a shoal is seen all is bustle and activity on board the ship, the grains and the harpoons are immediately **1** got ready, and those who are best skilled in throwing them take their stand at the bow and along the gunwale anxiously awaiting the welcome troop as they come gamboling and blowing around the vessel, in search of **2** food. When pierced with the harpoon and drawn on board, unless the fish is instantly killed by the stroke, which rarely happens, it utters most pitiful cries, greatly resembling those of an infant. The flesh cut into steaks and broiled, is not unlike very coarse beef, and the harslet in appearance and taste is so much like that of a **3** hog, that it would be no easy matter to distinguish the one from the other; from this circumstance the sailors have given the name of the herring hog to this fish; I **4** was told by some of the crew, that if one of them happens to free itself from the grains or harpoons, when struck, all the others, attracted by the blood, immediately quit the ship and give chase to the wounded one, and as soon as they overtake it immediately tear it in pieces. We also caught a large shark, which had followed the ship for several days with a hook which I made for the purpose, and although the flesh was by no means equal to that of the herring hog, yet to those destitute as we were of any thing fresh, I found it eat very well. After passing the Cape when the sea had become calm we saw great numbers of Albatrosses, a large brown and white bird of the goose kind, one of **5** which Captain Salter shot, whose wings measured from their extremities fifteen feet. One thing, however, I must not omit mentioning, as it struck me in a most singular and extraordinary manner. This was, that on passing Cape Horn in December, which was mid summer in that climate, the nights were so light, without any moon, that we found no difficulty whatever in reading small print which we frequently did during our watches.

Left: Albatross (Diomeda exultans), *often found great distances from land.* 23

Right: Grain, used for harpooning porpoise. 22

1 *the grains.* A grain was a five-pronged harpoon attached to a line, used especially for porpoise and dolphins. A seaman climbed out onto the jib boom at the bow of the ship and thrust the grain at the sea mammals flashing by beneath him.

2 *gamboling and blowing.* Porpoise are playful creatures and often cavort and leap around a moving vessel, though not in search of food.

3 *harslet.* This old English word, which refers to the edible viscera such as the heart and lungs, was mainly used in reference to the hog.

4 *I was told . . .* This statement is totally incorrect and shows the lack of knowledge of marine mammal behaviour that once existed. With their supportive social structure, porpoise swarm towards an injured animal to physically support it to prevent it from drowning, not to tear it to pieces.

5 *one of which Captain Salter shot.* Early mariners believed that killing an albatross, a bird thought to embody the souls of dead seamen, would bring misfortune. Would Captain Salter, then, shoot an albatross, or did Alsop, influenced by the recent (1798) publication of Samuel Coleridge's "Rime of the Ancient Mariner," deliberately add this foreboding event as a prophecy of the *Boston*'s fate?

Nootka Sound, looking north. 9

In this manner, with a fair wind and easy weather from the 28th of December, the period of our passing Cape Horn, we pursued our voyage to the Northward **1** until the 12th of March 1803, when we made Woody Point in Nootka Sound on the North West Coast of America. We immediately stood up the Sound for Nootka, where Captain Salter had determined to stop, in order to supply the ship with wood and water before proceeding up the coast to trade. But in order to avoid the risk of any molestation or interruption to his men from the Indians, while thus employed, he proceeded with the ship about five miles to the Northward of the village, which is situated on Friendly Cove, and sent out his chief mate with several of the crew in the boat to **2** find a good place for anchoring her.—After sounding for some time they returned with information that they had discovered a secure place for anchorage, on the Western side of an inlet or small bay at about half a mile from the coast, near a small island which protected it from the sea, and where there was a plenty of wood and excellent water. The ship accordingly came to anchor in

1 *until the 12th of March.* The *Boston's* passage from England to Nootka Sound took 190 days—more than half a year.

2 —*After sounding for some time* . . . This anchorage has never been ascertained in spite of extensive research and diving by David Griffiths of the Underwater Archaeological Society of British Columbia. Five miles north of the village is Marvinas Bay (in early times spelled Moweena or Mowenna), a popular anchorage for American vessels. It was known as Fort Washington by 1788, probably named for Capt. John Kendrick's ship, *Lady Washington.* Native history puts the anchorage closer to Abooksha; both places have sheltered bays and a small offshore island, as Jewitt describes.

The arrival of the Boston, at Nootka Sound.

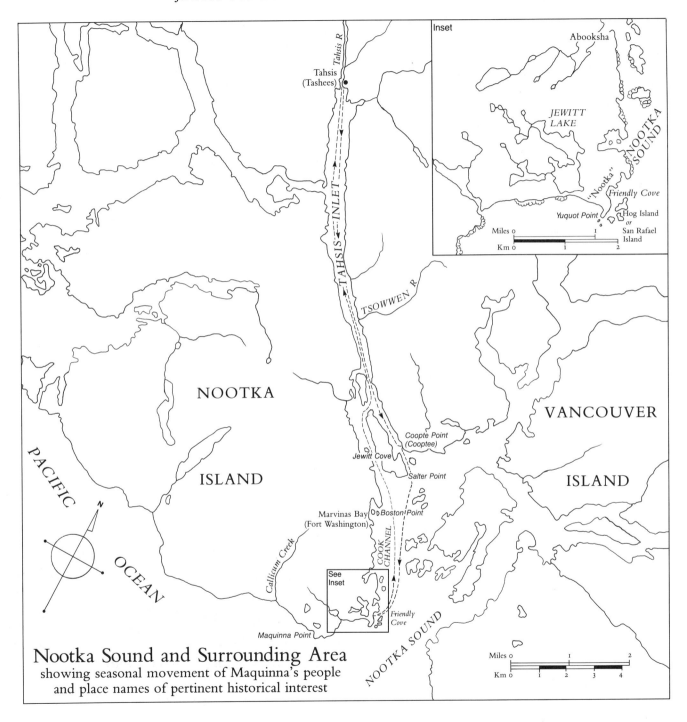

Inset

Abooksha

JEWITT LAKE

NOOTKA SOUND

"Nootka"

Friendly Cove

Yuquot Point

Hog Island or San Rafael Island

Miles 0 — 1
Km 0 — 1 — 2

Tahsis R

Tahsis (Tashees)

TAHSIS INLET

TSOWWEN R

NOOTKA

ISLAND

VANCOUVER

ISLAND

PACIFIC

OCEAN

Coopte Point (Cooptee)

Jewitt Cove

Salter Point

Marvinas Bay (Fort Washington)

Boston Point

Callicum Creek

COOK CHANNEL

See Inset

Friendly Cove

Maquinna Point

NOOTKA SOUND

N

Miles 0 — 1 — 2
Km 0 — 1 — 2 — 3 — 4

Nootka Sound and Surrounding Area
showing seasonal movement of Maquinna's people
and place names of pertinent historical interest

1 *twelve fathom.* A fathom is a nautical measurement equal to 1.8 m (6′).

2 *winding.* Winding is the action of a ship swinging around on her anchor in the wind.

3 *the village of Nootka.* Jewitt never refers to Maquinna's summer village as anything other than Nootka, even though seafarers before him knew it as Yuquot—in a variety of spellings. Once Cook established the name Nootka Sound, it seems to have come into use for the village also, perhaps one being considered synonymous with the other.

4 *king.* Jewitt's use of the terms king, queen and princess, all titles familiar to his frame of reference, shows his recognition of Maquinna and his family as the highest ranking in the village. Later, after becoming a working part of the household, Jewitt refers to Maquinna as "our chief." Linguistically, the correct word was *ha'wil* for a chief and *ha'qum* (which Jewitt writes as *Arcomah*) for his principal wife. While "chief" is not an exact translation of *ha'wil,* common usage of the title chief, especially by native people themselves, has given the word general acceptance.

5 *Maquina.* Now spelled Maquinna. The chief of the highest-ranking household at Yuquot actually had several names: *tsaxhw'sip,* meaning "harpooner," was his winter or ceremonial name, while *moquina,* a Kwakiutl word meaning "moon," was his summer name. The latter name was passed on to successive chiefs until the late eighteenth century, when, with increasing missionary influence, it became a surname—not without considerable prestige.

6 *white down.* The white down was most likely that of a young eagle. Symbolizing peace, friendship and good will, it usually formed part of the welcoming ceremonies of all the coast cultures.

7 *made from the bark of a tree.* The tree referred to was the red cedar (*Thuja plicata*) and/or the yellow cedar (*Chamaecyparis nootkatensis*), so named because it was first documented scientifically in Nootka Sound. Women shredded the inner bark into soft fibres and twined it at close intervals to create warm, flexible garments.

8 *two holes . . .* This description of the rectangular cedar bark "blanket" is unusual, since these garments did not have armholes. Both men and women wrapped the blanket around them in various ways, leaving the arms free; this may have given the appearance of armholes.

1 this place, at twelve o'clock at night, in twelve fathom water, muddy bottom, and so near the shore that to **2** prevent the ship from winding we secured her by a hauser to the trees. On the morning of the next day, the thirteenth, several of the natives came on board in a **3, 4** canoe from the village of Nootka, with their king, **5** called Maquina, who appeared much pleased on seeing us, and with great seeming cordiality, welcomed Capt. Salter and his officers to his country. As I had never before beheld a savage of any nation, it may readily be supposed that the novelty of their appearance, so different from any people that I had hitherto seen, excited in me strong feelings of surprise and curiosity. I was, however, particularly struck with the looks of their king, who was a man of a dignified aspect, about six feet in height and extremely strait and well proportioned; his features were in general good and his face was rendered remarkable by a large Roman nose, a very uncommon form of feature among these people; his complexion was of a dark copper hue, though his face, legs, and arms were on this occasion, so covered with red paint, that their natural colour could scarcely be perceived, his eye-brows were painted black in two broad stripes like a new moon, and his long black hair, which shone with oil, was fastened in a bunch on the top of his **6** head and strewed or powdered all over with white down, which gave him a most curious and extraordinary appearance. He was dressed in a large mantle or cloak of the black sea otter skin, which reached to his knees, and was fastened around his middle by a broad belt of the cloth of the country, wrought, or painted with figures of several colours; this dress was by no means unbecoming, but on the contrary had an air of savage magnificence. His men were habited in mantles **7** of the same cloth, which is made from the bark of a tree, and has some resemblance to straw matting, these are **8** nearly square and have two holes in the upper part large enough to admit the arms—they reach as low as the knees, and are fastened around their bodies with a belt about four inches broad of the same cloth.

From his having frequently visited the English and American ships that traded to the coast, Maquina had learned the signification of a number of English words, and in general could make himself pretty well understood by us in our own language. He was always the first to go on board such ships as came to Nootka, which he was much pleased in visiting, even when he had no trade to offer, as he almost always received some small present, and was in general extremely well treated by the commanders. He remained on board of us for some time during which the captain took him into the cabin and treated him with a glass of rum; these people being very fond of distilled spirits, and some biscuit and **1, 2** molasses which they prefer to any kind of food that we **3** can offer them.

As there are seldom many furs to be purchased at this place, and it was not fully the season, Capt. Salter had put in here not so much with an expectation of trading as to procure an ample stock of wood and water for the supply of the ship on the coast, thinking it more prudent to take it on board at Nootka, from the generally friendly disposition of the people, than to endanger the safety of his men in sending them on shore for that purpose among the more ferocious natives of the north. With this view, we immediately set about getting our water casks in readiness, and the next and two succeeding days part of the crew were sent on shore to cut pine **4** timber and assist the carpenter in making it into yards and spars for the ship, while those on board were employed in refitting the rigging, repairing the sails, &c. when we proceeded to take in our wood and water as expeditiously as possible, during which time I kept myself busily employed in repairing the muskets, making knives, tomaxes, &c. and doing such iron work as was

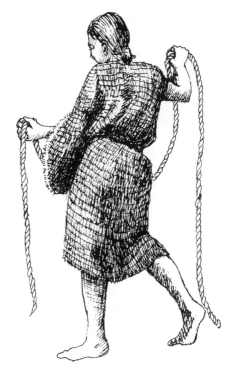

Method of wearing cedar bark blanket to leave both arms free for activity. *4

1 *fond of distilled spirits.* Prior to contact with Europeans, native people on the Northwest Coast had no fermented or distilled drinks. In fact, Captain Cook's journal noted: "They . . . rejected our spirituous liquor as being disgusting and unnatural."

2 *biscuit.* Ship biscuit, or hardtack, was a thin, flat cake made from flour and water but no salt, and baked hard for lengthy preservation.

3 *molasses.* With berries their only source of sweet flavour, native people relished molasses as a treat and welcomed it in trade.

4 *pine.* Pine, the generic name then used by the English to refer to all conifers, is frequently mentioned by Jewitt. It is more likely that spruce or fir trees were felled to make the ship's spars and yards.

Cedar bark clothing worn by an elder. *23

wanted for the ship. Meantime more or less of the natives came on board of us daily, bringing with them fresh salmon with which they supplied us in great plenty, receiving in return some trifling articles. Capt. Salter was always very particular before admitting these people on board to see that they had no arms about them, by obliging them indiscriminately to throw off their garments, so that he felt perfectly secure from any attack. On the fifteenth the king came on board with several of his chiefs; he was dressed as before in his magnificent otter skin robe, having his face highly painted, and his hair tossed off with the white down

1 which looked like snow; his chiefs were dressed in mantles of the country cloth of its natural colour, which is a pale yellow; these were ornamented with a broad border painted or wrought in figures of several colours representing men's heads, various animals, &c. and secured around them by a belt like that of the king from which it was distinguished only by being narrower: the

2 dress of the common people is of the same fashion and differs from that of the chiefs in being of a coarser texture and painted red, of one uniform colour.

Captain Salter invited Maquina and his chiefs to dine with him, and it was curious to see how these people (when they eat) seat themselves (in their country fashion upon our chairs) with their feet under them crossed like Turks. They cannot endure the taste of salt, and the only thing they would eat with us was the ship bread which they were very fond of, especially when dipped in molasses; they had also a great liking for tea and coffee when well sweetened. As iron weapons and tools of almost every kind are in much request among them, whenever they came on board they were always very attentive to me, crowding around me at the forge, as if to see in what manner I did my work, and in this way became quite familiar, a circumstance, as will be seen in the end, of great importance to me. The salmon which

1 *his chiefs were dressed* . . . Being of high rank, chiefs most likely wore garments made from the inner bark of the yellow cedar, which has a yellowed appearance compared with the bark of red cedar.

2 *dress of the common people* . . . Garments of a "coarser texture" would most probably have been made from the inner bark of red cedar, not finely shredded. Painting them helped shed rain.

they brought us furnished a most delicious treat to men who for a long time had lived wholly on salt provisions excepting such few sea fish as we had the good fortune occasionally to take. We indeed feasted most luxuriously, and flattered ourselves that we should not want while on the coast for plenty of fresh provisions, little imagining the fate that awaited us, and that this dainty food was to prove the unfortunate lure to our destruction! On the nineteenth, the king came again on board and was invited by the Captain to dine with him. He had much conversation with Capt. Salter, and informed him that there were plenty of wild ducks and geese near Friendly Cove, on which the Captain made him a present of a double-barreled fowling piece with which he appeared to be greatly pleased and soon after went on shore.

On the 20th we were nearly ready for our departure, having taken in what wood and water we were in want of.

The next day Maquina came on board with nine pair of wild ducks, as a present, at the same time he brought with him the gun, one of the locks of which he had broken, telling the Captain that it was *peshak,* that is bad; Capt. Salter was very much offended at this observation, and considering it as a mark of contempt for his present, he called the king a liar, adding other opprobrious terms, and taking the gun from him tossed it indignantly into the cabin and calling me to him said, 'John, this fellow has broken this beautiful fowling piece, see if you can mend it:' on examining it I told him that it could be done.—As I have already observed, Maquina knew a number of English words, and unfortunately understood but too well the meaning of the reproachful terms that the Captain addressed to him.—He said not a word in reply, but his countenance sufficiently expreseed the rage he felt, though he exerted himself to suppress it, and I observed him while the

*Canada goose (*Branta canadensis*).* 23

*Harlequin duck (*Histrionicus histrionicus*) inhabits rocky coast line, could have been one of several species taken for food.* 20

Captain was speaking repeatedly put his hand to his throat and rub it upon his bosom, which he afterwards told me was to keep down his heart which was rising into his throat and choaking him. He soon after went on shore with his men, evidently much discomposed.

On the morning of the 22d the natives came off to us as usual with salmon, and remained on board, when about noon Maquina came along side with a considerable number of his chiefs and men in their canoes, who, after going through the customary examination were admitted into the ship. He had a whistle in his hand, and over his face a very ugly mask of wood representing the head of some wild beast, appeared to be remarkably good humoured and gay, and whilst his people sung and capered about the deck, entertaining us with a variety of antic tricks and gestures, he blew his whistle to a kind of tune which seemed to regulate their motions. As Capt. Salter was walking on the quarter deck amusing himself with their dancing, the king came up to him and enquired when he intended to go to sea?—he answered, to-morrow.—Maquina then said, 'you love salmon—much in Friendly Cove, why not go then and catch some?'—The Captain thought that it would be very desirable to have a good supply of these fish for the voyage, and on consulting with Mr. Delouisa it was agreed to send part of the crew on shore after dinner with the seine in order to procure a quantity—Maquina and his chiefs staid and dined on board, and after dinner the

1   chief mate went off with nine men in the jolly boat and
2   yawl to fish at Friendly Cove, having set the steward on shore at our watering place to wash the captain's clothes. Shortly after the departure of the boats I went down to my vice-bench in the steerage, where I was employed in cleaning muskets. I had not been there more than an hour when I heard the men hoisting in the
3   long boat, which, in a few minutes after, was succeeded by a great bustle and confusion on deck. I immediately

1 *jolly boat.* A small craft used for general work and going ashore, the jolly boat probably derived its name from the Dutch *jol* or Danish *jolle,* meaning "boat."

2 *yawl.* Also from the Dutch word *jol,* the yawl was a heavily constructed, square-sterned work boat, about 5.5 m (18′) long. It could be rigged with sails.

3 *long boat.* The largest boat carried by a sailing ship, in this case the yawl.

ran up the steerage stairs, but scarcely was my head above deck, when I was caught by the hair by one of the savages, and lifted from my feet; fortunately for me, my hair being short, and the ribbon with which it was tied slipping, I fell from his hold into the steerage. As I was falling, he struck at me with an axe, which cut a deep gash in my forehead, and penetrated the skull, but in consequence of his losing his hold, I luckily escaped the full force of the blow; which, otherwise, would have cleft my head in two. I fell, stunned and senseless upon the floor—how long I continued in this situation I know not, but on recovering my senses the first thing that I did, was to try to get up; but so weak was I, from the loss of blood, that I fainted and fell. I was however soon recalled to my recollection by three loud shouts or yells from the savages, which convinced me that they had got possession of the ship. It is impossible for me to describe my feelings at this terrific sound.—Some faint idea may be formed of them by those who have known what it is to half waken from a hideous dream and still think it real. Never, no, never, shall I lose from my mind, the impression of that dreadful moment. I expected every instant to share the wretched fate of my unfortunate companions, and when I heard the song of triumph, by which these infernal yells was succeeded, my blood ran cold in my veins. Having at length sufficiently recovered my senses to look around me after wiping the blood from my eyes, I saw that the hatch of the steerage was shut. This was done, as I afterwards discovered, by order of Maquina, who, on seeing the savage strike at me with the axe, told him not to hurt me, for that I was the armourer, and would be useful to them in repairing their arms; while at the same time to prevent any of his men from injuring me, he had the hatch closed. But to me this circumstance wore a very different appearance, for I thought that these barbarians had only prolonged my life in order to deprive me of it by the most cruel tortures. I remained in this horrid state of suspense for a very long time, when at length the hatch was opened, and Maquina, calling me by name, ordered me to come up. I groped my way up as well as I was able, being almost blinded with the blood that flowed from my wound, and so weak as with difficulty to walk. The king, on perceiving my situation, ordered one of his men to bring a pot of water to wash the blood from my face, which having done, I was able to see distinctly with one of my eyes, but the other was so swollen from my wound, that it was closed. But what a terrific spectacle met my eyes; six naked savages, standing in a circle around me, covered with the blood of my murdered comrades, with their daggers uplifted in their hands, prepared to strike. I now thought my last moment had come, and recommended my soul to my Maker.—The king, who, as I have already observed, knew enough of English to make himself understood, entered the circle, and placing himself before me, addressed me nearly in the following words—"John—I speak—you no say no—You say no—daggers come!" He then asked me if I would be his slave during my life—If I would fight for him in his battles—If I would repair his muskets and make daggers and knives for him—with several other questions, to all of which I was careful to answer, yes. He then told me that he would spare my life, and ordered me to kiss his hands and feet to show my submission to him, which I did.—In the mean time his people were very clamorous to have me put to death, so that there should be none of us left to tell our story to our countrymen and prevent them from coming to trade with them; but the king, in the most determined manner opposed their wishes, and to his favour am I wholly indebted for my being yet among the living. As I was busy at work at the time of the attack, I was without my coat, and what with the coldness of the weather, my feebleness from loss of blood, the pain of my wound and the extreme agitation and terror that I still felt, I shook like a leaf, which the king observing, went into the cabin and bringing up a great coat that belonged to the captain, threw it over my shoulders, telling me to drink some rum from a bottle which he handed me at the same time, giving me to understand that it would be good for me and keep me from trembling as I did. I took a draught of it, after which, taking me by the hand, he led me to the quarter deck, where the most horrid sight presented itself that ever my eyes witnessed—the heads of our unfortunate Captain and his crew, to the number of twenty-five, were all arranged in a line, and Maquina ordering one of his people to bring a head, asked me whose it was: I answered, the Captain's; in like manner the others were showed me, and I told him the names, exepting a few that were so horribly mangled that I was not able to recognize them. I now discovered that all our unfortunate crew had been massacred, and learned that after getting possession of the ship, the savages had broke open the arm chest and magazine, and supplying themselves with ammunition **1** and arms, sent a party on shore to attack our men who had gone thither to fish, and being joined by numbers from the village, without difficulty overpowered and murdered them, and cutting off their heads, brought them on board, after throwing their bodies into the sea. On looking upon the deck, I saw it entirely covered with the blood of my poor comrades, whose throats had been cut with their own jack-knives, the savages having seized the opportunity while they were busy in hoisting in the boat to grapple with them and overpower them by their numbers; in the scuffle the captain was thrown overboard and despatched by those in the canoes, who immediately cut off his head: What I felt on this occasion, may be more readily conceived than expressed.

After I had answered his questions, Maquina took my

1 *magazine.* The part of a ship where ammunition is stored.

1 *tobacco*. Dubbed "the noble medicine," tobacco was hailed as a cure-all as early as 1560. Over the next three hundred years physicians, surgeons and quacks used it in many forms from powdered to boiled to treat wounds, toothache, gout, asthma and goitre, among other things—and even as a remedy against the plague and as a love potion. Considerable enquiries by this writer have failed to uncover any properties in tobacco that do promote healing, however.

2 *Maquina then ordered me . . .* Peter Webster, a native from Ahousat, believes that an Indian who had spent two years on a sailing ship was responsible for taking the *Boston* to Yuquot: "He got to know every movement of the ship, what could be tied and what could be knotted and what could be pulled, such as pulling up the sails. Then when they murdered this ship . . . this Indian commanded these people to do this, pull that, untie that and so the sails went up and they came down sailing with the north wind and hit the beach of Yuquot."

Substantiating this possibility is a comment by Ensign Alexander Walker, in 1787, regarding Capt. James Hanna's visit to Nootka Sound for sea otter furs: "They carried away with them a Boy, who was Brother to Mokquilla, and brought him in good health to China; this they acknowledged to have done secretly, but with the Lad's own consent." The lad, Comekela, returned to Yuquot in 1788 aboard Capt. John Meares's ship the *Felice*.

3 *drumming*. Roof drumming was a common method of expressing joy and was a celebratory gesture.

4 *pine torches*. The torches were probably made of several splints of spruce containing resin, lashed to the end of a stick.

5 *nine wives*. While monogamy was the general rule, men of high rank and wealth might have several wives. Having nine wives indicates the measure of Maquinna's position on the coast.

6 *to rejoice for their success*. The tumultuous welcome lay not only in the long-awaited revenge, but also, for the first time on the coast of Vancouver Island, the successful capture of a ship. Earlier attempts by various groups had failed.

1 silk handkerchief from my neck and bound it around my head, placing over the wound a leaf of tobacco, of which we had a quantity on board. This was done at my desire, as I had often found from personal experience the benefit of this application to cuts.

2 Maquina then ordered me to get the ship under weigh for Friendly Cove. This I did by cutting the cables and sending some of the natives aloft to loose the sails, which they performed in a very bungling manner. But they succeeded so far in loosing the jib and topsails, that, with the advantage of a fair wind, I succeeded in getting the ship into the Cove, where, by order of the King, I ran her ashore on a sandy beach, at 8 o'clock at night.

3 **4** We were received by the inhabitants of the village, men, women, and children, with loud shouts of joy, and a most horrible drumming with sticks upon the roofs and sides of their houses, in which they had also stuck a great number of lighted pine torches, to welcome their king's return and congratulate him on the success of his enterprize.

5 Maquina then took me on shore to his house, which was very large and filled with people—where I was received with much kindness by the women, particularly those belonging to the king, who had no less than nine wives, all of whom came around me expressing much sympathy for my misfortune, gently stroking and patting my head in an encouraging and soothing manner, with words expressive of condolence. How sweet is compassion even from savages?—Those who have been in a similar situation, can alone truly appreciate its value.

6 In the mean time, all the warriors of the tribe, to the number of five hundred, had assembled at the king's house to rejoice for their success. They exulted greatly in having taken our ship, and each one boasted of his own particular exploits in killing our men, but they were in general much dissatisfied with my having been suffered to live, and were very urgent with Maquina to deliver me to them to be put to death, which he obstinately refused to do, telling them that he had promised me my life and would not break his word; and that besides, I knew how to repair and to make arms, and should be of great use to them.

The king then seated me by him and ordered his women to bring him something to eat, when they set before him some dried clams and train oil, of which he **1** ate very heartily and encouraged me to follow his example, telling me to eat much and take a great deal of oil which would make me strong and fat; notwithstanding his praise of this new kind of food, I felt no disposition to indulge in it, both the smell and taste being loathsome to me; and had it been otherwise, such was the pain I endured, the agitation of my mind, and the gloominess of my reflections, that I should have felt very little inclination for eating. Not satisfied with his first refusal to deliver me up to them, the people again became clamorous that Maquina should consent to my being killed, saying that not one of us ought to be left alive to give information to others of our countrymen and prevent them from coming to trade or induce them to revenge the destruction of our ship, and they at length became so boisterous that he caught up a large club in a passion and drove them all out of the house. During this scene a son of the king, of about eleven years old, attracted no doubt by the singularity of my appearance came up to me: I caressed him; he returned my attentions with much apparent pleasure, and considering this as a fortunate opportunity to gain the good will of the father, I took the child on my knee, and cutting the metal buttons from off the coat I had on, I tied them around his neck. At this he was highly delighted, and became so much attached to me that he would not quit me.

Dried clams on strip of cedar bark. CMC/2

Left: Butter clam (Saxidomus giganteus) prefers well-protected sand and gravel beaches, in lower third of tidal range. Grows up to 13 cm (5″). 23

Right: Native little-neck clam (Protothaca staminea), mostly found at half-tide level on a variety of beaches, especially in mud-gravel of protected bays. Grows to about 6.4 cm (2½″). 23

1 *train oil.* The word train comes from the old Dutch word *traen*, meaning "oil rendered from blubber," especially that of whales. The Nuu-chah-nulth rendered the blubber of both whales and seals, while other groups along the coast made or traded for eulachon oil. Rich in nutrients and an important part of the diet, oil was used as a sort of sauce on almost all foods, even berries.

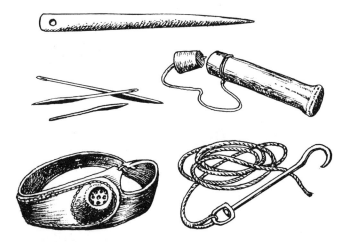

Sail-maker's tools include: top, marlin spike; centre, needles and needle case; bottom, sewing palm and bench hook. 24

The king appeared much pleased with my attention to his son, and telling me that it was time to go to sleep, directed me to lie with his son next to him, as he was afraid lest some of his people would come while he was asleep and kill me with their daggers. I lay down as he ordered me, but neither the state of my mind nor the pain I felt would allow me to sleep. About midnight I was greatly alarmed by the approach of one of the natives, who came to give information to the king that there was one of the white men alive, who had knocked him down as he went on board the ship at night. This Maquina communicated to me, giving me to understand that as soon as the sun rose he should kill him. I endeavoured to persuade him to spare his life, but he bade me be silent and go to sleep. I said nothing more but lay revolving in my mind what method I could devise to save the life of this man. What a consolation thought I, what a happiness would it prove to me in my forlorn state among these heathen, to have a Christian and one of my own countrymen for a companion, and how greatly would it alleviate and lighten the burden of my slavery. As I was thinking of some plan for his preservation, it all at once came into my mind that this man was probably the sail-maker of the ship, named Thompson, as I had not seen his head among those on deck, and knew that he was below at work upon the sails not long before the attack. The more I thought of it the more probable it appeared to me, and as Thompson was a man nearly forty years of age, and had an old look, I conceived it would be easy to make him pass for my father, and by this means prevail on Maquina to spare his life. Towards morning I fell into a doze, but was awakened with the first beams of the sun by the king, who told me that he was going to kill the man who was on board the ship, and ordered me to accompany him. I rose and followed him, leading with me the young prince his son.

On coming to the beach I found all the men of the tribe assembled. The king addressed them, saying that one of the white men had been found alive on board the ship, and requested their opinion as to saving his life or putting him to death. They were unanimously for the **1** first: This determination he made known to me. Having arranged my plan, I asked him, pointing to the boy whom I still held by the hand, if he loved his son, he answered that he did; I then asked the child if he loved his father, and on replying in the affirmative, I said and "I also love mine." I then threw myself on my knees at Maquina's feet, and implored him with tears in my eyes to spare my father's life, if the man on board should prove to be him, telling him that if he killed my father it was my wish that he should kill me too, and that if he did not I would kill myself,—and that he would thus lose my services; whereas, by sparing my father's life he would preserve mine, which would be of great advantage to him by my repairing and making arms for him. Maquina appeared moved by my entreaties and promised not to put the man to death if he should be my father. He then explained to his people what I had said, and ordered me to go on board and tell the man to come on shore. To my unspeakable joy on going into the hold, I found that my conjecture was true, Thompson was there, he had escaped without any injury, excepting a slight wound in the nose, given him by one of the savages with a knife as he attempted to come on deck, during the scuffle. Finding the savages in possession of the ship, as he afterwards informed me, he secreted himself in the hold, hoping for some chance to make his escape—but that the Indian who came on board in the night approaching the place where he was, he supposed himself discovered, and being determined to sell his life as dearly as possible, as soon as he came within his reach, he knocked him down, but the Indian immediately springing up, ran off at full speed.—I informed

1 *They were unanimously for the first.* The episode that follows indicates that this sentence should have read: "They were unanimously for the second," not the first.

Canoe rigged with sails. *13

him in a few words that all our men had been killed; that the king had preserved my life, and had consented to spare his on the supposition that he was my father, an opinion which he must be careful not to undeceive them in, as it was his only safety. After giving him his cue, I went on shore with him and presented him to Maquina, who immediately knew him to be the sail-maker and was much pleased, observing that he could make sails for his canoe.—He then took us to his house and ordered something for us to eat.

On the 24th and 25th the natives were busily employed in taking the cargo out of the ship, stripping her of her sails and rigging, cutting away the spars and masts, and in short rendering her as complete a wreck as possible, the muskets, ammunition, cloth and all the principal articles taken from her, being deposited in the king's house.

While they were thus occupied, each one taking what he liked, my companion and myself being obliged to aid them, I thought it best to secure the accounts and papers of the ship, in hopes that on some future day I might have it in my power to restore them to the owners. With this view I took possession of the Captain's writing desk which contained the most of them, together with some paper and implements for writing. I had also the good fortune to find a blank account book, in which I resolved, should it be permitted me to write an account of our capture and the most remarkable occurrences that I should meet with during my stay among these people, fondly indulging the hope that it would not be long before some vessel would arrive to release us. I likewise found in the cabin, a small volume of sermons, a bible, and a common prayer book of the Church of England, which furnished me and my comrade great consolation in the midst of our mournful servitude, and enabled me, under the favor of divine providence, to support, with firmness, the miseries of a life

1 *blank account book.* A ship's account book was for keeping an account of courses and distances run from noon to noon.

which I might otherwise have found beyond my strength to endure. As these people set no value upon things of this kind, I found no difficulty in appropriating them to myself, by putting them in my chest, which though it had been broken open and rifled by the savages, as I still had the key, I without much difficulty secured. In this I also put some small tools belonging to the ship, with several other articles, particularly a journal kept by the second mate, Mr. Ingraham, and a collection of drawings and views of places taken by him, which I had the good fortune to preserve, and on my arrival at Boston, I gave them to a connection of his, the honorable Judge Dawes, who sent them to his family in New-York.

On the 26th, two ships were seen standing in for Friendly Cove. At their first appearance the inhabitants were thrown into great confusion, but soon collecting a number of muskets and blunderbusses, ran to the shore, from whence they kept up so brisk a fire at them, that

Top: English musket, very early nineteenth century, probably similar to those on board the Boston. *Barrel length 106 cm (42"). 15*

Bottom: Blunderbuss, late eighteenth century, English. 71 cm (28").

1

they were evidently afraid to approach nearer, and after firing a few rounds of grape shot which did no harm to any one, they wore ship and stood out to sea. These

2

3, 4

1 The artist appears not to have read the manuscript since the threatening attack on the two ships was actually from shore by muskets and blunderbusses. The bowman is depicted as holding the bow vertically, European fashion, but on the Northwest Coast the bow was held horizontally.

2 *Grape shot.* This consisted of small cast-iron balls clustered together to form a charge for cannon.

3 *they wore ship.* To wear (or veer) a ship is to put the helm up so that the vessel's bow is turned away from, and the stern presented to, the wind. Turning until her sails fill on the other side, she is brought by the wind on the new tack.

4 *stood.* To stand is to maintain a course of direction.

1 *the Mary and Juno*. Trading ships often met up and sailed in pairs. The *Mary*, commanded by Capt. William Bowles, sailed from its home port of Boston in February 1802; the *Juno*, a 250-ton (254 t) vessel, sailed from Bristol, Rhode Island, the year before.

2 Although a number of these groups later amalgamated, the modern spellings of these names are as follows:

Jewitt's Spelling	Modern Spelling
Ai-tiz-zarts	Ehattesaht
Schoo-mad-its	not a known ethnographic name
Neu-wit-ties	Nawitti
Savin-nars	Tsowenach
Ah-owz-arts	Ahousaht
Mo-watch-its	Mowachaht
Suth-setts	not known
Neu-chad-lits	Nuchatlaht
Mich-la-its	Muchatlaht
Cay-u-quets	Kyuquot
Aytch-arts	Haachaht
Esquiates	Hesquiaht
Kla-oo-quates	Clayoquot
Wickanninish	not a known ethnographic group or place

The suffix "aht" means "people of" or "residing at." Some place names carry the "aht" sound but are spelled "at."

3 *and the Wickanninish . . .* Jewitt refers to Wickanninish as a tribe, but this was actually the name of a powerful chief, and may have been the name for his group. According to Capt. John Meares (1788), Wickanninish had political dominance of the villages from Clayoquot south to Nitinat. The distance was closer to one hundred miles (160 km), not two hundred (320 km).

4 *furnished with sails*. It is generally believed that canoes were not rigged with sails until after native people became acquainted with sailing ships. The sails Jewitt saw were likely made from trade cloth or ship's canvas, but cedar bark matting and even thin cedar boards lashed edge-to-edge served as sails for canoes.

5 *speaking trumpet*. Probably a European loud hailer such as those used on sailing ships. Maquinna would have seen them used and may have traded for his, or taken it from the *Boston*.

1 ships, as I afterwards learned, were the Mary and Juno of Boston.

They were scarcely out of sight when Maquina expressed much regret that he had permitted his people to fire at them, being apprehensive that they would give information to others in what manner they had been received, and prevent them from coming to trade with him.

A few days after hearing of the capture of the ship, there arrived at Nootka a great number of canoes filled with savages from no less than twenty tribes to the North and South. Among those from the North were **2** the Ai-tiz-zarts, Schoo-mad-its, Neu-wit-ties, Savin-nars, Ah-owz-arts, Mo-watch-its, Suth-setts, Neu-chad-lits, Mich-la-its and Cay-u-quets; the most of whom were considered as tributary to Nootka. From the South, the Aytch-arts and Esquiates also tributary, **3** with the Kla-oo-quates, and the Wickanninish, a large and powerful tribe about two hundred miles distant. These last were better clad than most of the others, and their canoes wrought with much greater skill; they are **4** furnished with sails as well as paddles, and with the advantage of a fair breeze, are usually but twenty-four hours on their passage.

Maquina, who was very proud of his new acquisition, was desirous of welcoming these visitors in the European manner. He accordingly ordered his men, as the canoes approached, to assemble on the beach with loaded muskets and blunderbusses, placing Thompson at the cannon which had been brought from the ship and laid upon two long sticks of timber in front of the **5** village, then taking a speaking trumpet in his hand he ascended with me the roof of his house, and began drumming or beating upon the boards with a stick most violently. Nothing could be more ludicrous than the appearance of this motley group of savages collected on the shore, dressed as they were, with their ill-gotten finery, in the most fantastic manner, some in women's smocks, taken from our cargo, others in *Kotsacks,* (or **1** cloaks) of blue, red or yellow broadcloth, with stockings drawn over their heads, and their necks hung round with numbers of powder-horns, shot-bags, and cartouch-boxes, some of them having no less than ten **2** muskets a piece on their shoulders, and five or six daggers in their girdles. Diverting indeed was it to see them all squatted upon the beach, holding their muskets perpendicularly, with the butt pressed upon the sand instead of against their shoulders, and in this position awaited the order to fire. Maquina, at last, called to them with his trumpet to fire, which they did in the most awkward and timid manner, with their muskets hard pressed upon the ground as above mentioned. At the same moment the cannon was fired by Thompson, immediately on which they threw themselves back and began to roll and tumble over the sand as if they had been shot, when suddenly springing up they began a song of triumph and running backward and forward upon the shore, with the wildest gesticulations, boasted of their exploits and exhibited as trophies what they had taken from us. Notwithstanding the unpleasantness of my situation, and the feelings that this display of our spoils excited, I could not avoid laughing at the strange appearance of these savages, their awkward movements, and the singular contrast of their dress and arms.

When the ceremony was concluded, Maquina invited the strangers to a feast at her house, consisting of whale blubber, smoked herring spawn, and dried fish **3** and train oil, of which they eat most plentifully. The feast being over, the trays out of which they eat, and other things were immediately removed to make room for the dance which was to close the entertainment. This was performed by Maquina's son, the young prince Sat-sat-sok-sis, whom I have already spoken of,

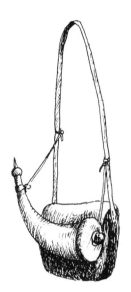

Powder horn (flask made of horn for carrying gunpowder) with shot pouch (leather bag for carrying lead shot); both used with muzzle-loading guns. 17

1 *Kotsacks, (or cloaks)*. The word *kotsack* (pluralized here with an s) refers to the rectangular cedar bark blanket that people wore in various ways. The coloured trade cloth that replaced it retained the same name but not the warmth or waterproofing needed. Various spellings of kotsack are used in the narrative.

2 *cartouch-boxes*. A box for storing and carrying cartridges; the word cartridge is derived from the French word *cartouche*.

3 *herring spawn*. Herring arrived on the coast in teeming millions in March, spawning on vegetation in quiet bays. Coast peoples set out hemlock branches weighted down with rocks, then lifted the branches to harvest the spawn that covered them.

Wolf mask worn on the forehead, about 38 cm (15″). BCPM/25

1 *a curious mask in imitation of a wolf's head.* The mask may well have been that of a wolf, but dancers also used a mask of the Feathered Serpent, whose wolflike head was plumed. Both were supernatural creatures. Whistles and rattles were generally featured in ceremonial dances.

2 *Tyee.* The word *tyee* comes from the native word *ti·yi,* meaning "elder brother" or "senior," and carries the meaning of chief, nobleman or person of high status. Capt. John Meares spelled it *Tighee,* Captain Cook and others as *Tyee.* Nowadays, sports fishermen refer to a large chinook salmon of 13.6 kg (30 lbs.) and over as a tyee or king salmon.

3 *European cloth.* This cloth was regarded as a valuable and prestigious item.

4 *fathom.* The fathom used to measure cloth was different from the nautical fathom and was the span of both arms fully stretched.

in the following manner—Three of the principal chiefs, drest in their otter-skin mantles, which they wore only on extraordinary occasions and at festivals, having their heads covered over with white down and their faces highly painted, came forward into the middle of the room, each furnished with a bag filled with the white down, which they scattered around in such a manner as to represent a fall of snow. These were followed by the young prince, who was dressed in a long piece of yellow cloth, wrapped loosely around him, and decorated with small bells, with a cap on his head, to which was **1** fastened a curious mask in imitation of a wolf's head, while the rear was brought up by the king himself in his robe of sea-otter skin, with a small whistle in his mouth and a rattle in his hand, with which he kept time to a sort of tune on his whistle. After passing very rapidly in this order around the house, each of them seated himself, except the prince, who immediately began his dance, which principally consisted in springing up into the air in a squat posture, and constantly turning around on his heels with great swiftness in a very narrow circle. This dance with a few intervals of rest, was continued for about two hours, during which the chiefs kept up a constant drumming with sticks of about a foot in length on a long hollow plank, which was, though a very noisy, a most doleful kind of music. This they accompanied with songs, the king himself acting as chorister, while the women applauded each feat of activity in the **2** dancer by repeating the words, *Wocash! Wocash Tyee!* that is good! very good prince. As soon as the dance was finished Maquina began to give presents to the strangers in the name of his son Sat-sat-sok-sis. These were pieces **3, 4** of European cloth generally of a fathom in length, muskets, powder, shot, &c. Whenever he gave them any thing, they had a peculiar manner of snatching it from him with a very stern and surly look, repeating each time the words, *Wocash Tyee.* This I understood to be their custom, and was considered as a compliment which if omitted would be supposed as a mark of disregard for the present. On this occasion Maquina gave away no less than one hundred muskets, the same number of looking glasses, four hundred yards of cloth, and twenty casks of powder, besides other things. **1**

After receiving these presents, the strangers retired **2** on board their canoes, for so numerous were they that Maquina would not suffer any but the chiefs to sleep in the houses; and in order to prevent the property from being pillaged by them, he ordered Thompson and myself to keep guard, during the night, armed with cutlasses and pistols.

In this manner tribes of savages from various parts of the coast, continued coming for several days, bringing with them, blubber, oil, herring spawn, dried fish and clams, for which they received in return, presents of cloth, &c. after which they in general immediately returned home. I observed that very few, if any of them, except the chiefs, had arms, which I afterwards learned is the custom with these people whenever they come upon a friendly visit or to trade, in order to show, on their approach, that their intentions are pacific.

Early on the morning of the 18th the ship was dis- **3** covered to be on fire. This was owing to one of the savages having gone on board with a fire brand at night for the purpose of plunder, some sparks from which fell into the hold, and communicating with some combustibles soon enveloped the whole in flames. The na- **4** tives regretted the loss of the ship the more as a great part of her cargo still remained on board. To my companion and myself it was a most melancholy sight, for with her disappeared from our eyes every trace of a civilized country; but the disappointment we experienced was still more severely felt, for we had calculated on having the provision to ourselves, which would have furnished us with a stock for years, as whatever is cured

1 *casks of powder.* A cask held 305 kg (672 lbs.) of gunpowder.

2 *After receiving these presents . . .* The ceremony that Jewitt and Thompson witnessed was a potlatch to validate Maquinna's acquisition of themselves as slaves. A Nuu-cha-nulth, Peter Webster from Ahousat, knew of this from the aural histories passed down through generations. In repeating the story of the capture of the two crewmen to Barbara Efrat and W. J. Langlois in 1978, Webster said: "These two men, Jewitt and Thompson, they became slaves. They were under the command of Maquinna then. They'd do anything they were told to do because they didn't want to get hurt, or be killed. And shortly after they became slaves Maquinna put on a potlatch party, to have the whole village as witness of Maquinna's ownership of these two white men."

3 *the 18th.* This date is likely a typographical error. Jewitt's journal entry for 29 March states: "Last night one of the natives having gone on board the ship with a lighted fire-brand in his hand with his intention to steal, dropt a spark of fire down the hold." This would make the date of the fire 28 March.

4 *in flames.* David Griffiths, a member of the Underwater Archaeological Society of British Columbia, made several dives in Friendly Cove during the late 1960s. At the east end of the bay, in about 7.6 m (25') of water, he found burned ship's timbers.

with salt, together with most of our other articles of food, are never eaten by these people. I had luckily saved all my tools excepting the anvil, and the bellows which was attached to the forge, and from their weight had not been brought on shore. We had also the good fortune in looking over what had been taken from the ship to discover a box of chocolate and a case of port wine, which as the Indians were not fond of it proved a great comfort to us for some time, and from one of the natives I obtained a nautical almanack, which had belonged to the Captain, and which was of great use to me in determining the time.

About two days after, on examining their booty, the savages found a tierce of rum with which they were highly delighted, as they have become very fond of spirituous liquors since their intercourse with the whites.—This was towards evening, and Maquina having assembled all the men at his house, gave a feast, at which they drank so freely of the rum, that in a short time, they became so extremely wild and frantic that Thompson and myself, apprehensive for our safety, thought it prudent to retire privately into the woods, where we continued till past midnight. On our return we found the women gone, who are always very temperate, drinking nothing but water, having quitted the house and gone to the other huts to sleep, so terrified were they at the conduct of the men, who all lay stretched out on the floor in a state of complete intoxication. How easy in this situation would it have been for us to have dispatched or made ourselves masters of our enemies, had there been any ship near to which we could have escaped, but as we were situated, the attempt would have been madness. The wish of revenge was however less strongly impressed on my mind, than what appeared to be so evident an interposition of divine Providence in our favour. How little can man penetrate its designs, and how frequently is that in-

1 *nautical almanack*. This was—and still is—an annual publication used as an aid to navigation. It tabulates the position of all celestial bodies in relation to the Greenwich meridian and the equator. Jewitt's journal states: "I happened to see one of the natives with an almanack, which I bought of him for a knife."

2 *tierce*. A tierce equals half a puncheon, 42 imperial gallons (191 L).

tended as a blessing which he views as a curse. The burning of our ship which we had lamented so much, as depriving us of so many comforts, now appeared to us in a very different light, for had the savages got possession of the rum of which there were nearly twenty **1** puncheons on board, we must inevitably have fallen a sacrifice to their fury in some of their moments of intoxication. This cask fortunately and a case of gin was all the spirits they obtained from the ship. To prevent the recurrence of similar danger I examined the cask, and finding still a considerable quantity remaining, I bored a small hole in the bottom with a gimblet, which **2** before morning to my great joy completely emptied it.

By this time the wound in my head began to be much better, so that I could enjoy some sleep, which I had been almost deprived of by the pain, and though I was still feeble from the loss of blood and my sufferings, I found myself sufficiently well to go to work at my trade, in making for the king and his wives bracelets and other small ornaments of copper or steel, and in re- **3** pairing the arms, making use of a large square stone for the anvil, and heating my metal in a common wood fire. This was very gratifying to Maquina and his women particularly, and secured me their good will.

In the mean time great numbers from the other tribes kept continually flocking to Nootka, bringing with them in exchange for the ship's plunder such quantities of provision, that notwithstanding the little success that Maquina met with in whaling this season, and their **4** gluttonous waste, always eating to excess when they have it, regardless of the morrow, seldom did the natives experience any want of food during the summer. As to myself and companion we fared as they did, never wanting for such provision as they had, though we were obliged to eat it cooked in their manner and with train oil as a sauce, a circumstance not a little unpleasant, both from their uncleanly mode of cooking, and

Gimlet, about 15 cm (6″). 23

1 *puncheons.* As a puncheon of spirits is only 12 per cent more than a hogshead, the previously mentioned twenty hogsheads of rum and the twenty puncheons of rum were probably the one and the same; Jewitt simply used the terms interchangeably.

2 *gimblet.* An alternate spelling of gimlet, this drilling tool was in prevalent use in the seventeenth to nineteenth centuries.

3 *copper.* Copper, a metal easy to work cold, was also a symbol of wealth connoting high rank and power. It was valued by all coastal peoples, and so desirous were they to obtain this metal that, on occasion, they would stealthily remove pieces from the hull of a ship at anchor.

4 *whaling.* At the Yuquot archaeological excavation of 1966, artifacts and whalebone fragments dating back about 3000 years were found in significant quantity. Whale hunting may or may not date that far back, since bones could have come from dead whales that drifted ashore.

*Skin of dogfish (*Squalus suckleyi*) used as sandpaper by woodworkers. Average fish measures 76 cm (30"), but species can grow to 1.5 m (5'). 20*

*Halibut (*Hippoglossus stenolapis*): males grow to 134.6 cm (53"), females larger. 19*

*Lingcod (*Ophiodon elongatus*), a good-sized fish, up to 1.5 m (5'), with a large mouth and big teeth. 19*

1 *dog fish.* The flesh of the dogfish or mud shark contains uric acid, which to Jewitt and Thompson gave it an unpalatable flavour.

2 *to cook them . . .* It is interesting to note that both the natives and the Europeans criticized each other's foods as being quite distasteful, and even certain methods of cooking by one group were unacceptable to the other.

many of the articles of their food which to an European are very disgusting, but, as the saying is, hunger will break through stone walls, and we found at times in the **1** blubber of sea animals and the flesh of the dog fish, loathsome as it in general was, a very acceptable repast. But much oftener would poor Thompson, who was no favorite with them, have suffered from hunger had it not been for my furnishing him with provision—This I was enabled to do from my work, Maquina allowing me the privilege, when not employed for him, to work for myself in making bracelets and other ornaments of copper, fish-hooks, daggers, &c. either to sell to the tribes who visited us, or for our own chiefs, who on these occasions, besides supplying me with as much as I wished to eat, and a sufficiency for Thompson, almost always made me a present of an European garment taken from the ship or some fathoms of cloth, which were made up by my comrade, and enabled us to go comfortably clad for some time, or small bundles of penknives, razors, scissors, &c. for one of which we could almost always procure from the natives two or three fresh salmon, cod, or halibut; or dried fish, clams and herring spawn from the stranger tribes; and had we **2** only been permitted to cook them after our own way, as we had pots, and other utensils belonging to the ship, we should not have had much cause of complaint in this respect; but so tenacious are these people of their customs, particularly in the article of food and cooking, that the king always obliged me to give whatever provisions I bought to the women to cook—and one day finding Thompson and myself on the shore employed in boiling down sea-water into salt, on being told what it was, he was very much displeased, and taking the little we had procured, threw it into the sea. In one instance alone, as a particular favor, he allowed me to boil some salmon in my own way, when I invited him and his queen to eat with me; they tasted it, but did not like it, and made their meal of some of it that I had cooked in their country fashion.

In May, the weather became uncommonly mild and pleasant, and so forward was vegetation that I picked a plenty of strawberries by the middle of the month. Of **1** this fruit there are great quantities on this coast, and I found them a most delicious treat.—My health had now become almost re-established, my wound being so far healed that it gave me no farther trouble. I had never failed to wash it regularly once a day in sea water, and to dress it with a fresh leaf of tobacco, which I obtained from the natives, who had taken it from the ship, but made no use of it. This was all the dressing I gave it, except applying to it two or three times, a little loaf sugar, **2** which Maquina gave me, in order to remove some proud flesh which prevented it from closing. My cure would doubtless have been much sooner effected had I have been in a civilized country, where I could have had it dressed by a surgeon and properly attended to. But alas! I had no good Samaritan with oil and wine to bind up my wounds, and fortunate might I even esteem myself, that I was permitted to dress it myself, for the utmost that I could expect from the natives was compassion for my misfortune, which I indeed experienced from the women, particularly the queen, or favorite wife of Maquina, the mother of Sat-sat-sox-sis, who used frequently to point to my head and manifest much kindness and solicitude for me. I must do Maquina the justice to acknowledge that he always appeared desirous of sparing me any labour which he believed might be hurtful to me, frequently enquiring in an affectionate manner, if my head pained me. As for the others, some of the chiefs excepted, they cared little what became of me, and probably would have been gratified with my death.

My health being at length re-established and my wound healed, Thompson became very importunate

Wild strawberry (Fragaria chiloensis). 21

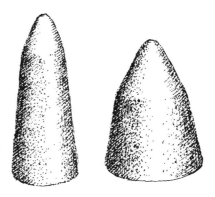

Two types of sugar loaf; the characteristic shape resulted from the method of manufacture. RSM

1 *strawberries.* Jewitt most probably picked wild strawberries, which were small but flavourful.

2 *loaf sugar.* A sugar loaf was a cone-shaped mass of hard sugar, no doubt taken from the *Boston*'s stores. Applied to the surface of an open wound, sugar sucked up fluid through osmosis, reducing the swelling of surrounding tissue and promoting healing.

Raven (Corvus corax). 23

for me to begin my journal, and as I had no ink, proposed to cut his finger to supply me with blood for the purpose whenever I should want it. On the first of June I accordingly commenced a regular diary, but had no occasion to make use of the expedient suggested by my comrade, having found a much better substitute in the expressed juice of a certain plant, which furnished me with a bright green colour, and after making a number of trials I at length succeeded in obtaining a very tolerable ink, by boiling the juice of the black-berry with a mixture of finely powdered charcoal and filtering it through a cloth. This I afterwards preserved in bottles and found it answer very well, so true is it that "necessity is the mother of invention." As for quills I found no difficulty in procuring them, whenever I wanted, from the crows and ravens with which the beach was almost always covered, attracted by the offal of whales, seals, &c. and which were so tame that I could easily kill them with stones, while a large clam shell furnished me with an ink stand.

The extreme solicitude of Thompson that I should begin my journal, might be considered as singular in a man, who neither knew how to write or read, a circumstance by the way, very uncommon in an American, were we less acquainted with the force of habit, he having been for many years at sea, and accustomed to consider the keeping of a journal as a thing indispensable. This man was born in Philadelphia, and at eight years old ran away from his friends, and entered as a cabin boy on board a ship bound to London; on his arrival there finding himself in distress, he engaged as an apprentice to the captain of a Collier, from whence he was impressed on board an English man of war, and continued in the British naval service about twenty-seven years, during which he was present at the engagement under Lord Howe with the French fleet in June, 1794, and when peace was made between England and France

1 *Collier.* A ship whose usual cargo was coal.

2 *impressed.* Being impressed on a war ship meant that Thompson was press ganged (as the practice came to be known) by a detachment of men, under command of an officer, empowered to force people into naval service.

3 *Lord Howe.* Lord Richard Howe, a famous naval officer in command of the Channel Fleet, won a decisive victory, known as the Glorious First of June, over the French in June 1794. Two years later Howe became Admiral of the Fleet.

was discharged. He was a very strong and powerful man, an expert boxer, and perfectly fearless; indeed so little was his dread of danger, that when irritated he was wholly regardless of his life. Of this the following will furnish a sufficient proof.

One evening about the middle of April, as I was at the house of one of the chiefs, where I had been employed on some work for him, word was brought me that Maquina was going to kill Thompson. I immediately hurried home, where I found the king in the act of presenting a loaded musket at Thompson, who was standing before him with his breast bared and calling on him to fire. I instantly stepped up to Maquina, who was foaming with rage, and addressing him in soothing words, begged him for my sake not to kill my father, and at length succeeded in taking the musket from him and persuading him to sit down. On enquiring into the cause of his anger, I learned that while Thompson was lighting the lamps in the king's room, Maquina having substituted our's for their pine torches, some of the boys began to teaze him, running around him and pulling him by the trowsers, among the most forward of whom was the young prince. This caused Thompson to spill the oil, which threw him into such a passion, that without caring what he did, he struck the prince so violent a blow in his face with his fist as to knock him down. The sensation excited among the savages by an act, which was considered as the highest indignity, and a profanation of the sacred person of majesty may be easily conceived. The king was immediately acquainted with it, who, on coming in and seeing his son's face covered with blood, seized a musket and began to load it, determined to take instant revenge on the audacious offender; and had I arrived a few minutes later than I did, my companion would certainly have paid with his life for his rash and violent conduct. I found the utmost difficulty in pacifying Maquina, who for a long time af-

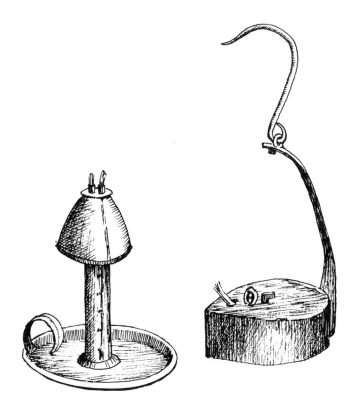

Two types of whale-oil lanterns. 26

ter could not forgive Thompson, but would repeatedly say, "John, *you* die—Thompson kill."—But to appease the king was not all that was necessary. In consequence of the insult offered to their prince, the whole tribe held a council, in which it was unanimously resolved that Thompson should be put to death in the most cruel manner. I however interceded so strenuously with Maquina, for his life, telling him that if my father was killed, I was determined not to survive him, that he refused to deliver him up to the vengeance of his people, saying, that for John's sake they must consent to let him live. The prince, who, after I had succeeded in calming his father, gave me an account of what had happened, told me that it was wholly out of regard to me, as Thompson was my father, that his life had been spared, for that if any one of the tribe should dare to lift a hand against him in anger, he would most certainly to put to death.

Yet even this narrow escape produced not much effect on Thompson, or induced him to restrain the violence of his temper. For not many weeks after, he was guilty of a similar indiscretion, in striking the eldest son of a chief, who was about eighteen years old, and according to their custom was considered as a Tyee, or chief himself, in consequence of his having provoked him by calling him a white slave. This affair caused great commotion in the village, and the tribe was very clamorous for his death, but Maquina would not consent. I used frequently to remonstrate with him on the imprudence of his conduct and beg him to govern his temper better, telling him, it was our duty, since our lives were in the power of these savages, to do nothing to exasperate them. But all I could say on this point availed little, for so bitter was the hate he felt for them, which he was no way backward in manifesting both by his looks and actions, that he declared he never would submit to their insults, and that he had much rather be

killed than be obliged to live among them, adding that
he only wished he had a good vessel and some guns, and
he would destroy the whole of the cursed race; for to a
brave sailor like him, who had fought the French and
Spaniards with glory, it was a punishment worse than
death to be a slave to such a poor, ignorant, despicable
set of beings.

As for myself I thought very differently. After returning thanks to that merciful Being who had in so
wonderful a manner softened the hearts of the savages
in my favour, I had determined from the first of my
capture to adopt a conciliating conduct towards them,
and conform myself, as far as was in my power, to their
customs and mode of thinking, trusting that the same
divine goodness that had rescued me from death, would
not always suffer me to languish in captivity among
these heathen. With this view I sought to gain their
good will by always endeavouring to assume a cheerful
countenance, appearing pleased with their sports and
buffoon tricks, making little ornaments for the wives
and children of the chiefs, by which means I became
quite a favorite with them, and fish hooks, daggers, &c.
for themselves. As a farther recommendation to their
favour, and what might eventually prove of the utmost
importance to us, I resolved to learn their language,
which in the course of a few months residence, I so far
succeeded in acquiring, as to be able in general to make
myself well understood. I likewise tried to persuade
Thompson to learn it as what might prove necessary to
him. But he refused, saying, that he hated both them
and their cursed lingo, and would have nothing to do
with it.

By pursuing this conciliatory plan, so far did I gain
the good will of the savages, particularly the chiefs, that
I scarcely ever failed experiencing kind treatment from
them, and was received with a smile of welcome at their
houses, where I was always sure of having something

*Ornaments found in Yuquot excavation. Left: Child's bracelet of
copper alloy, 4.6 cm (1 ⅞") diameter. Right: Nose ring of copper
alloy, 2.5 cm (1") diameter. Both are post-1790 and could have been
made by Jewitt. PC/11*

*Nose and ear ornaments worn by Sheshaht man. *10*

Looking east across Nootka Sound, from north end of Yuquot; Hog Island in middle distance. 23

given me to eat, whenever they had it, and many a good meal have I had from them, when they themselves were short of provisions and suffering for the want of them.

1 And it was a common practice with me when we had nothing to eat at home which happened not unfrequently during my stay among them, to go around the village, and on noticing a smoke from any of the houses, which denoted that they were cooking, enter in without ceremony and ask them for something, which I was never refused. Few nations indeed, are there, so very rude and unfeeling, whom constant mild treatment and an attention to please, will not mollify and obtain from them some return of kind attention. This, the treatment I received from these people may exemplify, for not numerous, even among those calling themselves civilized, are there instances to be found of persons depriving themselves of food to give it to a stranger, whatever may be his merits.

It may perhaps be as well in this place to give a description of Nootka, some accounts of the tribes who were accustomed to visit us, and the manners and customs of the people, as far as I hitherto had an opportunity of observing them.

2 The village of Nootka, is situated in between 49 and 50 deg. N. lat. at the bottom of Friendly Cove, on the 3 West or North West side. It consists of about twenty houses or huts, on a small hill which rises with a gentle ascent from the shore. Friendly Cove which affords good and secure anchorage for ships close in with the shore is a small harbour of not more than a quarter or half a mile in length, and about half a mile or three quarters broad, formed by the line of coast on the East, and a long point, or headland which extends as much as 4 three leagues into the sound in nearly a Westerly direction. This as well as I can judge from what I have seen of it, is in general from one to two miles in breadth, and mostly a rocky and unproductive soil with but few

1 *And it was a common practice* . . . Jewitt's journal entry for 9 June 1803: "Fine weather. Walked from house to house begging for something to eat, we went into one house and they asked us to eat cockles, we accepted, thanked them, and returned home."

2 *The village of Nootka* . . . Archaeological excavations of Yuquot in 1966 (under the direction of William Folan) show that originally the village site was little more than a spit of sand connecting the shore to the nearby rocky outcrops. The accumulation of midden deposits over at least 4300 years of continuous habitation built up the land by about 5.5 m (18′), giving it the "gentle ascent from the shore."

3 *twenty houses.* The number of inhabitants in each house varied, but generally there were several extended families, all related to the highest-ranking chief of the house, as well as slaves.

4 *three leagues.* A league is an old measure of distance equal to three miles (4.8 km).

trees. The Eastern and Western shores of this harbour are steep, and in many parts rocky, the trees growing quite to the water's edge, but the bottom to the North and North-West is a fine sandy beach of half a mile or more in extent. From the village to the North and North-East extends a plain, the soil of which is very excellent, and with proper cultivation may be made to produce almost any of our European vegetables; this is but little more than half a mile in breadth, and is terminated by the sea coast, which in this place is lined with rocks and reefs and cannot be approached by ships. The coast in the neighbourhood of Nootka is in general low and but little broken into hills and vallies. The soil is good, well covered with fine forests of pine, spruce, beach and other trees, and abounds with streams of the **1** finest water, the general appearance being the same for many miles round.

The village is situated on the ground occupied by the Spaniards, when they kept a garrison here; the founda- **2** tions of the church and the governor's house are yet visible, and a few European plants are still to be found, which continue to be self-propagated, such as onions, peas, and turnips, but the two last are quite small, particularly the turnips, which afford us nothing but the tops for eating. Their former village stood on the same **3** spot, but the Spaniards finding it a commodious situation, demolished the houses and forced the inhabitants to retire five or six miles into the country. With great sorrow, as Maquina told me, did they find themselves compelled to quit their ancient place of residence, but with equal joy did they repossess themselves of it when the Spanish garrison was expelled by the English.

The houses as I have observed are above twenty in number, built nearly in a line. These are of different sizes according to the rank or quality of the *Tyee,* or chief, who lives in them, each having one, of which he is considered as the lord. They vary not much in width,

Spanish garrison on Hog Island at Friendly Cove, 1791. Redrawn from illustration by Joseph Cardero. VPL

1 *beach.* Early spellings for the beech tree (*Alnus rubra*) include beetch, bech, beche, bece and boech—but not beach, which may be a misspelling or a typographical error.

2 *garrison.* In 1789 the Spanish built a small settlement as an adjunct to their armed garrison on an island at one end of the cove. They abandoned it in 1795.

3 *Their former village . . .* Maquinna and his people probably camped at the village west of the Beano River in the summer, and wintered at Tahsis and Cooptee.

Top: Framework of large house (carved house posts not shown); upright posts set into ground. Bottom: Exterior of house. 2

1 *that of the king* . . . In September 1792, Capt. George Vancouver sailed "about seven leagues up the sound, at a place called Tahsheis" and recorded: "Maquinna's habitation was considerably larger than any of the others. . . . On the house of Maquinna were three . . . immense spars; the middle piece was the largest and measured at the butt-end nearly five feet [1.5 m] in diameter; this extended the whole length of the habitation, which was about an hundred feet [30 m] long."

2 *feather edge.* A plank with a feather edge is tapered in a way similar to well-made cedar shakes. In overlapping, the thin edge is uppermost.

being usually from thirty-six to forty feet wide, but are **1** of very different lengths, that of the king which is much the longest being about one hundred and fifty feet, while the smallest which contain only two families do not exceed forty feet in length, the house of the king is also distinguished from the others by being higher.

Their method of building, is as follows, they erect in the ground two very large posts at such a distance apart as is intended for the length of the house. On these, which are of equal height, and hollowed out at the upper end, they lay a large spar for the ridgepole of the building, or if the length of the house requires it, two or more, supporting their ends by similar upright posts; these spars are sometimes of an almost incredible size, having myself measured one in Maquina's house which I found to be one hundred feet long and eight feet four inches in circumference. At equal distances from these two posts two others are placed on each side, to form the width of the building; these are rather shorter than the first, and on them are laid in like manner spars, but of a smaller size, having the upper part hewed flat, with a narrow ridge on the outer side to support the ends of the planks. The roof is formed of pine planks with a **2** broad feather edge, so as to lap well over each other, which are laid lengthwise from the ridgepole in the centre, to the beams at the sides, after which the top is covered with planks of eight feet broad, which form a kind of covering projecting so far over the ends of the planks, that form the roof, as completely to exclude the rain. On these they lay large stones to prevent their being displaced by the wind. The ends of the planks are not secured to the beams on which they are laid by any fastening, so that in a high storm I have often known all the men obliged to turn out and go upon the roof to prevent them from being blown off, carrying large stones and pieces of rock with them to secure the boards, always stripping themselves naked on these occasions whatever may be the severity of the weather, to prevent their garments from being wet and muddied, as these storms are almost always accompanied with heavy rains. The sides of their houses are much more open and exposed to the weather; this proceeds from their not being so easily made close as the roof, being built with planks of about ten feet long and four or five **1** wide, which they place between stancheons or small posts of the height of the roof, of these there are four to each range of boards, two at each end and so near each other as to leave space enough for admitting a plank. The planks or boards which they make use of for building their houses, and for other uses, they procure of different lengths as occasion requires, by splitting them out, with hard wooden wedges from pine logs, and afterwards dubbing them down with their chizzels, with much patience, to the thickness wanted, rendering them quite smooth.

There is but one entrance; this is placed usually at the end, though sometimes in the middle as was that of Maquina's. Through the middle of the building from one end to the other, runs a passage of about eight or nine feet broad, on each side of which, the several families that occupy it, live, each having its particular fire-place, but without any kind of wall or separation to mark their respective limits; the chief having his apartment at the upper end, and the next in rank opposite on the other side. They have no other floor than the ground; the fire-place or hearth consists of a number of stones loosely put together, but they are wholly without a chimney, nor is there any opening left in the roof, but whenever a fire is made, the plank immediately over it is thrust aside, by means of a pole, to give vent to the smoke. The height of the houses in general, from the ground to the centre of the roof does not exceed ten feet, that of Maquina's was not far from fourteen; the spar forming the ridgepole of the latter was painted in red and black

*Frame of house at Yuquot (photographed in 1874), with carved post at rear and central beam with end carved as sea lion, could have been occupied in Jewitt's time. *10*

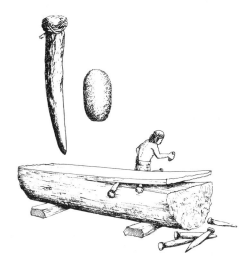

Splitting off planks from cedar log, using wooden wedges and hammer stone. 2

1 *ten feet long and four or five wide.* These measurements are no exaggeration. To the south of Yuquot, in Barkley Sound, is a fallen cedar tree that had planks split from it while it stood. The face of the scarred trunk, measuring close to 2.7 m × 1.2 m (9′ × 4′), is evidence of the size of planks split from cedars.

circles alternately by way of ornament, and the large

1 posts that supported it had their tops curiously wrought or carved, so as to represent human heads of a monstrous size, which were painted in their manner. These were not, however, considered as objects of adoration, but merely as ornaments.

The furniture of these people is very simple, and consists only of boxes in which they put their clothes, furs, and such things as they hold most valuable; tubs for keeping their provision of spawn and blubber in; trays from which they eat; baskets for their dried fish and other purposes, and bags made of bark matting, of which they also make their beds, spreading a piece of it upon the ground when they lie down, and using no other bed covering than their garments. The boxes are of pine, with a top that shuts over, and instead of nails

2 or pegs are fastened with flexible twigs, they are extremely smooth and high polished, and sometimes

3 ornamented with rows of very small white shells. The

4 tubs are of a square form, secured in the like manner, and of various sizes, some being extremely large, hav-

5 ing seen them that were six feet long by four broad and five deep. The Trays are hollowed out with their chiz-

6 zels from a solid block of wood, and the baskets and mats are made from the bark of trees. From this they likewise make the cloth for their garments, in the fol-

7 lowing manner. A quantity of this bark is taken and put into fresh water where it is kept for a fortnight to give it time to completely soften; it is then taken out and beaten upon a plank, with an instrument made of bone or some very hard wood, having grooves or hollows on one side of it, care being taken to keep the mass constantly moistened with water, in order to separate with more ease the hard and woody from the soft and fibrous parts, which, when completed, they parcel out into skeins, like thread. These they lay in the air to bleach, and afterwards dye them black or red as suits their fan-

1 *tops curiously wrought or carved*. Carved figures on the house posts were not simply for ornament. They depicted the inherited crests of the family within and were a great source of pride to the residents.

2 *flexible twigs*. These are the slender branches or withes of the red cedar, made more pliable by removing the bark and by twisting. The tensile strength of this material is nearly 69 000 kPa (10,000 lbs. p.s.i.). See illustration for manner of fastening.

3 *white shells*. Usually inlaid in rows around the edge of the box lid, the "shells" were most probably not shells but the opercula of red turban snails, which are found in local waters.

4 *tubs*. Jewitt uses the word tub for a large wooden container without a lid and for a box with a lid. Both are bentwood boxes unique to the people of the Northwest Coast, made by steambending a single plank to form the four sides, requiring only one corner to be joined; then attaching a base, usually by pegging.

5 *six feet long by four broad and five deep*. The dimensions of this box seem somewhat exaggerated; if these measurements are correct, this would be an exceptionally large container.

6 *baskets and mats*. These and many other household and ceremonial items were made from the inner bark of the red cedar.

7 *A quantity of this bark . . .* This description of bark preparation is correct for yellow cedar inner bark, not red, but very likely Jewitt did not recognize the difference. Because of its finer texture and pale colour, yellow cedar bark provided superior garments for high-ranking people.

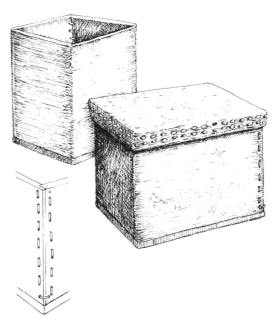

Bentwood box and chest, used for cooking, for storage of dried foods, oil, equipment and ceremonial regalia, or as coffin, etc. Detail shows corner sewn with cedar withe. 2

*Carved house post from old house at Kyuquot. *BCPM*

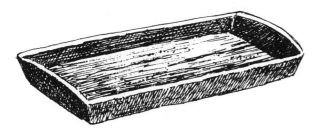

Wooden food tray, carved from a block of red alder, probably similar to those mentioned by Jewitt. About 46 cm (18"). MCRC

Red turban snail (Astraea gibberosa), found at low tide attached to rocks; its operculum was inlaid for decoration on carved wooden items. Average size about 16 mm (⁵⁄₈"). 23

Cedar bark mat, 80 cm × 117 cm (31½″ × 46″). Private collection.

Elderly woman, known as an expert basketmaker. *10

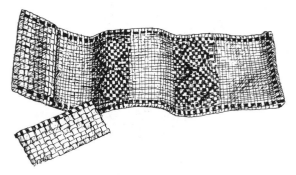

Cedar bark fishhook bag, with pouch that folded several times for extra protection. 56 cm (22″). BCPM/2

Basket of cedar bark and grass (probably swamp grass, Carex obnupta) from Nootka Sound. Designs made with grass dyed red and black. Diameter 21 cm (8¼″). VM

Whaler's bag held whaling equipment and also served as a drogue if harpooned whale towed canoe out to sea. 106 cm (42″). FMNH/2

cies, their natural colour being a pale yellow. In order to form the cloth, the women by whom the whole of this process is performed, take a certain number of these skeins and twist them together by rolling them with their hands upon their knees, into hard rolls, which are afterwards connected by means of a strong thread made **1** for the purpose.

Their dress usually consists of but a single garment, which is a loose cloak or mantle (called *Kutsack*) in one piece, reaching nearly to the feet. This is tied loosely over the right or left shoulder so as to leave the arms at full liberty.

Those of the common people are painted red with ochre the better to keep out the rain, but the chiefs wear them of their native colour, which is a pale yellow, ornamenting them with borders of the sea otter skin, a kind of grey cloth made of the hair of some animal **2** which they procure from the tribes to the South, or their own cloth wrought or painted with various figures in red or black, representing men's heads, the sun and moon, fish and animals, which are frequently executed with much skill. They have also a girdle of the same kind for securing this mantle, or *Kutsack,* around them, which is in general still more highly ornamented, and serves them to wear their daggers and knives in. In winter however, they sometimes make use of an additional garment, which is a kind of hood, with a hole in it for the purpose of admitting the head, and falls over the breast and back as low as the shoulders; this is bordered both at top and bottom with fur, and is never worn except when they go out. The garments of the women vary not essentially from those of the men, the mantle having holes in it for the purpose of admitting **3** the arms, and being tied close under the chin, instead of over the shoulder. The chiefs have also mantles of the sea otter skin, but these are only put on upon extraordinary occasions, and one that is made from the skin of a

*Woman weaving cedar bark blanket on wooden frame. *10*

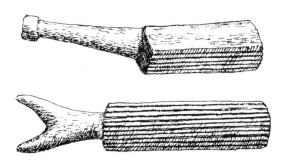

Bark beaters made of whalebone for shredding cedar bark for clothing and other uses. Each about 26 cm (10″). Top, HMG/1. Bottom, BM/5

1 *connected.* The method of "connecting" the rolls of bark was by twining done with cedar bark string.

2 *the hair of some animal.* The animal may well have been a dog bred specially for its wool by the Coast Salish of southern Vancouver Island and Puget Sound. Such wool, often mixed with that of the mountain goat, was traded to southern Nuu-chah-nulth groups who likely traded it (or finished blankets) to their northern neighbours at Yuquot.

3 *having holes.* As noted earlier, no garments with armholes have been collected or appear in historical illustrations, so this description is somewhat baffling.

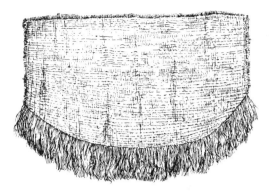

Fringed cedar bark blanket collected in 1778 by Cook expedition.
157.5 cm (62"). BM/2

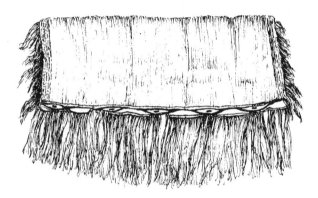

Cedar bark blanket with border woven in yellow and black wool;
design components are similar to eyes on wolf masks. Collected from
Nootka Sound by Cook expedition, 1778. 1.33 m (52½") BM/5

Double-layered cape of yellow cedar bark having traces of red pigment.
73.5 cm (29") long. NMI/2

Mountain goat (Oreamnos americanus), enjoys steep rocky terrain
at and above timber line. Its coat consists of long guard hairs over dense
white wool, the latter ideally suited to spinning and weaving.
Although hunted for its wool and meat, the wool was more easily
gathered from shrubs after the moult. Height at shoulder 91.5 cm
(36"). 23

Wool-bearing dog, as depicted in Paul Kane's 1855 oil painting
Clallam Woman Weaving a Blanket. ROM/23

Shredded cedar bark cape with red and black designs which include sea
mammals. 61 cm (24") long. ROM/2

certain large animal, which is brought from the South by the Wickanninish and Kla-iz-zarts. This they prepare by dressing it in warm water, scraping off the hair and what flesh adheres to it carefully with sharp muscle **1** shells, and spreading it out in the sun to dry, on a wooden frame, so as to preserve the shape. When dressed in this manner it becomes perfectly white and as pliable as the best deer's leather, but almost as thick again. They then paint it in different figures with such paints as they usually employ in decorating their persons: these figures mostly represent human heads, canoes employed in catching whales, &c. This skin is called Metamelth and is probably got from an animal of the moose kind, it is highly prized by these people, is **2** their great war dress, and only worn when they wish to make the best possible display of themselves. Strips or bands of it, painted as above, are also sometimes used by them for girdles or the bordering of their cloaks, and also for bracelets and ancle ornaments by some of the inferior class.

On their heads when they go out upon any excursion, particularly whaling or fishing, they wear a kind of cap or bonnet in form not unlike a large sugar loaf with the top cut off. This is made of the same materials with their cloth, but is in general of a closer texture and by way of tassel has a long strip of the skin of the Metamelth attached to it, covered with rows of small white shells or beads. Those worn by the common people are painted entirely red, the chiefs having theirs of different colours. The one worn by the king and **3** which serves to designate him from all the others, is longer and broader at the bottom; the top, instead of being flat, having upon it an ornament in the figure of a small urn. It is also of a much finer texture than the others and plaited or wrought in black and white stripes with the representation in front of a canoe in pursuit of a whale with the harpooner standing in the prow pre-

Elk or wapiti (Cervus canadensis), *source of* metamelth. 18

Rainproof hat tightly woven in double layer. Diameter 35.6 cm (14″). GM/2

1 *muscle shells.* Jewitt's spelling of this marine bivalve is incorrect. The mussel referred to is the large variety (*Mytilus californianus*) with thick, strong shells, which can grow to about 25 cm (10″) and more. Edge grinding made the shell sharp enough for use as a scraper, fish-cutting knife or harpoon head.

2 *moose.* The animal referred to here was very likely the elk (wapiti).

3 *The one worn by the king . . .* The hat was woven of fine spruce root, overlaid with a tall grass which the weaver dried and split into fine strands. Generally she used either basket sedge, which grew locally, or bear grass, traded from the Olympic Peninsula to the south. The weaver created the whale hunt scene by using strands of grass that she had coloured with vegetable dyes. A few Nuu-cha-nulth woman still make similar hats, now referred to as "Maquinna hats," using a different, less complex weaving technique.

Bulbous topped, conical hat woven from natural and dyed grass (probably swamp grass, Carex obnupta); *multicoloured design depicted whale hunt. Worn only by whaling chiefs. BM*

1 *berries.* Captain Cook's botanist recorded finding "plenty of elder, gooseberry and currant bushes" in Nootka Sound.

2 *raspberries.* Jewitt must have been mistaken in his identification, as the wild raspberry does not grow on that part of the coast.

pared to strike. This bonnet is called *Seeya-poks.*

Their mode of living is very simple—their food consisting almost wholly of fish, or fish spawn fresh or dried, the blubber of the whale, seal, or sea-cow, mus-
1 cles, clams, and berries of various kinds; all of which are eaten with a profusion of train oil for sauce, not excepting even the most delicate fruit, as strawberries and
2 raspberries. With so little variety in their food, no great can be expected, in their cookery. Of this, indeed, they may be said to know but two methods, viz. by boiling and steaming, and even the latter is not very frequently practised by them. Their mode of boiling is as follows: into one of their tubs, they pour water sufficient to cook the quantity of provision wanted. A number of heated stones are then put in to make it boil, when the salmon or other fish are put in without any other preparation than sometimes cutting off the heads, tails and fins, the boiling in the mean time being kept up by the application of the hot stones, after which it is left to cook until the whole is nearly reduced to one mass. It is then taken out and distributed in the trays. In a similar manner they cook their blubber and spawn, smoked or dried fish, and in fine, almost every thing they eat, nothing going down with them like broth.

When they cook their fish by steam, which are usually the heads, tails, and fins of the salmon, cod and halibut, a large fire is kindled, upon which they place a bed of stones, which, when the wood is burnt down, becomes perfectly heated. Layers of green leaves or pine boughs, are then placed upon the stones, and the fish, clams, &c. being laid upon them, water is poured over them, and the whole closely covered with mats to keep in the steam. This is much the best mode of cooking, and clams and muscles done in this manner, are really excellent. These, as I have said, may be considered as their only kinds of cookery; though I have in a very few instances known them dress the roe or spawn of the salmon and the herring, when first taken, in a different manner; this was by roasting them, the former being supported between two split pieces of pine, and the other having a sharp stick run through it, with one end fixed in the ground; sprats are also roasted by them in this way, a number being spitted on one stick; and this kind of food, with a little salt, would be found no contemptible eating even to a European.

At their meals they seat themselves upon the ground, with their feet curled up under them, around their trays, which are generally about three feet long by one board, **1** and from six to eight inches deep. In eating they make use of nothing but their fingers, except for the soup or oil, which they lade out with clam shells. Around one **2** of these trays, from four to six persons will seat themselves, constantly dipping in their fingers or clam shells, one after the other.—The king and chiefs alone have separate trays, from which no one is permitted to eat **3** with them, except the queen, or principal wife of the chief, and whenever the king or one of the chiefs wishes to distinguish any of his people with a special mark of favour on these occasions, he calls him and gives him some of the choice bits from his tray. The slaves eat at the same time, and of the same provisions, faring in this respect as well as their masters, being seated with the family and only feeding from separate trays. Whenever a feast is given by the king or any of the chiefs, there is a person who acts as a master of ceremonies, and whose business it is to receive the guests as they enter the house and point out to them their respective seats, which is **4** regulated with great punctiliousness as regards rank; the king occupying the highest or the seat of honour, his son or brother sitting next him, and so on with the chiefs according to their quality; the private persons belonging to the same family being always placed together to prevent any confusion. The women are seldom invited to their feasts, and only at those times when a gen-

Two cooking methods: box cooking using hot rocks to boil water in the box, and roasting small fish placed on sticks close to fire. Redrawn from a watercolour sketch by John Webber, 1778.

*Shells of horse clam (*Schizothaerus nuttalli*), used as food dishes and ladles, grow to 20.3 cm (8″). 24*

1 *board.* This is a typographical error; it should read "broad."

2 *clam shells.* These were likely a species of horse clam or the geoduck, both of which have large, deep shells.

3 *trays.* On important occasions, a chief used a large carved feast dish that had a name. He might sing a song about the dish telling how he had acquired it.

4 *respective seats.* The order of seating, which had great importance throughout the coast, was a way of acknowledging and confirming the rank and status of individuals. The order of rank for seating members of a family at a feast also held for seating them in a canoe.

Carved bowl collected by Cook expedition from Nootka Sound, 1778. 29.2 cm (11½"). BM

eral invitation is given to the village.

As whenever they cook, they always calculate to have an abundance for all the guests, a profusion in this respect being considered as the highest luxury, much more is usually set before them than they can eat. That which is left in the king's tray he sends to his house for his family, by one of his slaves, as do the chiefs theirs, while those who eat from the same tray and who generally belong to the same family, take it home as common **1** stock, or each one receives his portion, which is distributed on the spot. This custom appeared very singular to my companion and myself, and it was a most awkward thing for us at first, to have to lug home with us, in our hands or arms, the blubber or fish that we received at these times; but we soon became reconciled to it, and were very glad of an opportunity to do it.

In point of personal appearance the people of Nootka are among the best looking of any of the tribes that I have seen. The men are in general from about five feet six to five feet eight inches in height; remarkably straight, of a good form, robust, and strong, with their limbs in general well turned and proportioned excepting the legs and feet, which are clumsy and ill formed, owing no doubt to their practice of sitting on them, though I have seen instances in which they were very well shaped; this defect is more particularly apparent in the women, who are for the most part of the time within doors, and constantly sitting while employed in their cooking and other occupations. The only instance of deformity that I saw among them was a man of dwarfish stature; he was thirty years old and but three feet three inches high; he had however no other defect than this diminutive size, being well made, and as strong and able to bear fatigue as what they were in general. Their complexion, when freed from the paint and oil with which their skins are generally covered, is a brown, somewhat inclining to a copper cast. The shape of the

1 *each one receives his portion.* The custom of giving guests a quantity of food demonstrated the host's wealth and generosity and provided sustenance for those travelling often long distances home. The recipient of a large amount of food was, in turn, expected to give a feast when he returned to his village; thus distribution of surplus foods to others was ensured. Not to accept the food would be an insult to the host.

face is oval; the features are tolerably regular, the lips being thin and the teeth very white and even: their eyes are black but rather small, and the nose pretty well formed, being neither flat nor very prominent: their hair is black, long and coarse, but they have no beard, completely extirpating it, as well as the hair from their bodies, Maquina being the only exception, who suffered his beard to grow on his upper lip, in the manner of mustachios, which was considered as a mark of dignity. As to the women they are much whiter, many of them not being darker than those in some of the Southern parts of Europe. They are in general very well looking and some quite handsome. Maquina's favorite wife in particular, who was a Wickinninish princess, would be considered as a beautiful woman in any country. She was uncommonly well formed, tall, and of a majestic appearance: her skin remarkably fair for one of these people, with considerable colour, her features handsome and her eyes black, soft, and languishing; her hair was very long, thick, and black, as is that of the females in general, which is much softer than that of the men; in this they take much pride, frequently oiling and plaiting it carefully into two broad plaits, tying the ends with a strip of the cloth of the country and letting it hang down before on each side of the face.

The women keep their garments much neater and cleaner than the men, and are extremely modest in their deportment and dress; their mantle or Katsack, which is longer than that of the men, reaching quite to their feet, and completely enveloping them, being tied close under the chin, and bound with a girdle of the same cloth or of sea otter skin around their waists; it has also loose sleeves which reach to the elbows. Though fond of ornamenting their persons they are by no means so partial to paint as the men, merely colouring their eyebrows black and drawing a bright red stripe from each corner of the mouth towards the ear. Their ornaments

*Young man of the Nuu-chah-nulth people. *VPL*

*Man wearing bearskin. *VPL*

Girl from Hesquiat. *13

Left: Woman wearing clothing of shredded cedar bark, with hat of woven grass. Redrawn from an early Spanish watercolour. 5

Right: Young child of the Nuu-chah-nulth people. *OHS

Young girl wearing bark blanket. *10

High-class woman adorned with shell nose-ring, copper earrings, necklace and bracelet of dentalia shells. 23

Woman of Nootka Sound wearing cedar bark blanket. *BCPM

consist chiefly of ear-rings, necklaces, bracelets, rings for the fingers and ankles, and small nose jewels, (the latter are however wholly confined to the wives of the king or chiefs) these are principally made out of copper or brass, highly polished and of various forms and sizes; the nose jewel is usually a small white shell or bead suspended to a thread. The wives of the common people frequently wear for bracelets and ankle rings, strips of the country cloth or skin of the Metamelth painted in figures, and those of the king or principal chiefs bracelets and necklaces, consisting of a number of strings of *Ife-waw,* an article much prized by them, and **1** which makes a very handsome appearance. This *Ife-waw,* as they term it, is a kind of shell of a dazzling whiteness, and as smooth as ivory, it is of a cylindrical form, in a slight degree curved, about the size of a goose quill, hollow, three inches in length and gradually tapering to a point, which is broken off by the natives as it is taken from the water; this they afterwards string upon threads of bark, and sell it by the fathom; it forms a kind of circulating medium among these nations, five fathoms being considered as the price of a slave their most valuable species of property. It is principally obtained from the Aitizzarts, a people living about thirty or forty miles to the Northward, who collect it from the reefs and sunken rocks with which their coast **2** abounds, though it is also brought in considerable quantity from the South. Their mode of taking it has been thus described to me. To one end of a pole is fastened a piece of plank in which a considerable number of pine pegs are inserted, made sharp at the ends; above the plank in order to sink it, a stone or some weight is tied, and the other end of the pole suspended to a long rope; this is let down perpendicularly by the *Ife-waw* fishers in those places where that substance is found, which are usually from fifty to sixty fathoms deep; on finding the bottom they raise the pole up a few

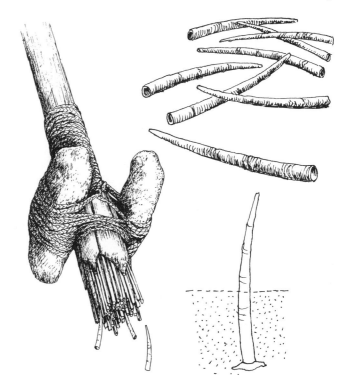

Left: Model of spear used by Nuu-chah-nulth to gather dentalia shells, though this one not exactly as described by Jewitt. Length of stones about 30.5 cm (12"). BCPM 8

Right: Dentalia shells (Dentalium pretiosum), also known as tusk shells and tooth shells. Up to 7 cm (2¾"). 23

1 *Ife-waw.* Spelled various ways by Jewitt, this refers to *Dentalium pretiosum,* the larger of two species of dentalium found on the Northwest Coast. Also called tooth shell, tusk shell and tusk money, these delicate white shells were an important trade item for many of the Nuu-chah-nulth prior to the availability of goods from white traders. West coast people had a monopoly on dentalia, trading it (sorted by size) in standard lengths or containers, to people all up the Pacific coast. Through successive trading, the shells found their way over the coastal mountains and inland as far as the Great Plains.

2 *reefs and sunken rocks.* Jewitt is mistaken; dentalia live partially buried in the sand, not on rocks and reefs, though the beds of these shellfish may lie in association with rocks.

feet and let it fall, this they repeat a number of times as if sounding, when they draw it up and take off the *Ife-waw* which is found adhering to the points. This method of procuring it is very laborious and fatiguing, especially as they seldom take more than two or three of these shells at a time, and frequently none.

Though the women, as I have said, make but little use of paint, the very reverse is the case with the men. In decorating their heads and faces they place their principal pride, and none of our most fashionable beaus, when preparing for a grand ball can be more particular: For I have known Maquina after having been employed for more than an hour in painting his face, rub the whole off and recommence the operation anew when it did not entirely please him. The manner in which they paint themselves frequently varies, according to the occasion, but it oftener is the mere dictate of whim.—The most usual method is to paint the eye-brows black, in form of a half moon, and the face red in small squares, with the arms and legs and part of the body red; sometimes one half of the face is painted red in squares, and the other black; at others, dotted with red spots, or red and black instead of squares, with a variety of other devices, such as painting one half of the face and body red, and the other black. But a method of painting which they sometimes employed, and which they were much more particular in, was by laying on the face a quantity of bear's grease of about one eighth of an inch thick; this they raised up into ridges resembling a small bead in joiner's work, with a stick prepared for the purpose, and then painted them red, which gave the face a very singular appearance. On extraordinary occasions, the king and principal chiefs used to strew over their faces, after painting, a fine black shining powder, procured from some mineral, as Maquina told me it was got from the rocks. This they call *pelpelth,* and value it highly, as, in their opinion, it serves to set off

1 *adhering to the points.* The dentalia shells became lodged between the splints, not on the points, because the opening at the top of the shell was much too small for the point to enter.

2 *pelpelth.* This is black mica (known as biotite), which is generally found in exposed veins and often in streambeds. It differs from white mica in having iron as one of its constituents.

their looks to great advantage, glittering, especially in the sun, like silver.—This article is brought them in bags by the *Newchemass,* a very savage nation who live a [1] long way to the North, from whom they likewise receive a superior kind of red paint, a species of very fine and rich ochre, which they hold in much estimation. [2]

Notwithstanding this custom of painting themselves, they make it an invariable practice, both in summer and winter, to bathe once a day, and sometimes oftener; but [3] as the paint is put on with oil, it is not much discomposed thereby, and whenever they wish to wash it off, they repair to some piece of fresh water and scour themselves with sand or rushes.

In dressing their heads on occasion of a festival or visit, they are full as particular, and almost as long, as in painting. The hair, after being well oiled, is carefully gathered upon the top of the head and secured by a piece of pine or spruce bough with the green leaves upon it. After having it properly fixed in this manner, the king and principal chiefs used to strew all over it the white down obtained from a species of large brown eagle, [4] which abounds on this coast, which they are very particular in arranging so as not to have a single feather out of place, occasionally wetting the hair to make it adhere. This, together with the bough, which is sometimes of considerable size, and stuck over the feathers by means of turpentine, gives them a very singular and grotesque [5] appearance, which they, however, think very becoming, and the first thing they do on learning the arrival of strangers is to go and decorate themselves in this manner.

The men also wear bracelets of painted leather or copper, and large ear-rings of the latter—but the ornament on which they appear to set the most value, is the nose-jewel, if such an appellation may be given to the wooden stick, which some of them employ for this purpose. The king and chiefs, however, wear them of a dif-

Bald eagle (Haliaeetus leucocephalus); *white head and tail indicate a mature bird. Wingspan can measure up to 2 m (6′).* 23

1 *Newchemass.* These were probably the Nimpkish, who lived on the Nimpkish River, in the northeastern part of Vancouver Island. Inland trading trails, linked by rivers and lakes, connected these people with those on the west coast of the island.

2 *ochre.* During the Spanish occuptation of the village, seamen bought red ochre from the native people, mixed it with whale oil and used it to paint their ships.

3 *bathe.* In 1868, Gilbert Sproat wrote that "till beyond middle age many of the natives bathe every day in the sea, and in winter rub their bodies with oil after coming out of the sea."

4 *large brown eagle.* The bald eagle is abundant along the coast of British Columbia. The immature bird is brown and develops the distinctive white head and tail at maturity—about five years of age.

5 *turpentine.* Although turpentine is extracted from a resinous substance exuded by certain conifers, Jewitt is referring here to a glue made from the resin of (most likely) the spruce tree. The sticky resin liquifies when heated to boiling point, then solidifies when cool. It is also waterproof.

Barkley Sound man with a wooden or bone ornament worn through septum of nose. *10

1 *twisted conical shell.* Most likely the purple olivella found on the west coast of Vancouver Island, from Cape Scott south to Juan de Fuca Strait.

2 *pipe stem.* The pipe referred to is the European clay pipe with a long, slender stem about 7 mm (¼″) thick.

3 *sprit-sail yard.* The sprit-sail is a small, square sail set beneath the bowsprit of a square-rigged sailing ship. The yard is the timber that spreads the sail.

4 *brace him up sharp to the wind.* A ship doing this would turn about thirty degrees in another direction.

5 *The sea-otter is . . .* This is a somewhat strange description of the sea otter. The largest adult measures up to 1.5 m (5′), including the tail; its ears are inconspicuous and it has no central tuft of head fur, though possibly grooming the wet fur gave it that appearance. Sea otters of all ages have head fur of a lighter colour than the rest of the body, so perhaps Jewitt saw this as a broad band of white.

ferent form, being either small pieces of polished copper or brass, of which I made many for them, in the shape

1 of hearts and diamonds, or a twisted conical shell about half an inch in length of a blueish colour and very bright, which is brought from the South. These are suspended by a small wire or string to the hole, in the gristle of the nose, which is formed in infancy, by boring it with a pin, the hole being afterwards enlarged by the repeated insertion of wooden pegs of an increased size, until it becomes about the diameter of a

2 pipe stem, though some have them of a size nearly sufficient to admit the little finger.—The common class who cannot readily procure the more expensive jewels that I have mentioned, substitute for them, usually a smooth round stick, some of which are of an almost incredible length, for I have seen them projecting not less than eight or nine inches beyond the face on each side; this is made fast or secured in its place by little wedges on each

3 side of it. These sprit-sail-yard fellows, as my messmate used to call them, when rigged out in this manner made quite a strange show, and it was his delight whenever he saw one of them coming towards us with an air of consequence proportioned to the length of his stick, to put up his hand suddenly as he was passing him, so as to strike the stick, in order, as he said, to

4 brace him up sharp to the wind; this used to make them very angry, but nothing was more remote from Thompson's ideas than the wish to cultivate their favour.

The natives of Nootka appear to have but little inclination for the chase, though some of them were expert marksmen, and used sometimes to shoot ducks and geese, but the seal and the sea-otter form the principal objects of their hunting, particularly the latter. Of this animal, so much noted for its valuable skin, the follow-

5 ing description may not be uninteresting. The sea-otter is nearly five feet in length, exclusive of the tail, which

Sea otter hunter. *13

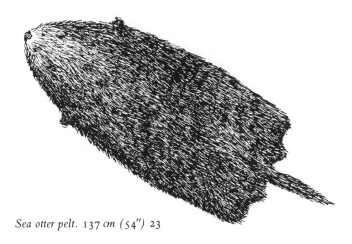

Sea otter pelt. 137 cm (54″) 23

Sea otter (Enhydra lutris lutris)*, prized by fur traders, spends most of its life in sea. Its fur, sleek when wet, needs constant grooming to maintain insulating qualities.* 23

Northern sea lion (Eumetopias jubata) *hunted by native peoples.* 18

Harbour seal, also called hair seal (Phoca vitulina)*, often basks on rocks close to water, presenting vulnerable target for hunters silently approaching by canoe.* 18

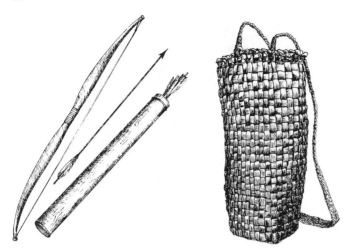

*Left: Bow, arrow and quiver, used in hunting sea otter. Bow was generally made from western yew (*Taxus brevifolia*) or wild crabapple (*Pyrus fusca*). Average bow about 106 cm (42"). 8*

Right: Hunter's quiver with shoulder strap. 35 cm (13¾"). VM/2

1 *the fur.* Sea otter fur has more than 100 800 hairs per square centimetre (650,000 per square inch), twice the density of the fur seal.

2 *a prime skin.* A celebrated trader, Capt. William Sturgis of Boston, Massachusetts, described a top sea otter skin thus: "A full grown, prime, which has been stretched before drying, is about five feet long and twenty four to thirty inches wide, covered with very fine hair, three fourths of an inch in length, having a rich jet black, glossy surface, and exhibiting a silver colour when blown open."

3 *The food of the sea-otter . . .* This sea mammal's staple food is sea urchins, but it also eats crabs, mollusks, shrimp and worms. It must eat 20 to 25 per cent of its body weight in food each day in order to maintain its high metabolic rate.

4 *three or four young . . .* Sea otters produce only one pup every second year, another factor that contributed to their swift decline and eventual extinction on the coast of Vancouver Island. The mother does not deposit her young anywhere; it clings to her body by its teeth, or she holds it in her front paws on her chest while she swims on her back. A young cub cannot swim until it is several months old.

is about twelve inches, and is very thick and broad where it joins the body, but gradually tapers to the end, which is tipped with white. The colour of the rest is a shining silky black, with the exception of a broad white stripe on the top of the head. Nothing can be more beautiful than one of these animals when seen swimming, especially when on the lookout for any object. At such times it raises its head quite above the surface, and the contrast between the shining black and the white, together with its sharp ears and a long tuft of hair rising from the middle of its forehead, which look like three small horns, render it quite a novel and attractive object. They are in general very tame, and will permit a canoe or boat to approach very near before they dive. I was told, however, that they are become much more shy since they have been accustomed to shoot them with muskets, than when they used only arrows. The skin is held in great estimation in China, more espe- **1** cially that of the tail, the fur of which is finer and closer set than that on the body. This is always cut off and sold separately by the natives. The value of a skin is deter- **2** mined by its size, that being considered as a prime skin which will reach, in length, from a man's chin to his **3** feet. The food of the sea-otter is fish, which he is very dexterous in taking, being an excellent swimmer, with feet webbed like those of a goose.—They appear to be wholly confined to the sea-coast, at least to the salt **4** water. They have usually three or four young at a time, but I know not how often they breed, nor in what places they deposit their young, though I have frequently seen them swimming around the mother when no larger than rats. The flesh is eaten by the natives, cooked in their usual mode by boiling, and is far preferable to that of the seal of which they make much account.

But if not great hunters there are few people more expert in fishing. Their lines are generally made from the

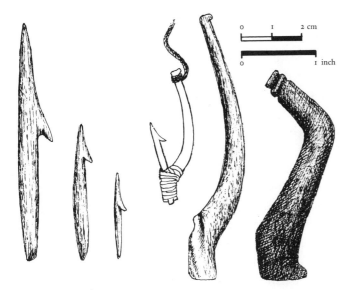

Fishhook barbs and shanks from the Yuquot excavation. Left: three barbed bone points of varying size. Right: shank of bone (note groove for holding barb) and one of stone. Centre: assembled hook, with leader for attaching to fish line. PC

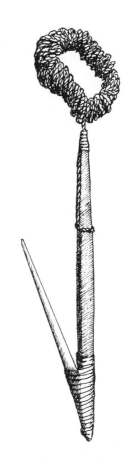

Fishhook with bone barb and cedar bark line, from Nootka Sound. BM/5

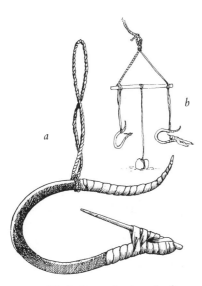

Halibut fishing gear. a. Hook of steam-bent wood, often yew (Taxus brevifolia) with bone point. b. Method of rigging baited hooks, with line going to surface float. 4

Fisherman returning with load of flounder or small halibut. *WSHS

Humpback whale (Megaptera novaeangliae), which reaches 15.2 m
(50′), was probably the species hunted by Maquinna in summer
months. 23

Grey whale (Eschrichtius glaucus) hunted off the coast by
Maquinna in spring, could reach 13.7 m *(45′).* 22

1 *Bearded.* An old word for barbed.

2 *muscle shell.* The mussel shell used for the whaling harpoon
blade was *Mytilus californianus,* a large species that can grow to
about 25.4 cm (10″). Spruce resin filled and covered the shell,
except for its cutting edge.

sinew of the whale, and are extremely strong. For the
hook, they usually make use of a straight piece of hard
wood, in the lower part of which is inserted and well
secured, with thread or whale sinew, a bit of bone made
1   very sharp at the point and bearded; but I used to make
for them hooks from iron, which they preferred, not
only as being less liable to break, but more certain of
securing the fish. Cod, halibut, and other seafish were
not only caught by them with hooks, but even salmon.
To take this latter fish, they practise the following
method—One person seats himself in a small canoe, and
baiting his hook with a sprat, which they are always
careful to procure as fresh as possible, fastens his line to
the handle of the paddle; this, as he plies it in the water,
keeps the fish in constant motion, so as to give it the appearance of life, which the salmon seeing, leaps at it and
is instantly hooked, and by a sudden and dexterous motion of the paddle, drawn on board. I have known some
of the natives to take no less than eight or ten salmon of
a morning in this manner, and have seen from twenty to
thirty canoes at a time in Friendly Cove thus employed.
They are likewise little less skilful in taking the whale.
This they kill with a kind of javelin or harpoon, thus
constructed and fitted. The barbs are formed of bone
which are sharpened on the outer side and hollowed
within for the purpose of forming a socket for the staff;
these are then secured firmly together with whale
sinew, the point being fitted so as to receive a piece of
2   muscle shell which is ground to a very sharp edge, and
secured in its place by means of turpentine. To this head
or prong is fastened a strong line of whale sinew about
nine feet in length, to the end of which is tied a bark
rope from fifty to sixty fathoms long, having from
twenty to thirty seal skin floats or buoys, attached to it
at certain intervals, in order to check the motion of the
whale and obstruct his diving. In the socket of the harpoon a staff or pole of about ten feet long, gradually

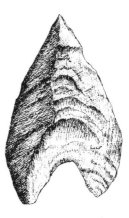

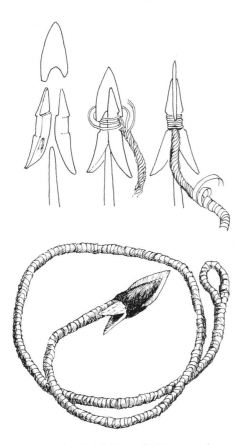

Metal whaling harpoon head with lanyard. Diagrams show
components and assemblage of composite toggling harpoon head. 8

Sealskin floats used in whaling. Seal hide, turned inside out, was well
scraped and lashed tightly where head, flippers and tail had been cut
off. Painted designs at these points identified owner of float. *23

Shell of sea or California mussel (Mytilus californianus) used for
blade of whaling harpoon head. These shellfish can grow to about 25.4
cm (10"). 23

Harpoon point cut and ground from large mussel shell. 8.3 cm (3¼").
MCRC/3

Whaling harpoon head in protective cedar bark cover. 23 cm (9"). 8

Large canoes held many people and possessions while travelling between villages. 23

1 *The whale is . . .* Another precept of the hunt was that whaling villages should keep within their own recognized whaling grounds, which were each some distance apart.

2 *sea cow.* The Steller's sea cow, known as the dugong, was a large herbivorous marine mammal, native to the Alaskan coast, already hunted to extinction by early fur traders who relished its beeflike meat and sweet-tasting oil. Jewitt probably is referring to the northern sea lion; males can attain a length of 3.4 m (11′) and weigh up to 998 k (2,200 lbs.).

3 *the use of iron.* It is not known exactly how far back iron was used by Northwest Coast peoples, nor from where or whom it originally came. Captain Cook noted in 1778 that the use of iron was already widespread, and an archaeological excavation directed by Richard Daugherty at Ozette, on the Olympic Peninsula, Washington, revealed the rusted iron blades of high-quality tools that date to 500 years ago.

tapering from the middle to each end, is placed: this the harpooner holds in his hand in order to strike the whale, and immediately detaches it as soon as the fish is struck.

1 The whale is considered as the king's fish, and no other person, when he is present, is permitted to touch him until the royal harpoon has first drawn his blood, however near he may approach; and it would be considered almost as sacrilege for any of the common people to strike a whale, before he is killed, particularly if any of the chiefs should be present. They also kill the porpoise

2 and sea cow with harpoons, but this inferior game is not interdicted the lower class.

With regard to their canoes, some of the handsomest to be found on the whole coast are made at Nootka, though very fine ones are brought by the Wickanninish and the Klaiz-zarts, who have them more highly ornamented. They are of all sizes, from such as are capable of holding only one person to their largest war canoes which will carry forty men, and are extremely light. Of these, the largest of any that I ever saw, was one belonging to Maquina, which I measured and found to be *forty-two* feet *six* inches in length at the bottom, and *forty-six* feet from stem to stern. These are made of pine hollowed out from a tree with their chisels solely, which are about three inches broad and six in length, and set into a handle of very hard wood. This instrument was formerly made of flint or some hard stone ground down to as sharp an edge as possible, but since they have

3 learned the use of iron, they have almost all of them of that metal. Instead of a mallet for striking this chisel, they make use of a smooth round stone, which they hold in the palm of the hand. With this same awkward instrument they not only excavate their canoes and trays and smooth their plank, but cut down such trees as they want, either for building, fuel, or other purposes, a labour which is mostly done by their slaves.

The falling of trees as practised by them is a slow and

most tedious process, three of them being generally from two to three days in cutting down a large one, yet so attached were they to their own method, that notwithstanding they saw Thompson frequently with one of our axes, of which there was a number saved, fall **1** a tree in less time than they could have gone round it with their chisels, still they could not be persuaded to make use of them.

After hollowing out their canoes, which they do very neatly, they fashion the outside, and slightly burn it for **2** the purpose of removing any splinters or small points that might obstruct its passage through the water, after which they rub it over thoroughly, with rushes or **3** coarse mats, in order to smooth it, which not only renders it almost as smooth as glass, but forms a better security for it from the weather; this operation of burning and rubbing down the bottoms of their canoes is practised as often as they acquire any considerable degree of roughness from use. The outside, by this means becomes quite black, and to complete their work they paint the inside of a bright red, with ochre or some other similar substance; the prows and sterns are almost always ornamented with figures of ducks or some other kind of bird, the former being so fashioned as to represent the head and the latter the tail, these are separate pieces from the canoe, and are fastened to it with small flexible twigs or bark cord. Some of these canoes, par- **4** ticularly those employed in whaling, which will hold about ten men, are ornamented within about two inches below the gunwale, with two parallel lines on each side of very small white shells running fore and aft, which **5** has a very pretty effect. Their war canoes have no ornament of this kind but are painted on the outside with figures in white chalk representing eagles, whales, hu- **6** man heads, &c. They are very dexterous in the use of their paddles, which are very neatly wrought, and are five feet long with a short handle and a blade seven

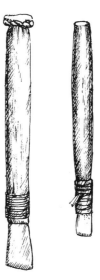

Chisels. Left: with bone blade, 40.6 cm (16″) Right: with iron blade, cherry bark lashing, 84 cm (33″). BCPM

1 *axes.* Native people quickly recognized the advantage of iron blades over stone blades on their cutting tools, but were reluctant to use the axe, an unfamiliar tool.

2 *slightly burn it . . .* Scorching the canoe hull also hardened the wood and helped to protect it from splitting.

3 *rushes.* These may well have been scouring rush, which contains natural silica, a fine abrasive, and which was often used by native carvers for a fine, smooth finish.

4 *bark cord.* The bark cord would no doubt have been made from inner cedar bark.

5 *white shells.* These could have been the opercula of red turban snails or sea otter teeth.

6 *white chalk.* Obviously chalk would not have been suitable for ornamenting a canoe. Jewitt is probably referring to a white paint made from mixing calcined clamshells with a binding agent, most likely the albumen of salmon eggs.

Left: Common scouring rush (Equisetum hiemale) *abounds along streams, swampy places and other moist ground. Grows to a height of about 1.5 m (5').* 23

Right: Paddle, probably of yew wood or yellow cedar. 10

1 *The language of . . .* That Jewitt noticed the difference between the language used for conversation and that used for songs indicates the depth of his acute interest in and observation of the culture. Some songs may have been an old form of the language or may have been learned from a group speaking a different dialect.

inches broad in the middle tapering to a sharp point. With these they will make a canoe skim very swiftly on the water with scarcely any noise, while they keep time to the stroke of the paddle with their songs.

With regard to these they have a number which they sing on various occasions; as war* whaling, and fishing, at their marriages and feasts, and at public festivals or **1** solemnities. The language of the most of these appears to be very different, in many respects, from that used in their common conversation, which leads me to believe either that they have a different mode of expressing themselves in poetry, or that they borrow their songs from their neighbors, and what the more particularly induces me to the latter opinion, is, that whenever any of the Newchemass, a people from the Northward and who speak a very different language, arrived, they used to tell me that they expected a new song, and were almost always sure to have one.

Their tunes are generally soft and plaintive, and though not possessing great variety, are not deficient in harmony.—Their singing is generally accompanied with several rude kinds of instrumental music; among the most prominent of which is a kind of drum. This is nothing more than a long plank hollowed out on the under side and made quite thin, which is beat upon by a stick of about a foot long and renders a sound not unlike beating on the head of an empty cask, but much louder. But the two most favorite instruments are the rattle and the pipe or whistle; these are however only used by the king, the chiefs, or some particular persons; the former is made of dried seal-skin, so as to represent a fish, and is filled with a number of small smooth pebbles, it has a short handle and is painted red. The whistle is made of bone, generally the leg of a deer, it is short but emits a

* A specimen of one of their war songs will be found at the end of this work.

very shrill sound. They have likewise another kind of music, which they make use of in dancing, in the manner of castanets, this is produced by a number of muscle or cockle shells tied together and shaken to a kind of tune, which is accompanied with the voice.

Their slaves, as I have observed, form their most valuable species of property.—These are of both sexes, being either captives taken by themselves in war, or purchased from the neighboring tribes, and who reside in the same house, forming as it were a part of the family, are usually kindly treated, eat of the same food, and live as well as their masters. They are compelled however at times to labour severely, as not only all the menial offices are performed by them, such as bringing water, cutting wood and a variety of others, but they are obliged to make the canoes, to assist in building and repairing the houses, to supply their masters with fish, and to attend them to war and to fight for them. None **2** but the king and chiefs have slaves, the common people being prevented from holding them either from their inability to purchase them, or as I am the rather inclined to think from its being considered as the privilege of the former alone to have them, especially as all those made prisoners in war belong either to the king or the chiefs, who have captured them, each one holding such as have been taken by himself or his slaves. There is probably however some little distinction in favour of the king, who is always the commander of the expedition, as Maquina had nearly fifty, male and female, in his house, a number constituting about one half of its inhabitants, comprehending those obtained by war and purchase, whereas none of the other chiefs had more than twelve. The females are employed principally in manufacturing cloth, in cooking, collecting berries, &c. and with regard to food and living in general have not a much harder lot than their mistresses, the principal difference consisting, in these poor unfortunate creatures being

Ceremonial rattle made of deer hoofs, with sections of bird quills attached to cedar withe. 12.7 cm (5"). GM/2

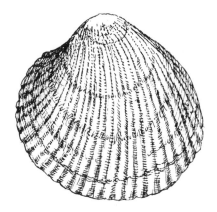

Cockle shell (Clinocardium nuttalli), average size 7.6 cm (3"). 23

1 *slaves.* Gilbert Sproat wrote of the Nuu-chah-nulth in 1868: "A slave was considered a useful and honourable possession, and if lost or sold, was replaced immediately with another."

2 *None but the king and chief have slaves . . .* Almost every well-born person owned a slave, and chiefs generally had from five to twelve, depending on their status. For Maquinna to have fifty slaves was certainly a reflection of his uncommonly high position, wealth and power.

96

*Left: Woman from a southern people, her head flattened by steady pressure of board in a specially rigged cradle. *VPL*

*Right: Woman with sugar-loaf shaped head comes from a northern people. *8*

1 *to visit Nootka.* In his journal, Jewitt records more than ninety canoe visits.

2 *Kla-iz-zarts.* Nuu-chah-nulth people used the name Kla-iz-zarts to refer to the Makah of Cape Flattery on the Olympic Peninsula, Washington, though that name was not used by the people themselves. It translates as "southerly people," with the literal meaning based on a word stem meaning "outside, towards the sea," an appropiate description of the Makah's position on the Olympic Peninsula, as compared to others along the coast. The distance from Nootka Sound to the Kla-iz-zarts is only about half that given by Jewitt—who did not go there.

considered as free to any one, their masters prostituting them whenever they think proper for the purpose of gain. In this way many of them are brought on board the ships and offered to the crews, from whence an opinion appears to have been formed by some of our navigators, injurious to the chastity of their females, than which nothing can be more generally untrue, as perhaps in no part of the world is that virtue more prized.

The houses at Nootka as already stated, are about twenty, without comprising those inhabited by the Klahars, a small tribe that has been conquered and incorporated into that of Nootka, though they must be considered as in a state of vassalage as they are not permitted to have any chiefs among them, and live by themselves in a cluster of small houses at a little distance from the village. The Nootka tribe which consists of about five hundred warriors, is not only more numerous than almost any of the neighbouring tribes, but far exceeds them in the strength and martial spirit of its people; and in fact there are but few nations within a hundred miles either to the North or South but are considered as tributary to them.

1 In giving some account of the tribes that were accustomed to visit Nootka, I shall commence at the Southward with the Kla-iz-zarts, and the Wickinninish, premising that in point of personal appearance there prevails a wonderful diversity between the various tribes on the coast, with the exception of the feet and legs, which are badly shaped in almost all of them from **2** their practice of sitting on them. The Kla-iz-zarts are a numerous and powerful tribe, living nearly three hundred miles to the South, and are said to consist of more than a thousand warriors. They appear to be more civilized than any of the others, being better and more neatly dressed, more mild and affable in their manners, remarkable for their sprightliness and vivacity, and celebrated for their singing and dancing. They exhibit also great marks of improvement in whatever is wrought by them; their canoes, though not superior to those of Nootka in point of form and lightness, being more highly ornamented, and their weapons and tools of every kind have a much higher finish and display more skill in the workmanship. Their cast of countenance is very different from that of the Nootkians, their faces being very broad, with a less prominent nose and smaller eyes, and the top of the head flattened as if it had **1** been pressed down with a weight. Their complexion is also much fairer, and their stature shorter, though they are well formed and strongly set. They have a custom which appears to be peculiar to them, as I never observed it in any of the other tribes, which is to pluck out **2** not only their beards, and the hair from their bodies, but also their eye-brows, so as not to leave a vestige remaining. They were also in general more skilful in painting and decorating themselves, and I have seen some of them with no less than a dozen holes in each of their ears to which were suspended strings of small beads about two inches in length. Their language is the **3** same as spoken at Nootka, but their pronunciation is much more hoarse and guttural. These people are not only very expert in whaling, but are great hunters of the sea otter and other animals with which their country is said to abound, as the Metamelth a large animal of the deer kind, the skin of which I have already spoken of, another of a light grey colour, with very fine hair from which they manufacture a handsome cloth, the beaver and a species of large wild cat, or tyger cat. **4**

The Wickinninish, their neighbours on the North, are about two hundred miles from Nootka. They are a robust, strong and warlike people, but considered by the Nootkians as their inferiors in courage. This tribe is more numerous than that of Nootka, amounting to between six and seven hundred warriors. Though not so

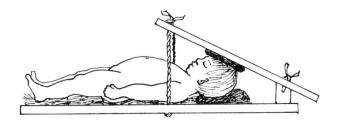

Cradle board in position for flattening an infant's head. 7

To achieve sugar-loaf head shape, cradle was rigged with soft hide straps and shredded cedar bark pads that applied gentle, constant pressure to top and sides of an infant's skull. 2

1 *the top of the head flattened . . .* Many coastal peoples practised cranial deformation—a mark of high rank. One method involved gentle and constant pressure of a board on an infant's head during the first few months after birth, in a cradle equipped for this procedure. The result was a broad, flattened head, as Jewitt describes.

2 *to pluck out . . .* Tweezers for plucking out facial hair consisted of a pair of small mussel shells.

3 *Their language is the same . . .* Originally the Kla-iz-zarts, or Makah, were Nuu-chah-nulth living, it is said, on the Jordan River. Crowded conditions led to a migration south to Cape Alava, where the village of Ozette was established over 2000 years ago; hence the similarity of language.

4 *wild cat, or tyger cat.* This was most likely a cougar, also known as a mountain lion or puma, and still abundant on Vancouver Island.

Left: Cougar, also called mountain lion and puma (Felis concolor). 18

Right: Beaver (Castor canadensis) inhabits streams and lakes in forested areas; its meat was eaten by many native peoples. Total length 112 cm (44"). 18

1 *the shape of a sugar loaf.* This description better fits the Koskimo people who lived north of Yuquot. To achieve the sugar-loaf shape, a sign of high birth, the cradle was rigged with soft deerhide straps and cedar bark pads to apply gentle but constant pressure to top and sides of the infant's skull. In 1868, Gilbert Sproat wrote of "a girl with a sugar-loaf head, measuring eighteen inches from the eyes to the summit."

2 *Maqunia's* Arcomah, *or Queen* . . . Maquinna's marriage to the daughter of the chief of a strong and powerful group is typical of marriages made for the purpose of forming or strengthening an alliance with a potential enemy, particularly one whose warriors outnumber one's own, as in this case.

3 *rivers, creeks, and marshes.* Such an environment would account for the 20 February entry in Jewitt's journal: "Arrived a canoe from Esquates with forty pair of wild geese, employed attending upon the strangers."

4 *forty miles.* Forty miles (64.3 km) is the correct distance, but since Jewitt did not go there, it is interesting to speculate whether the native people by this time had a knowledge of miles, or whether Jewitt calculated distance by the time it took for paddlers to travel it. Some of his other mileages are incorrect.

civilized as the Kla-iz-zarts and less skilful in their manufactures, like them they employ themselves in hunting as well as in whaling and fishing. Their faces are broad but less so than the Kla-iz-zarts, with a darker complexion, and a much less open and pleasing expression of countenance, while their heads present a very different form, being pressed in at the sides and lengthened towards the top, somewhat in the shape of a sugar loaf. **1** These people are very frequent visitors at Nootka, a close friendship subsisting between the two nations, Maqunia's *Arcomah,* or Queen, *Y-ya-tintla-no,* being the **2** daughter of the Wickinninish king. The Kla-oo-quates adjoining them on the North are much less numerous, their force not exceeding four hundred fighting men; they are also behind them in the arts of life. These are a fierce, bold, and enterprizing people, and there were none that visited Nootka, whom Maquina used to be more on his guard against, or viewed with so much suspicion. The Eshquates are about the same number; these are considered as tributary to Maquina: Their coast abounds with rivers, creeks, and marshes. To the North **3** the nearest tribe of any importance is the Aitizzarts; these however do not exceed three hundred warriors. In appearance they greatly resemble the people of Nootka, to whom they are considered as tributary, their manners, dress, and style of living also being very similar. They reside at about forty miles distance up the sound. **4** A considerable way further to the northward are the *Cayuquets;* these are a much more numerous tribe than that of Nootka, but thought by the latter to be deficient in courage and martial spirit, Maquina having frequently told me that their hearts were little like those of birds.

There are also both at the North and South many other intervening tribes, but in general small in number and insignificant, all of whom as well as the above mentioned speak the same language. But the Newchemass who come from a great way to the Northward, and from some distance inland, as I was told by Maquina, speak quite a different language, although it is well understood by those of Nootka. These were the most savage looking and ugly men that I ever saw, their complexion being much darker, their stature shorter, and their hair coarser, than that of the other nations, and their dress and appearance dirty in an extreme. They wear their beards long like Jews, and have a very morose and surly countenance. Their usual dress is a *Kootsuck* made of wolk skin, with a number of the tails attached to it, of which I have seen no less than ten on one garment, hanging from the top to the bottom; though they sometimes wear a similar mantle of bark cloth, of a much coarser texture than that of Nootka, the original colour of which appears to be the same, though from their very great filthiness, it was almost impossible to discover what it had been. Their mode of dressing their hair also varies essentially from that of the other tribes, for they suffer that on the back of the head to hang loose, and bind the other over their foreheads in the manner of a fillet, with a strip of their country cloth, **2** ornamented with small white shells. Their weapons are the *Cheetoolth,* or war club, which is made from whale bone, daggers, bows and arrows, and a kind of spear pointed with bone or copper. They brought with them no furs for sale, excepting a few wolf skins, their merchandize consisting principally of the black shining mineral called pelpelth, and the fine red paint which they carefully kept in close mat bags, some small dried salmon, clams, and roes of fish, with occasionally a little coarse matting cloth. They were accustomed to remain a much longer time at Nootka than the other tribes, in order to recover from the fatigue of a long journey, part of which was over land, and on these occasions taught their songs to our savages. The trade of most of the other tribes with Nootka was principally

1

2

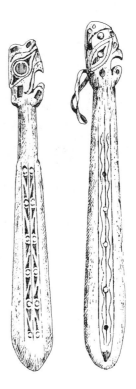

Whalebone clubs used in warfare. Vancouver expedition collected these two from Nootka Sound, 1792. Left, 54 cm (21¼"), UM. Right, RAM.

War club of whalebone, carved with eagle, two animals (possibly bear and wolf) and human: not a traditional design and possibly used ceremonially. BCPM/13

1 *a different language . . .* The language would be a dialect of Kwakiutl, another of the Wakashan language groups, and most probably understood by the people of Yuquot because of frequent trading over a long period of time, and possibly intermarriage.

2 *fillet.* A narrow headband.

Young Clayoquot girl. *23

1 *yama.* The salal plant has purple-black berries much favoured among all the Northwest Coast peoples who had access to them. Women mashed and boiled the fruit, often with other berries, and dried them in cake form for winter use.

2 *whale sinew.* Strong and flexible, whale sinew was especially useful for the harpoon lines used in whaling and other sea mammal hunting.

3 *Quawnoose.* The 6 July 1805 entry in Jewitt's journal states: "This day arrived canoes from Clar-zarts with nine skins and three large baskets of an excellent fruit, called by the natives Quawnoose." The fuller description here of a root food identifies it as the blue camas (either *Camassia leichtlinii* or *C. quamash,* the latter having a smaller bulb). The word quamash is derived from the native name for this food plant, once an important staple of the Coast Salish and other southern people in whose area it grew in great abundance.

4 *tributary offerings.* A portion of the foods taken from territories owned by a chief were given to him as tribute and served to confirm his owner's rights to those lands.

5 *a great feast is always made . . .* "An Indian who thinks anything of himself, never gets a deer or a seal, or even a quantity of flour, without inviting his friends to a feast," wrote Gilbert Sproat in 1868.

train oil, seal or whale's blubber, fish fresh or dried, herring or salmon spawn, clams, and muscles, and the **1** *yama,* a species of fruit which is pressed and dried, cloth, sea otter skins, and slaves. From the Aitizzarts, and the Cayuquets, particularly the former, the best I-whaw and in the greatest quantities was obtained. The Eshquates furnished us with wild ducks and geese, particularly the latter. The Wickinninish and Kla-iz-zarts brought to market many slaves, the best sea otter skins, **2** great quantities of oil, whale sinew, and cakes of the *yama,* highly ornamented canoes, some I-whaw, red ochre and pelpelth of an inferior quality to that obtained from the Newchemass, but particularly the so much valued *Metamelth,* and an excellent root called by the **3** Kla-iz-zarts *Quawnoose.* This is the size of a small onion, but rather longer, being of a tapering form like a pear, and of a brownish colour. It is cooked by steam, is always brought in baskets ready prepared for eating, and is in truth a very fine vegetable, being sweet, mealy and of a most agreeable flavour. It was highly esteemed by the natives who used to eat it as they did everything else with train oil.—From the Kla-iz-zarts was also received, though in no great quantity, a cloth manufactured by them from the fur already spoken of, which feels like wool and is of a grey colour.

Many of the articles thus brought, particularly the **4** provisions, were considered as presents, or tributary offerings, but this must be viewed as little more than a nominal acknowledgment of superiority, as they rarely failed to get the full amount of the value of their presents. I have known eighteen of the great tubs, in which they keep their provisions, filled with spawn **5** brought in this way. On these occasions a great feast is always made, to which not only the strangers, but the whole village, men, women, and children are generally invited, and I have seen five of the largest tubs employed at such time in cooking at the king's house. At these feasts they generally indulge in eating to an excess, making up in this respect for their want of inebriating liquors, which they know no method of preparing in any form, their only drink being water.

Whenever they came to visit or trade it was their general custom, to stop a few miles distant under the lee of some bluff or rock, and rig themselves out in their best manner, by painting and dressing their heads. On their **1** first coming on shore, they were invited to eat by the king, when they brought to him, such articles as he wanted, after which the rest of the inhabitants were permitted to purchase, the strangers being careful to keep them in their canoes until sold, under strict guard to prevent their being stolen, the disposition of these people for thieving being so great, that it is necessary to keep a watchful eye upon them.

This was their usual mode of traffick, but whenever they wished to purchase any particular object, as for instance, a certain slave, or some other thing of which they were very desirous, the canoe that came for this purpose would lie off at a little distance from the shore, and a kind of embassador or representative of the king or chief by whom it was sent, dressed in their best manner, and with his head covered with the white down, would rise, and after making known the object of his mission in a pompous speech, hold up specimens of such articles as he was instructed to offer in payment, mentioning the number or quantity of each, when if the bargain was concluded, the exchange was immediately made.

On their visits of friendship or traffick, the chiefs alone used to sleep on shore, this was generally at the house of the king or head chief, the others passing the night on board of their canoes, which was done not only for the preservation of their property, but because they were not permitted to remain on shore, lest they might excite some disturbance or commit depredations.

*Flowers and edible bulbs of blue camas (*Camassia quamash*). Bulbs about 5 cm (2"). 23*

1 *On their first coming on shore . . .* This description of traditional buying and selling substantiates the experiences of early ships' captains who found the native people to be skilled and shrewd traders.

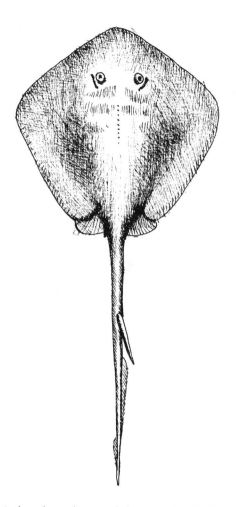

*Kyuquot is about the northernmost habitat boundary for the sting ray (*Dasyatis dipterurus)*. It measures up to 1.8 m (6′) and carries a viciously sharp bone barb on its tail. 19*

1 *the bone of the sting ray.* The diamond stingray inhabits the waters off the west coast of Vancouver Island and south to California. The single spine on its whiplike tail is long, sharp and serrated, making it ideal for a spearhead, though Jewitt's reference to such a weapon is unique.

All these people generally go armed, the common class wearing only a dagger, suspended from their neck behind, with a string of metamelth, and sometimes thrust in their girdles. The chiefs in addition to the dagger carry the *Cheetoolth,* or war-club suspended in the same manner beneath their mantles; this in the hands of a strong man is a powerful weapon, in the management of which, some of the older chiefs are very dexterous. It is made from the bone of a whale, and is very heavy. The blade is about eighteen inches long and three broad, till it approaches near the point, where it expands to the breadth of four inches. In the middle, from whence it slopes off gradually to an edge on each side, it is from one to two inches in thickness. This blade is usually covered with figures of the sun and moon, a man's head, &c. and the hilt which is made to represent the head of a man or some animal, is curiously set with small white shells, and has a band of metamelth fastened to it in order to sling it over the shoulder. Some of the tribes have also a kind of spear headed with copper or **1** the bone of the sting ray, which is a dangerous weapon; this is however not usual, and only carried by the chiefs. The bow and arrow are still used by a few, but since the introduction of fire arms among them, this weapon has been mostly laid aside.

But to return to our unhappy situation. Though my comrade and myself fared as well, and even better than we could have expected among these people, considering their customs and mode of living, yet our fears lest no ship would come to our release, and that we should never more behold a Christian country, were to us a source of constant pain. Our principal consolation in this gloomy state, was to go on Sundays, whenever the weather would permit, to the borders of a fresh water pond, about a mile from the village, where, after bathing, and putting on clean clothes, we would seat ourselves under the shade of a beautiful pine, while I read some chapters in the Bible, and the prayers appointed by our Church for the day, ending our devotions with a fervent prayer to the Almighty that he would deign still to watch over and preserve our lives, rescue us from the hands of the savages, and permit us once more to behold a Christian land. In this manner were the greater part of our Sundays passed at Nootka; and I felt grateful to heaven, that amidst our other sufferings, we were at least allowed the pleasure of offering up our devotions unmolested, for Maquina, on my explaining to him as well as was in my power the reason of our thus retiring at this time, far from objecting, readily consented to it. The pond above mentioned was small, not more than a **1** quarter of a mile in breadth and of no great length, the water being very clear, though not of great depth, and bordered by a beautiful forest of pine, fir, elm, and **2** beach, free from bushes and underwood—a most delightful retreat, which was rendered still more attractive by a great number of birds that frequented it, particularly the humming bird. Thither we used to go to wash our clothes, and felt secure from any intrusion from the natives, as they rarely visited it except for the purpose of cleansing themselves of their paint.

In July we at length thought that the hope of delivery we had so long anxiously indulged, was on the point of being gratified. A ship appeared in the offing, but alas, our fond hopes vanished almost as soon as formed; for instead of standing in for the shore she passed to the northward and soon disappeared. I shall not attempt to describe our disappointment—my heart sunk within me, and I felt as though it was my destiny never more to behold a Christian face. Four days after there occurred a tremendous storm of thunder and lightning, during which the natives manifest great alarm and terror, the whole tribe, hurrying to Maquina's house, where, instead of keeping within, they seated themselves on the roof amid the severest of the tempest, drumming upon

Jewitt Lake. 23

1 *The pond.* This "pond" is larger than Jewitt realized, as most of it is hidden by a mountain ridge. Perhaps it would have been a further consolation to the captive had he known that this body of water would one day bear the name of Jewitt Lake.

2 *elm, and beach.* Botany seems not to have been Jewitt's strong point, as he is again mistaken in his tree identification. Neither elm nor beech grow in the area, though he might have mistaken large alders for elms.

*Stinging nettle (*Urtica doica*).* 21

1 *Quahootze.* Several early historic accounts refer to Quahootze (spelling varies) as a single deity to whom people prayed. Twentieth-century consultants have told of the Four Chiefs: Above Chief, Horizon Chief, Land Chief and Undersea Chief, called on in prayers during ritual bathing. Andy Callicum contends that Quahootze was the grandson of the Great Spirit comprising the Four Grandfathers. Representing the four winds, they were the Grandfather in the east, in the west, in the south and in the north.

2 *Spanish garden.* Growing in rich midden earth, this vegetable garden evidently perpetuated itself for quite some time after the Spanish pulled out in 1795. In August of that year John Boit, aboard the *Union,* wrote about "A vast many canoes, with Green Peas & Beans, Cabbages etc, which they collected from ye remains of the Spanish gardens." Jewitt and Thompson harvested from the abandoned garden eight years later.

3 *young nettles.* When steamed or boiled, the young tops of stinging nettles lose their sting and make a tasty potherb.

the boards, and looking up to heaven, while the king beat the long hollow plank, singing, and as he afterwards told me, begging *Quahootze,* the name they gave to God, not to kill them, in which he was accompanied by the whole tribe; this singing and drumming was continued until the storm abated.

1

As the summer drew near its close, we began to suffer from the frequent want of food, which was principally owing to Maquina and the chiefs being out whaling, in which he would not permit Thompson and myself to join, lest we should make our escape to some of the neighbouring tribes. At these times the women seldom or ever cook any provision, and we were often hungry, but were sometimes fortunate enough to procure secretly, a piece of salmon, some other fish, spawn, or even blubber, which, by boiling in salt water, with a few onions and turnips, the remains of the Spanish garden, or young nettles and other herbs, furnished us a delicious repast in private. In the mean time, we frequently received accounts from the tribes who came to Nootka, both from the north and south, of there being vessels on the coast, and were advised by their chiefs to make our escape, who also promised us their aid, and to put us on board. These stories, however, as I afterwards learned, were almost all of them without any foundation, and merely invented by these people with a view to get us into their power in order to make slaves of us themselves, or to sell us to others. But I was still more strongly solicited to leave Nootka by a woman. This was a Wickinninish princess, a younger sister of Maquina's wife, who was there on a visit. I had the good fortune, if it may be so called, to become quite a favourite with her. She appeared much interested for me—asked me many questions respecting my country, if I had a mother and sister at home, and if they would not grieve for my absence. Her complexion was fairer

2, 3

than that of the women in general, and her features more regular, and she would have been quite handsome had it not been for a defect in one of her eyes, the sight of which had been injured by some accident, the reason, as Maquina told me, why she had not been married, a defect of this kind being by these savages considered as almost an insuperable objection. She urged me repeatedly to return with her, telling me that the Wickinninish were much better than the Nootkians; that her father would treat me more kindly than Maquina, give me better food and clothes, and finally put me on board one of my own country vessels. I felt, however, little disposed to accompany her, considering my situation with Maquina full as eligible as it would be with the Wickinninish, if not better, notwithstanding all she said to the contrary.

On the third of September, the whole tribe quitted Nootka, according to their constant practice, in order to pass the autumn and winter at Tashees and Cooptee, the **1** latter lying about thirty miles up the Sound in a deep bay, the navigation of which is very dangerous from the great number of reefs and rocks with which it abounds. On these occasions every thing is taken with them, even **2** the planks of their houses, in order to cover their new dwellings. To an European, such a removal exhibits a scene quite novel and strange: canoes piled up with boards and boxes, and filled with men, women and children of all ranks and sizes, making the air resound with their cries and songs. At these times, as well as when they have occasion to go some distance from their houses, the infants are usually suspended across the mother's shoulders, in a kind of cradle or hammock, formed of bark, of about six inches in depth, and of the length of the child, by means of a leather band inserted through loops on its edges; this they also keep them in when at home, in order to preserve them in a straight

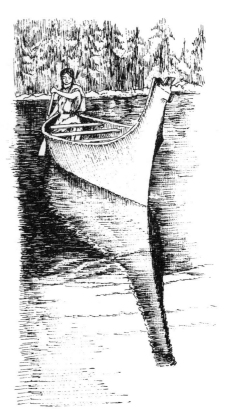

*Women were equally as skilled in paddling as men. *BCPM*

1 *the latter lying about thirty miles up the Sound.* It is not the latter but Tashees that lies about thirty miles [9 km] up the sound. Tashees was a major salmon fishing village for Maquinna's people, who spent considerable time there taking and preserving provisions for winter. A logging company town established in 1944 at the head of the inlet bears the name Tahsis, as do the inlet, the narrows and the river. The name is derived from the Wakashan word *taci* or *taxi*, meaning "doorway" or "entrance," referring to the start of an overland trading trail from the village to Kwakiutl territory lying to the northwest.

2 *On these occasions . . .* One practical advantage of leaving a village for a period of time was that its nonoccupation allowed birds, animals and the weather to clean up any fish remains and other organic trash lying about, both indoors and out.

Site of Coopte (or Cooptee), DksSp 1, 1975. Note canoe runways (pathways cleared of rocks) along beach. Drawn from photograph, courtesy Alan McMillan.

1 *Cooptee.* This account of the location of Cooptee is puzzling. Jewitt was there at least twice, yet his description of it does not in any way match the present village site known as Coopte (Indian Reserve No. 9), which is not on a south bank, a deep bay or a river as described. However, Tahsis is about 24 km (15 mi.) from Cooptee and through such wilderness as Jewitt describes; but it is a long narrow inlet, not a river, though it does end with a river flowing into it. Possibly Alsop added the imagined landscape as an afterthought.

2 *trees of the country.* These are principally red cedar, western hemlock, spruce and species of fir—all conifers.

3 *twenty rods.* A rod is an old English linear measurement, also known as a pole or a perch, equal to 16′6″ (5 m). Thus, the width of the river at the village site was about 100 m (330′). The exact site of Maquinna's fishing village has not yet been located, but a large pulp mill, a lumber mill and the town of Tahsis at the head of the inlet may have obliterated any remains.

position, and prevent any distortion of the limbs, most probably a principal cause of these people being so seldom deformed or crooked.

The long boat of our ship having been repaired and furnished with a sail by Thompson, Maquina gave us the direction of it, we being better acquainted with managing it than his people, and after loading her as deep as she could swim, we proceeded in company with them to the north, quitting Nootka with heavy hearts, as we could entertain no hopes of release until our return, no ships ever coming to that part of the coast. **1** Passing Cooptee, which is situated on the southern bank, just within the mouth of a small river flowing from the east in a narrow valley at the foot of a mountain, we proceeded about fifteen miles up this stream to Tashees, between a range of lofty hills on each side, which extend a great distance in-land, and are covered **2** with the finest forest trees of the country. Immediately on our arrival, we all went to work very diligently in covering the houses with the planks we had brought, the frames being ready erected, these people never pretending to remove the timber. In a very short time the work was completed, and we were established in our new residence.

Tashees is pleasantly situated and in a most secure position from the winter storms, in a small vale or hollow on the south shore, at the foot of a mountain. The spot on which it stands is level, and the soil very fine, the country in its vicinity abounding with the most romantic views, charmingly diversified, and fine streams of water falling in beautiful cascades from the **3** mountains. The river at this place is about twenty rods in width, and in its deepest part, from nine to twelve feet. This village is the extreme point of navigation, as immediately beyond, the river becomes much more shallow, and is broken into rapids and falls. The houses here are placed in a line like those at Nootka, but closer together, the situation being more confined they are also smaller, in consequence of which we were much crowded, and incommoded for room.

The principal object in coming to this place, is the facility it affords these people of providing their winter stock of provisions, which consists principally of salmon, and the spawn of that fish; to which may be added herring and sprats, and herring spawn. The latter, however, is always procured by them at Nootka, previous to their quitting it. At the seasons of spawning, which are early in the spring and the last of August, they collect a great quantity of pine branches, which they place **1** in different parts of the Cove at the depth of about ten feet and secure them by means of heavy stones. On these the herring deposit their spawn in immense quantities; the bushes are then taken up, the spawn stripped from the branches, and after being washed and freed from the pine leaves by the women, is dried and put up in baskets for use. It is considered as their greatest delicacy, and eaten both cooked and raw: in the former case, being boiled and eaten with train oil, and in the latter, mixed up with cold water alone.

The salmon are taken at Tashees, principally in pots or wears. Their method of taking them in wears is thus:—A pot of twenty feet in length, and from four to **2** five feet diameter at the mouth, is formed of a great number of pine splinters which are strongly secured, an inch and a half from each other, by means of hoops made of flexible twigs, and placed about eight inches apart. At the end it tapers almost to a point, near which is a small wicker door, for the purpose of taking out the fish. This pot or wear is placed at the foot of a fall or rapid, where the water is not very deep, and the fish driven from above with long poles, are intercepted and caught in the wear, from whence they are taken into the canoes. In this manner I have seen more than seven hundred salmon caught in the space of fifteen minutes. I

Herring spawn on hemlock boughs. Jewitt's journal for 2 April states: "This day the natives employed in putting down pine bushes in the salt water for herring to spawn on." 23

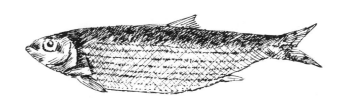

Herring (Culpea pallasii) *grow up to 30.5 cm (12″).* 20

1 *pine branches.* The branches were probably western hemlock, as the flat surface of the needled boughs made it easier to remove the spawn after it dried.

2 *A pot . . .* The pot described was a very efficient basket trap made of cedar wood slats, held in place by cedar withe hoops. The wicker door mentioned likely refers to the weave—a rigid warp and a flexible weft. The basket trap was used with weirs, which were fencelike constructions that guided the salmon into the mouth of the trap.

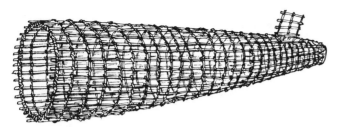

Fish trap used with fence weirs in river; weirs guided salmon migrating upriver into trap, 6 m (20') in length, 1.2 to 1.5 m (4' to 5') in diameter at mouth. 4

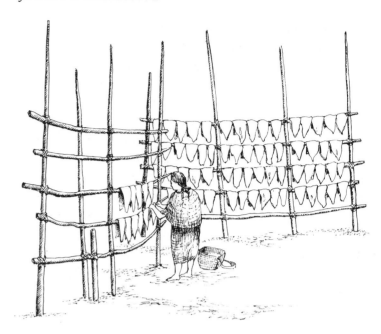

*Women cut halibut into thin fillets to facilitate drying, then hung them on rack outdoors before taking them in for final drying over fire. *TBM*

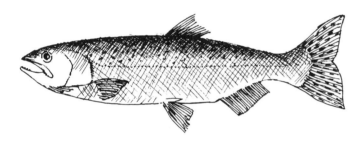

Coho or silver salmon (Oncorhynchus kisutch), *one of several species on the coast. Average size 76 cm (30″).* 19

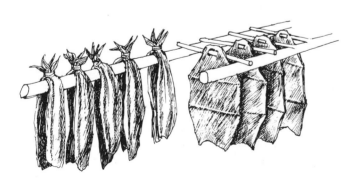

Salmon hanging to dry; backs were cut out with flesh on and dried separately. 10

*Harpooning salmon as they congregate near river or creek mouth prior to ascending to spawning grounds. *VPL*

have also sometimes known a few of the striped bass **1** taken in this manner but rarely.

At such times there is great feasting and merriment among them. The women and female slaves being busily employed in cooking, or in curing the fish for their winter stock, which is done by cutting off the heads and tails, splitting them, taking out the back bone, and hanging them up in their houses to dry. They also dry the halibut and cod, but these instead of curing whole they cut up into small pieces for that purpose, and expose to the sun. The spawn of the salmon, which is a principal article of their provision, they take out, and without any other preparation, throw it into their tubs, where they leave it to stand and ferment, for though they frequently eat it fresh, they esteem it much more when it has acquired a strong taste, and one of the greatest favours they can confer on any person, is to invite him to eat *Quakamiss,* the name they give this food, though scarcely any thing can be more repugnant to a European palate, than it is in this state; and whenever they took it out of these large receptacles, which they are always careful to fill, such was the stench which it exhaled, on being moved, that it was almost impossible for me to abide it, even after habit, had in a great degree dulled the delicacy of my senses.—When boiled it became less offensive, though it still retained much of the putrid smell and something of the taste.

Such is the immense quantity of these fish, and they are taken with such facility, that I have known upwards of twenty-five hundred brought into Maquina's house at once, and at one of their great feasts, have seen one hundred or more cooked in one of their largest tubs.

I used frequently to go out with Maquina upon these fishing parties, and was always sure to receive a handsome present of salmon, which I had the privilege of calling mine; I also went with him several times in a canoe, to strike the salmon, which I have attempted to **2**

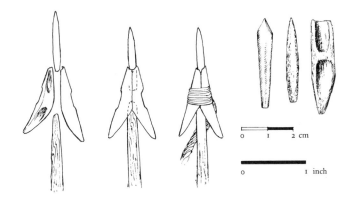

Left: Assemblage of composite toggling harpoon heads for salmon fishing, from Yuquot. PC/14. Right: Bone points and valve for this assemblage, from Yuquot. 4

1 *striped bass.* The striped bass is generally found in coastal waters to the south. If Jewitt's identification was correct, an upswelling of a warm current (El Niño) could account for its presence in the Nootka Sound area.

2 *fishing parties.* Jewitt's journal entries for July include:
"July 13th. This day I went fishing with our chief in a canoe, caught four salmon and returned.
"July 14th. Employed fishing with our chief; caught five salmon.
"July 15th. We are pleased at seeing the chiefs brought so low as to be obliged themselves to go a fishing."

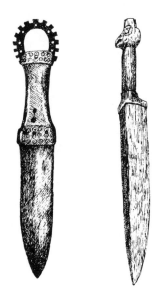

Left: Knife with iron blade, bone haft and top decoration of brass, collected from Yuquot by Mr. Fish, lighthouse keeper at Nootka light (Friendly Cove) from 1928 to 1936, who was told it had been made by John Jewitt. Knife is typical of those tied to thigh of wolf dancer. 32 cm (12⅝"). VM

Right: Dagger of whalebone, with carved eagle head, collected from Yuquot early in twentieth century, 41 cm (16⅛"). VM

1 *if he ever saw me writing* . . . Writing about this in his journal, Jewitt says: "Notwithstanding his threats I shall continue to avail myself of every opportunity to fill it up when he is fishing."

2 *daggers.* Jewitt's journal entry for 10 January 1804: "Our chief bought my dagger for which he gave me a coat that was made and another that was not." This gesture shows the kindly side of Maquinna's nature.

do myself, but could never succeed, it requiring a degree of adroitness that I did not possess. I was also permitted to go out with a gun, and was several times very successful in shooting wild ducks, and teal, which are very numerous here, though rather shy. These they cooked in their usual manner, by boiling, without any farther dressing than skinning them. In many respects, however, our situation was less pleasant here than at Nootka. We were more incommoded for room, the houses not being so spacious, nor so well arranged, and as it was colder, we were compelled to be much more within doors. We however, did not neglect on Sundays, when the weather would admit, to retire into the woods, and by the side of some stream, after bathing, return our thanks to God for preserving us, and offer up to him our customary devotions. I was however, very apprehensive, soon after our arrival at this place, that I should be deprived of the satisfaction of keeping my journal, as Maquina one day observing me writing in it, enquired of me what I was doing, and when I endeavoured to explain it, by telling him that I was keeping an account of the weather, he said it was not so, and that I was speaking bad about him and telling how he had taken our ship and killed the crew, so as to inform my **1** countrymen, and that if he ever saw me writing in it again, he would throw it into the fire. I was much rejoiced that he did no more than threaten, and became very cautious afterwards not to let him see me write.

2 Not long after I finished some daggers for him, which I polished highly; these pleased him much, and he gave me directions to make a cheetoolth, in which I succeeded so far to his satisfaction, that he gave me a present of cloth sufficient to make me a complete suit of raiment, besides other things. Thompson, also, who had become rather more of a favourite than formerly, since he had made a fine sail for his canoe, and some garments for him out of European cloth, about this time completed another, which was thought by the savages a most superb dress. This was a *Kootsuk* or mantle, a fathom square, made entirely of European vest patterns of the gayest colours. These were sewed together, in a manner to make the best show, and bound with a deep trimming of the finest otter skin, with which the arm-holes were also bordered; while the bottom was farther embellished with five or six rows of gilt buttons, placed as near as possible to each other. Nothing could exceed the pride of Maquina when he first put on this royal robe, decorated like the coat of Joseph, with all the colours of the rainbow, and glittering with the buttons, which as he strutted about made a tinkling, while he repeatedly exclaimed in a transport of exultation, *Klew shish Katsuck —wick kum atack Nootka.* A fine garment— Nootka cant make him.   **1**

Maquina, who knew that the chiefs of the tribes who came to visit us, had endeavoured to persuade me to es-cape, frequently cautioned me not to listen to them, saying that should I make the attempt, and he were to take me, he should certainly put me to death. While here he gave me a book in which I found the names of seven persons belonging to the ship Manchester of **2** Philadelphia, Capt. Brian, viz.—Daniel Smith, Lewis Gillon, James Tom, Clark, Johnson, Ben and Jack. These men, as Maquina informed me, ran away from the ship, and came to him, but that six of them soon af-ter went off in the night, with an intention to go to the Wickinninish, but were stopped by the Eshquiates, and sent back to him, and that he ordered them to be put to death; and a most cruel death it was, as I was told by one the natives, four men holding one of them on the ground, and forcing open his mouth, while they choaked him by ramming stones down his throat. As to Jack the boy, who made no attempt to go off, Maquina afterwards sold him to the Wickinninish. I was in-formed by the princess *Yuqua,* that he was quite a small

1 *Nootka.* If, indeed, Maquinna used the word Nootka, it might have been because all the European seamen, Jewitt included, called the village by that name. It is interesting to speculate why, even after more than two years of living with Maquinna and his people, Jewitt did not learn the actual name of the village. Had he done so, surely he would have noted it.

2 *the ship Manchester.* The *Manchester* a 285-ton (290-t) vessel from Bristol, Philadelphia, was trading on the coast in 1801 when this incident occurred. The captain's name was Brice, not Brian.

boy, who cried a great deal, being put to hard labour beyond his strength by the natives, in cutting wood and bringing water, and that when he heard of the murder of our crew, it had such an effect on him that he fell sick and died shortly after. On learning the melancholy fate of this unfortunate lad, it again awakened in my bosom those feelings that I had experienced at the shocking death of my poor comrades.

The king finding that I was desirous of learning their language, was much delighted, and took great pleasure in conversing with me. On one of these occasions, he explained to me his reasons for cutting off our ship, saying that he bore no ill will to my countrymen, but that he had been several times treated very ill by them. The first injury of which he had cause to complain, was **1** done him by a Captain Tawnington, who commanded a schooner which passed a winter at Friendly Cove, where he was well treated by the inhabitants. This man taking advantage of Maquina's absence, who had gone to the Wickinninish to procure a wife, armed himself and crew, and entered the house where there were none but women, whom he threw into the greatest consternation, and searching the chests, took away all the skins, of which Maquina had no less than forty of the best; and that about the same time, four of their chiefs **2** were barbarously killed by a Captain Martinez, a Span-**3** iard. That soon after Captain Hanna, of the Sea-Otter, in consequence of one of the natives having stolen a chisel from the carpenter, fired upon their canoes which were along side, and killed upwards of twenty of the natives, of whom several were *Tyees* or chiefs, and that he himself being on board the vessel, in order to escape was obliged to leap from the quarter deck, and swim for a long way under water.

These injuries had excited in the breast of Maquina, an ardent desire of revenge, the strongest passion of the savage heart, and though many years had elapsed since

1 *Captain Tawnington.* Shipping records for the Northwest Coast do not include a Captain Tawnington, nor any name similar. Possibly Jewitt's version of a name already mispronounced by the native people rendered it unrecognizable.

2 *Captain Martinez.* Estevan Martinez, commander of the Spanish corvette *Princesa,* arrived in Nootka Sound in May 1789 and established a small fort on an island close by Yuquot. Estevan Point, about 27 km (17 mi.) to the south and now the site of a lighthouse, was named after him.

3 *Captain Hanna.* Capt. James Hanna, who outfitted the *Sea Otter* in 1785 at Macao, was the first of many fur traders to ply the Pacific Northwest Coast.

The Sea Otter firing upon the Natives.

their commission, still they were not forgotten, and the want of a favourable opportunity alone prevented him from sooner avenging them. Unfortunately for us, the long wished for opportunity at length presented itself in our ship, which Maquina finding not guarded with the usual vigilance of the North West Traders, and feeling his desire of revenge rekindled by the insult offered by Capt. Salter, formed a plan for attacking, and on his return, called a council of his chiefs, and communicated it to them, acquainting them with the manner in which he had been treated. No less desirous of avenging this affront offered their king, than the former injuries, they readily agreed to his proposal, which was to go on board without arms as usual, but under different pretexts, in greater numbers, and wait his signal for the moment of attacking their unsuspecting victims. The execution of this scheme, as the reader knows, was unhappily too successful.—And here I cannot but indulge a reflection that has frequently occurred to me on the manner in which our people behave towards the na-

Picking salalberries (Gaultheria shallon). *BCPM

Salalberry (Gaultheria shallon). 21

tives. For though they are a thievish race, yet I have no doubt that many of the melancholy disasters have principally arisen from the imprudent conduct of some of the captains and crews of the ships employed in this trade, in exasperating them by insulting, plundering, and even killing them on slight grounds. This, as nothing is more sacred with a savage than the principle of revenge, and no people are so impatient under insult, induces them to wreak their vengeance upon the first vessel or boat's crew that offers, making the innocent too frequently suffer for the wrongs of the guilty, as few of them know to discriminate between persons of the same general appearance, more especially when speaking the same language. And to this cause do I believe, must principally be ascribed the sanguinary disposition with which these people are reproached, as Maquina repeatedly told me that it was not his wish to hurt a white man, and that he never should have done it, though ever so much in his power, had they not injured him. And were the commanders of our ships to treat the savages with rather more civility than they sometimes do, I am inclined to think they would find their account in it; not that I should recommend to them a confidence in the good faith and friendly professions of these people, so as in any degree to remit their vigilance, but on the contrary, to be strictly on their guard, and suffer but a very few of them to come on board the ship, and admit not many of their canoes along side at a time; a precaution that would have been the means of preventing some of the unfortunate events that have occurred, and if attended to, may in future, preserve many a valuable life. Such a regulation too, from what I know of their disposition and wants, would produce no serious difficulty in trading with the savages, and they would soon become perfectly reconciled to it.

Among the provisions which the Indians procure at Tashees, I must not omit mentioning a fruit that is very important, as forming a great article of their food. That is what is called by them the *Yama,* a species of berry that grows in bunches like currants, upon a bush from two to three feet high, with a large, round and smooth leaf. This berry is black, and about the size of a pistol shot, but of rather an oblong shape, and open at the top like the blue whortleberry. The taste is sweet but a little **1** acrid, and when first gathered, if eaten in any great quantity, especially without oil, is apt to produce cholics. To procure it, large companies of women go out on the mountains, accompanied by armed men, to protect them against wild beasts, where they frequently remain for several days, kindling a fire at night, and sheltering themselves under sheds constructed of boughs. At these parties, they collect great quantities. I have known Maquina's queen and her women return loaded, bringing with them upwards of twelve bushels. In order to preseve it, it is pressed in the bunches between two planks, and dried and put away in baskets for use. It is always eaten with oil.

Of berries of various kinds, such as strawberries, rasp-berries, black-berries, &c. there are great quanti- **2** ties in the country, of which the natives are very fond, gathering them in their seasons, and eating them with oil, but the yama is the only one that they preserve.

Fish is, however, their great article of food, as almost all the others, excepting the yama, may be considered as accidental.—They nevertheless are far from disrelishing meat, for instance, venison and bear's flesh. With regard to the latter, they have a most singular custom, which is, that any one who eats of it is obliged to abstain from eating any kind of fresh fish whatever, for the term of two months, as they have a superstitious belief, that should any of their people after tasting bear's flesh, eat of fresh salmon, cod, &c. the fish, though at ever so great a distance off, would come to the knowledge of it, and be so much offended thereat, as not to al-

*Trailing blackberry (*Rubus ursinus), *abundant in Jewitt's area.* 21

*Salmonberry (*Rubus spectabilis), *early ripening fruit important to all coastal Indian people.* 21

1 *whortleberry.* An old English name for blueberry.

2 *rasp-berries.* As the wild raspberry does not grow on that part of the coast, these were most probably salmonberries or thimbleberries, both of which resemble the raspberry of Jewitt's homeland.

*Black bear (*Ursus americanus vancouveri)*, average length 167.6 cm (66″).* 23

low themselves to be taken by any of the inhabitants. This I had an opportunity of observing while at Tashees, a bear having been killed early in December, of which not more than ten of the natives would eat, being prevented by the prohibition annexed to it, which also was the reason of my comrade and myself not tasting it, on being told by Maquina the consequence.

As there is something quite curious in their management of this animal, when they have killed one, I shall give a description of it. After well cleansing the bear from the dirt and blood, with which it is generally covered when killed, it is brought in and seated opposite the king in an upright posture, with a chief's bonnet, wrought in figures on its head, and its fur powdered over with the white down. A tray of provision is then set before it, and it is invited by words and gestures to

1 eat. This mock ceremony over, the reason of which I could never learn, the animal is taken and skinned, and the flesh and entrails boiled up into a soup, no part, but the paunch being rejected.

2

Thompson and one of the Indians shooting a Bear.

This dressing the bear as they call it, is an occasion of great rejoicing throughout the village, all the in-

1 *This mock ceremony.* The special ceremony of welcome accorded the bear may have been because of the animal's great power and its strong resemblance to humans, with its upright stance and humanlike footprints.

2 The gun and bow and arrow in this illustration again indicate that the artist seems not to have read the manuscript, which describes how native people did trap bears.

habitants being invited to a great feast at the king's house, though but few of them, in consequence of the penalty, will venture to eat of the flesh, but generally content themselves with their favourite dish of herring spawn and water. The feast on this occasion was closed by a dance from *Sat-sat-sak-sis,* in the manner I have already described, in the course of which he repeatedly shifted his mask for another of a different form.

A few days after a second bear was taken like the for-**1** mer, by means of a trap. This I had the curiosity to go and see at the place where it was caught, which was in the following manner. On the edge of a small stream of water in the mountains, which the salmon ascend, and near the spot where the bear is accustomed to watch for them, which is known by its track, a trap or box about the heighth of a man's head is built of posts and planks with a flat top, on which are laid a number of large stones or rocks. The top and sides are then carefully covered with turf, so as to resemble a little mound, and wholly to exclude the light, a narrow entrance of the height of the building only being left, just sufficient to admit the head and shoulders of the beast. On the inside, to a large plank that covers the top, is suspended by a strong cord a salmon, the plank being left loose so that a forcible pull will bring it down. On coming to its usual haunt, the bear enters the trap, and in endeavouring to pull away the fish, brings down the whole covering with its load of stones upon its head, and is almost always crushed to death on the spot, or so wounded as to be unable to escape. They are always careful to examine these traps every day, in order if a bear be caught, to bring it away, and cook it immediately, for it is not a little singular, that these people will eat no kind of meat that is in the least tainted, or not perfectly fresh, while, on the contrary, it is hardly possible for fish to be in too putrid a state for them, and I have frequently known them when a whale has been driven ashore, bring pieces

Mask of northern Nuu-chah-nulth. 38.4 *cm* (15⅛″). 9

1 *repeatedly shifted his mask for another of a different form.* Maquinna's son very likely danced with both a human mask and a bear mask; repeatedly changing from one to the other would depict his transformation from bear to human and back again.

*Man from Ucluelet wearing brow mask representing wolf snout; made of wood, with shredded cedar bark and eagle down. *13*

1 *a most singular farce . . .* The Shamans' or Wolf Dance was the most dramatic and important ceremonial in Nuu-chah-nulth culture. Everyone, of all ranks, took part in this type of tribal initiation at least once in their lives. Usually staged in midwinter, the ceremony was characterized by the abduction of children (the initiates) by supernatural wolf spirits. Rescued later by their relatives, the initiates were then ceremonially purified. Such ceremonies often marked an event of importance in a chief's life. Perhaps the capture of the *Boston* was such an event.

2 *seven days.* Maquinna probably sent the two novices into the woods for the seven-day seclusion period required for the initiation that was part of the annual Winter Ceremonial, rather than simply banishing them. Doubtless the captives failed to recognize the significance of the edict.

of it home with them in a state of offensiveness insupportable to any thing but a crow, and devour it with high relish, considering it as preferable to that which is fresh.

1 On the morning of the 13th of December, commenced what appeared to us a most singular farce. Apparently without any previous notice, Maquina discharged a pistol close to his son's ear, who immediately fell down as if killed, upon which all the women of the house set up a most lamentable cry, tearing handfulls of hair from their heads, and exclaiming that the prince was dead, at the same time a great number of the inhabitants, rushed into the house armed with their daggers, muskets, &c. enquiring the cause of their outcry; these were immediately followed by two others dressed in wolf skins, with masks over their faces representing the head of that animal; the latter came in on their hands and feet in the manner of a beast, and taking up the prince carried him off upon their backs, retiring in the same manner they entered. We saw nothing more of the ceremony, as Maquina came to us, and giving us a quantity of dried provision, ordered us to quit the house and not return to the village before the expiration of **2** seven days, for that if we appeared within that period, he should kill us.

At any other season of the year such an order would by us have been considered as an indulgence, in enabling us to pass our time in whatever way we wished, and even now, furnished as we were, with sufficient provision for that term, it was not very unpleasant to us, more particularly Thompson, who was always desirous to keep as much as possible out of the society and sight of the natives, whom he detested. Taking with us our provisions, a bundle of clothes, and our axes, we obeyed the directions of Maquina, and withdrew into the woods, where we built ourselves a cabin to shelter us, with the branches of trees, and keeping up a good fire, secured ourselves pretty well from the cold. Here we passed the prescribed period of our exile, with more content than much of the time while with them, employing the day in reading and praying for our release, or in rambling around and exploring the country, the soil of which we found to be very good, and the face of it, beautifully diversified with hills and valleys, refreshed with the finest streams of water, and at night enjoyed comfortable repose upon a bed of soft leaves, with our garments spread over us to protect us from the cold.

At the end of seven days we returned and found several of the poeple of A-i-tiz-zart with their king or chief at Tashees, who had been invited by Maquina to attend the close of this performance, which I now learn was a celebration, held by them annually, in honour of their God, whom they call *Quahootze,* to return him their thanks for his past, and implore his future favours. It terminated on the 21st, the day after our return, with a most extraordinary exhibition. Three men, each of **1** whom had two bayonets run through his sides, between the ribs, apparently regardless of the pain, traversed the room, backwards and forwards, singing war songs, and exulting in this display of firmness.

On the arrival of the 25th, we could not but call to mind, that this being Christmas, was in our country a day of the greatest festivity, when our fellow countrymen assembled in their churches, were celebrating the goodness of God, and the praises of the Saviour. What a reverse did our situation offer—captives in a savage land, and slaves to a set of ignorant beings unacquainted with religion or humanity, hardly were we permitted to offer up our devotions by ourselves in the woods, while we felt even grateful for this privilege. Thither with the king's permission, we withdrew, and after reading the service appointed for the day, sung the hymn of the Nativity, fervently praying that heaven in

Headdress mask representing supernatural wolf. AMNH/6

1 *Three men . . .* They were possibly war chiefs showing a display of fortitude and would later receive payment for their suffering. Although in later years such displays of bravery were often convincingly faked, in this time period Jewitt may have witnessed the real thing.

*Bundle of dried rhizomes, or "roots," of the clover (*Trifolium wormskjoldii*). BCPM*

its goodness, would permit us to celebrate the next festival of this kind in some Christian land. On our return, in order to conform as much as was in our power to the custom of our country, we were desirous of having a better supper than usual. With this view we bought from one of the natives, some dried clams and oil, and a **1** root called *Kletsup,* which we cooked by steaming, and found it very palatable. This root consists of many fibres, of about six inches long, and of the size of a crow quill. It is sweet, of an agreeable taste, not unlike the *Quanoose,* and it is eaten with oil. The plant that produces it I have never seen.

On the 31st, all the tribe quitted Tashees for Cooptee, whither they go to pass the remainder of the winter, and complete their fishing, taking off every thing with them in the same manner as at Nootka. We arrived in a few hours at Cooptee, which is about fifteen miles, and immediately set about covering the houses, which was soon completed.

This place, which is their great herring and sprat fishery, stands just within the mouth of the river, on the same side with Tashees, in a very narrow valley at the foot of a high mountain. Though nearly as secure as Tashees from the winter storms, it is by means so pleasantly situated, though to us it was a much more agreeable residence, as it brought us nearer Nootka, where we were impatient to return, in hopes of finding some vessel there, or hearing of the arrival of one near.

2 The first snow that fell this season, was the day after our arrival, on New-Years; a day that like Christmas, brought with it, painful reccollections, but at the same time led us to indulge the hope of a more fortunate year than the last.

Early on the morning of the 7th of January, Maquina took me with him in his canoe on a visit to *Upquesta,* chief of the A-i-tiz-zarts, who had invited him to attend an exhibition at his village, similar to the one with

1 *Kletsup*. This may well be the rhizomes of clover, an important food for many coastal Indians. Where the plant grew in abundance, often along river flats, individuals or families harvested them on sections which they owned. Or kletsup may come from a fern called licorice root because of its licorice flavour. The rhizomes of both are the thickness of "a crow's quill." Archibald Menzies, Cook's botanist who spent considerable time in Nootka Sound, commented on "two sorts of roots, of a mild, sweetish taste, which are eaten raw." Although roots were generally steamed or roasted, and eaten with oil, licorice root is tasty raw.

2 *The first snow . . .* Although it has a temperate climate, the west coast of Vancouver Island has occasional cold spells in the winter. For November and December of 1803, nine of Jewitt's journal entries begin with "Frosty weather." On 1 January 1804, he writes: "The new year comes in with snow which is the first we have had this season."

which he had been entertained at Tashees. This place is between twenty and thirty miles distant up the sound, and stands on the banks of a small river about the size of that of Cooptee, just within its entrance, in a valley of much greater extent than that of Tashees; it consists of fourteen or fifteen houses, built and disposed in the manner of those at Nootka. The tribe, which is considered as tributary to Maquina, amounts to about three hundred warriors, and the inhabitants, both men and women, are among the best looking of any people on the coast.

On our arrival we were received at the shore by the inhabitants, a few of whom were armed with muskets, which they fired, with loud shouts and exclamations of *Wocash, wocash.*

We were welcomed by the chief's messenger, or master of ceremonies, dressed in his best garments, with his hair powdered with white down, and holding in his hand the cheetoolth, the badge of his office. This man preceded us to the chief's house, where he introduced and pointed out to us our respective seats. On entering, the visitors took off their hats, which they always wear on similar occasions, and Maquina his outer robes, of which he has several on whenever he pays a visit, and seated himself near the chief. As I was dressed in European clothes I became quite an object of curiosity to these people, very few of whom had ever seen a white man. They crowded around me in numbers, taking hold of my clothes, examining my face, hands and feet, and even opening my mouth to see if I had a tongue, for notwithstanding I had by this time become well acquainted with their language, I preserved the strictest silence, Maquina on our first landing having enjoined me not to speak, until he should direct. Having undergone this examination for some time, Maquina at length made a sign to me to speak to them. On hearing me address them in their own language, they were

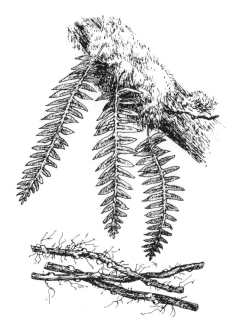

Licorice fern (Polypodium glycyrrhiza) *and rhizomes.* 23

Woman carrying root-digging stick, wearing cedar bark cape as back protector against burden basket. *11

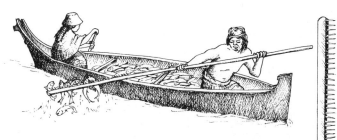

Herring rake and method of use. 4

greatly astonished and delighted, and told Maquina that they now perceived that I was a man like themselves, except that I was white and looked like a seal, alluding to my blue jacket and trowsers, which they wanted to persuade me to take off, as they did not like their appearance. Maquina in the mean time gave an account to the chief, of the scheme he had formed for surprising our ship, and the manner in which he and his people had carried it into execution, with such particular and horrid details of that transaction as chilled the blood in my veins. Trays of boiled herring spawn and train oil were soon after brought in and placed before us, neither the chief or any of his people eating at the same time, it being contrary to the ideas of hospitality entertained by these nations, to eat any part of the food that is provided for strangers, always waiting until their visitors have finished, before they have their own brought in.

The following day closed their festival with an exhibition of a similar kind, to that which had been given at Tashees, but still more cruel, the different tribes appearing on these occasions to endeavour to surpass each other, in their proofs of fortitude and endurance of pain. In the morning twenty men entered the chief's house, with each an arrow run through the flesh of his sides, and either arm, with a cord fastened to the end, which as the performers advanced, singing and boasting, was forcibly drawn back by a person having hold of it. After this performance was closed we returned to Cooptee, which we reached at midnight, our men keeping time with their songs to the stroke of their paddles.

The natives now began to take the herring and sprat in immense quantities, with some salmon, and there was nothing but feasting from morning till night. The following is the method they employ to take the herring. **1** ring. A stick of about seven feet long, two inches broad, and half an inch thick, is formed from some hard wood, one side of which is set with sharp teeth, made from

1 *A stick . . .* This implement is the herring rake, used by many Northwest Coast peoples. It is uncertain what fish Jewitt means when he refers to sprats, though they may have been the sardines (young pilchards) he mentions elsewhere.

whale bone, at about half an inch apart. Provided with this instrument, the fisherman seats himself in the prow of a canoe, which is paddled by another, and whenever he comes to a shoal of herring, which cover the water in great quantities, he strikes it with both hands upon them, and at the same moment turning it up, brings it over the side of the canoe, into which he lets those that are taken drop. It is astonishing to see how many are caught by those who are dexterous at this kind of fishing, as they seldom fail when the shoals are numerous, of taking as many as ten to twelve at a stroke, and in a very short time will fill a canoe with them. Sprats are likewise caught in a similar manner.

About the beginning of February, Maquina gave a great feast, at which were present not only all the inhabitants, but one hundred persons from A-i-tiz-zart, and a number from Wickinninish, who had been invited to attend it. It is customary with them to give an annual entertainment of this kind, and it is astonishing to see what a quantity of provision is expended, or rather wasted on such an occasion, when they always eat to the greatest excess. It was at this feast that I saw upwards of a hundred salmon cooked in one tub. The whole residence at Cooptee presents an almost uninterrupted succession of feasting and gormondizing, and it would seem as if the principal object of these people was to consume their whole stock of provision before leaving it, trusting entirely to their success in fishing and whaling, for a supply at Nootka.

On the 25th of February, we quitted Cooptee, and returned to Nootka.[1] With much joy did Thompson and myself again find ourselves in a place, where notwithstanding the melancholy recollections which it excited, we hoped before long to see some vessel arrive to our relief; and for this we became the more solicitous, as of late we had become much more apprehensive of our safety in consequence of information brought Maquina

1 *On the 25th of February* . . . Jewitt's journal entry for that same day reads: "Frosty weather. This day we left Cooptee to return to Nootka, which is about twenty miles [32 km] distance, having been there almost two months; arrived at Nootka, 4 o'clock, P.M. having had hard work and nothing to eat."

a few days before we left Cooptee, by some of the Cayuquets, that there were twenty ships at the northward preparing to come against him, with an intention of destroying him and his whole tribe, for cutting off the Boston. This story which was wholly without foundation, and discovered afterwards to have been invented by these people, for the purpose of disquieting him, threw him into great alarm, and notwithstanding all I could say to convince him that it was an unfounded report, so great was his jealousy of us, especially after it had been confirmed to him by some others of the same nation, that he treated us with much harshness, and kept a very suspicious eye upon us. Nothing indeed could be more unpleasant than our present situation, when I reflected that our lives were altogether dependent on the will of a savage, on whose caprice and suspicions no rational calculation could be made.

Not long after our return, a son of Maquina's sister, a boy about eleven years old, who had been for some time declining, died. Immediately on his death, which was about midnight, all the men and women in the house, set up loud cries and shrieks, which awakening Thompson and myself, so disturbed us that we left the house. This lamentation was kept up during the remainder of the night. In the morning, a great fire was kindled, in which Maquina burned in honour of the deceased, ten fathoms of cloth, and buried with him ten fathoms more, eight of I-whaw, four prime sea otter skins, and two small trunks, containing our unfortunate captain's clothes and watch. This boy was considered as a Tyee or chief, being the only son of *Tootoosch,* one of their principal chiefs, who had married Maquina's sister, whence arose this ceremony on his interment; it being an established custom with these people, that whenever a chief dies, his most valuable property is **1** burned or buried with him; it is, however, wholly confined to the chiefs, and appears to be a mark of honour

1 *burned or buried with him.* A deceased person was not actually buried in the ground. The body, wrapped in cedar bark matting, or sea otter furs for high-ranking chiefs, was put into a box and placed in a cave or rock shelter, together with grave goods.

appropriate to them. In this instance Maquina furnished the articles, in order that his nephew might have the proper honours rendered him. Tootoosch his father was esteemed the first warrior of the tribe, and was one who had been particularly active in the destruction of our ship, having killed two of our poor comrades, who were ashore, whose names were Hall and Wood. About the time of our removal to Tashees, while in the enjoyment of the highest health, he was suddenly seized with a fit of delirium, in which he fancied that he saw the ghosts of those two men constantly standing by him, and threatening him, so that he would take no food, except what was forced into his mouth. A short time before this, he had lost a daughter of about fifteen years of age, which afflicted him greatly, and whether his insanity, a disorder very uncommon amongst these savages, no instance of the kind having occurred within the memory of the oldest man amongst them, proceeded from this cause, or that it was the special interposition of an all merciful God in our favour, who by this means thought proper to induce these barbarians still farther to respect our lives, or that for hidden purposes, the Supreme Disposer of events, sometimes permits the spirits of the dead to revisit the world, and haunt the murderer I know not, but his mind from this period until his death, which took place but a few weeks after that of his son was incessantly occupied with the images of the men whom he had killed. This circumstance made much impression upon the tribe, particularly the chiefs, whose uniform opposition to putting us to death, at the various councils that were held on our account, I could not but in part attribute to this cause, and Maquina used frequently in speaking of Tootoosch's sickness, to express much satisfaction that his hands had not been stained with the blood of any of our men. When Maquina was first informed by his sister, of the strange conduct of her husband, he immediately went to his house, taking us with him; suspecting that his disease had been caused by us, and that the ghosts of our countrymen had been called thither by us, to torment him. We found him raving about Hall and Wood, saying that they were *peshak,* that is bad. Maquina then placed some provision before him to see if he would eat. On perceiving it, he put forth his hand to take some, but instantly withdrew it with signs of horror, saying that Hall and Wood were there, and would not let him eat. Maquina then pointing to us, asked if it was not John and Thompson who troubled him. *Wik,* he replied, that is, no, *John klushish—Thompson klushish—*John and Thompson are both good; then turning to me, and patting me on the shoulder, he made signs to me to eat. I tried to persuade him that Hall and Wood were not there, and that none were near him but ourselves: he said, I know very well you do not see them, but I do. At first Maquina endeavoured to convince him that he saw nothing, and to laugh him out of his belief, but finding that all was to no purpose, he at length became serious, and asked me if I had ever seen any one affected in this manner, and what was the matter with him. I gave him to understand, pointing to his head, that his brain was injured, and that he did not see things as formerly. Being convinced by Tootoosch's conduct, that we had no agency in his indisposition, on our return home, Maquina asked me what was done in my country in similar cases. I told him that such persons were closely con-

1 fined, and sometimes tied up and whipped, in order to make them better. After pondering for some time, he said that he should be glad to do any thing to relieve him, and that he should be whipped, and immediately gave orders to some of his men, to go to Tootoosch's house, bind him, and bring him to his, in order to undergo the operation. Thompson was the person selected to administer this remedy, which he undertook very

1 *whipped.* Whipping was then a commonly used method of dealing with the mentally disturbed in England, but the practice of whipping was unknown among the Nuu-chah-nulth. Nor were native children ever struck or punished, for to do so, it was believed, would make them aggressive and bad natured.

readily, and for that purpose provided himself with a good number of spruce branches, with which he whipped him most severely, laying it on with the best will imaginable, while Tootoosch displayed the greatest rage, kicking, spitting, and attempting to bite all who came near him. This was too much for Maquina, who, at length, unable to endure it longer, ordered Thompson to desist, and Tootoosch to be carried back, saying that if there was no other way of curing him but by whipping, he must remain mad.

The application of the whip produced no beneficial effect on Tootoosch, for he afterwards became still more deranged; in his fits of fury sometimes seizing a club, and beating his slaves in a most dreadful manner, and striking and spitting at all who came near him, till at length his wife no longer daring to remain in the house with him, came with her son to Maquina's.

The whaling season now commenced, and Maquina **1** was out almost every day in his canoe in pursuit of them, but for a considerable time, with no success, one day breaking the staff of his harpoon, another, after having been a long time fast to a whale, the weapon **2** drawing, owing to the breaking of the shell which formed its point, with several such like accidents, arising from the imperfection of the instrument. At these times he always returned very morose and out of temper, upbraiding his men with having violated their obligation to continence preparatory to whaling. In this **3** state of ill humour he would give us very little to eat, which added to the women not cooking when the men are away, reduced us to very low fare.

In consequence of the repeated occurrence of similar accidents, I proposed to Maquina to make him a harpoon or foreganger of steel, which would be less liable **4** to fail him. The idea pleased him, and in a short time I completed one for him, with which he was much de-

*This whaler, shown wearing a bearskin and carrying a whaling harpoon and sealskin floats, was drawn from a posed photo. In reality, after his harpoon lodged firmly in the whale, the whaler crouched down in the bow of the canoe and covered himself with the bearskin. *23*

1 *The whaling season . . .* Jewitt's journal frequently records that Maquinna went out whaling and returned without success. For 22 June 1803, he writes: "Our chief out whaling, struck one and was near to him one day and one night, and then his line parted. Returned and was very cross." A later entry states: "Our chief out whaling; struck one, but there being only one canoe fast to him, it filled, and our chief was drawn into the water, so that he was obliged to cut from him."

2 *a whale.* According to Jewitt's journal, Maquinna's first day of whaling was always in the first week of April; therefore, he would likely have been after the grey whale, which migrates up the coast at that time, coming fairly close to shore. The average male of this species measures 12.2 m (40'), the female slightly larger.

3 *continence.* Part of the whaling crew's ritual preparations for the hunt included a period of abstinence from marital relations.

4 *foreganger.* The shaft attached to the end of the harpoon shaft, onto which the socketed harpoon head was fixed.

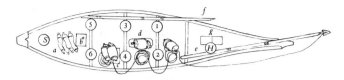

Diagram shows placement of crew and gear in whaling canoe.
H. Harpooner stood at bow with left foot on thwart, right foot on
gunwale 1. through 6. Paddlers (paddlers 2, 4 and 6 paid out harpoon
line and floats when whale was struck) S. Steersman a. Spare floats,
deflated b. Box of drinking water c. Boxes of food beneath float
d. Whaler's bag beneath float e. Rigged harpoon f. Spare harpoon
shaft and lance for final killing of whale g. Whaler's tackle boxes. 9

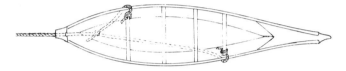

Tow hitch, used in towing dead whale back to village, ensured even
pull on canoe. 9

1 *towing it in*. To prepare the whale for towing, one of the crew
dived into the water, cut slits in the whale's jaw and tied the mouth
shut to prevent sea water from entering the carcass and sinking the
animal. Floats were added to help buoy the whale up, and it was
attached to the canoe with a special tow hitch to ensure an even
pull. Towing was a task that could take many hours—even days—
and to help the journey along, the crew sang towing songs and
chants.

2 *cut up*. The whaler had the privilege of making the first cut in the
whale. He cut out the saddle (the dorsal fin and the blubber in
front, behind and down each side), which was decorated and
honoured in a ritual celebration. Taking directions from the
whaler, the first paddler cut off the rest of the blubber in long
strips; certain portions went to the whaler's crew, then the assisting
canoe leaders and their crews, according to their importance. The
flesh of the whale was generally left for anyone who wanted it.

lighted, and the very next day went out to make trial of
it. He succeeded with it in taking a whale. Great was the
joy throughout the village as soon as it was known that
the king had secured the whale, by notice from a person
stationed at the head-land in the offing. All the canoes
were immediately launched, and, furnished with harpoons and seal skin floats, hastened to assist in buoying
1 it up and in towing it in. The bringing in of this fish exhibited a scene of universal festivity. As soon as the
canoes appeared at the mouth of the cove, those on
board of them singing a song of triumph to a slow air,
to which they kept time with their paddles, all who
were on shore, men, women, and children, mounted
the roofs of their houses, to congratulate the king on his
success, drumming most furiously on the planks, and
exclaiming *Wocash*—*wocash Tyee*.

The whale on being drawn on shore, was immedi-
2 ately cut up, and a great feast of the blubber given at
Maquina's house, to which all the village were invited,
who indemnified themselves for their lent, by eating as
usual to excess. I was highly praised for the goodness of
my harpoon, and a quantity of blubber given me, which
I was permitted to cook as I pleased, this I boiled in salt
water with some young nettles and other greens for
Thompson and myself, and in this way we found it tolerable food.

Their method of procuring the oil, is to skim it from
the water in which the blubber is boiled, and when
cool, put it up into whale bladders for use, and of these I
have seen them so large as, when filled, would require
no less than five or six men to carry. Several of the
chiefs, among whom were Maquina's brothers, who after the king has caught the first whale, are privileged to
take them also, were very desirous, on discovering the
superiority of my harpoon, that I should make some for
them, but this Maquina would not permit, reserving for
himself this improved weapon. He however gave me

directions to make a number more for himself, which I executed, and also made him several lances, with which he was greatly pleased.

As these people have some very singular observances preparatory to whaling, an account of them will, I presume, not prove uninteresting, especially as it may serve to give a better idea of their manners. A short time before leaving Tashees, the king makes a point of passing a day alone on the mountain, whither he goes very privately early in the morning, and does not return till late in the evening. This is done, as I afterwards learned, for the purpose of singing and praying to his God for **1** success in whaling the ensuing season. At Cooptee the same ceremony is performed, and at Nootka after the return thither, with still greater solemnity, as for the next two days he appears very thoughtful and gloomy, scarcely speaking to any one, and observes a most rigid fast. On these occasions, he has always a broad red fillet **2** made of bark, bound around his head, in token of humiliation, with a large branch of green spruce on the top, and his great rattle in his hand. In addition to this, for a week before commencing their whaling, both himself and the crew of his canoe observe a fast, eating but very little, and going into the water several times in the course of each day to bathe, singing and rubbing **3** their bodies, limbs and faces with shells and bushes, so that on their return I have seen them look as though they had been severely torn with briers. They are likewise obliged to abstain from any commerce with their women for the like period, the latter restriction being considered as indispensable to their success.

Early in June Tootoosch, the crazy chief, died. On being acquainted with his death the whole village, men, women, and children set up a loud cry, with every testimony of the greatest grief, which they contined for more than three hours. As soon as he was dead, the body, according to their custom, was laid out on a

Stripping blubber, a valuable part of a whale. *10

1 *singing and praying.* Here Jewitt interpreted Maquinna's ritual through the practices of his own religion. The whaler was most likely communicating with ancestor spirits, particularly those who had been successful whalers, in order to receive their powers for the forthcoming hunt.

2 *red fillet.* People wore headdresses of cedar bark dyed red on many ceremonial occasions.

3 *rubbing their bodies . . .* Such harsh ritualistic bathing served to toughen the whaling crew for the rigours of the hunt. They also bathed whilst at sea, submerging, and surfacing and blowing spouts of water in imitation of the whale, getting close to its spirit.

Whaler bathing ceremonially. *8

1 *Kinneclimmets.* This man held the important position of Maquinna's speaker. All chiefs of sufficiently high rank traditionally had a speaker, whose function was roughly comparable to that of a master of ceremonies. Today, Ray Williams, who lives at Yuquot, is the hereditary speaker for Ambrose Maquinna, and on occasion still acts in that capacity.

plank, having the head bound round with a red bark fillet, which is with them an emblem of mourning and sorrow. After laying some time in this manner, he was wrapped in an otter skin robe, and three fathoms of I-whaw being put about his neck, he was placed in a large coffin or box about three feet deep, which was ornamented on the outside with two rows of the small white shells. In this, the most valuable articles of his property were placed with him, among which were no less than twenty-four prime sea-otter skins. At night, which is their time for interring the dead, the coffin was borne by eight men with two poles, thrust through ropes passed around it, to the place of burial, accompanied by his wife and family, with their hair cut short, in token of grief, all the inhabitants joining the procession. The place of burial was a large cavern on the side of a hill at a little distance from the village, in which, after depositing the coffin carefully, all the attendants repaired to Maquina's house, where a number of articles belonging to the deceased, consisting of blankets, pieces of cloth, &c. were burned by a person appointed by Maquina for that purpose, dressed and painted in the highest style, with his head covered with white down, who, as he put in the several pieces, one by one, poured upon them a quantity of oil to increase the flame, in the intervals between, making a speech and playing off a variety of buffoon tricks, and the whole closed with a feast and dance from Sat-sat-sak-sis, the king's son.

The man who performed the ceremony of burning on this occasion, was a very singular character, named 1 *Kinneclimmets.* He was held in high estimation by the king, though only of the common class, probably from his talent for mimicry and buffoonry, and might be considered as a kind of king's jester, or rather as combining in his person the character of a buffoon with that of master of ceremonies, and public orator to his majesty, as he was the one who at feasts always regulated the place of the guests, delivered speeches on receiving or returning visits, besides amusing the company at all their entertainments, with a variety of monkey pranks and antic gestures, which appeared to these savages the height of wit and humour, but would be considered as extremely low by the least polished people. Almost all the kings or head chiefs of the principal tribes, were accompanied by a similar character who appeared to be attached to their dignity, and are called in their language, *Climmer-habbee*.

This man, *Kinneclimmets,* was particularly odious to Thompson, who would never join in the laugh at his tricks, but when he began, would almost always quit the house with a very surly look, and an exclamation of, cursed fool! which Maquina, who thought nothing could equal the cleverness of his *Climmer-habbee,* used to remark with much dissatisfaction, asking me why Thompson never laughed, observing that I must have had a very good tempered woman indeed for my mother, as my father was so very ill-natured a man. Among those performances that gained him the greatest applause, was his talent of eating to excess, for I have **1** known him devour at one meal, no less than seventy-five large herring, and at another time when a great feast was given by Maquina, he undertook, after drinking three pints of oil by way of whet, to eat four dried salmon, and five quarts of spawn, mixed up with a gallon of train oil, and actually succeeded in swallowing the greater part of this mess, until his stomach became so overloaded, as to discharge its contents in the dish. One of his exhibitions, however, had nearly cost him his life, this was on occasion of *Kla-quak-ee-na,* one of the chiefs, having bought him a new wife, in celebration of which he ran three times through a large fire, and burned himself in such a manner, that he was not able to stir for more than four weeks. These feats of savage skill were much praised by Maquina, who never failed to

1 *eating to excess.* It was traditional for speakers and warrior chiefs to eat enormous quantities of food.

Wild peas (Lathyrus japonicus). Profusion of small green pods carry ripened peas in summer, flavour is quite acceptable. 23

make him a present, of cloth, muskets, &c. on such occasions.

The death of Tootoosch increased still more the disquietude which his delirium had excited among the savages, and all those chiefs who had killed our men became much alarmed, lest they should be seized with the same disorder and die like him; more particularly, as I had told Maquina, that I believed his insantiy was a punishment inflicted on him by *Quahootze,* for his cruelty in murdering two innocent men, who had never injured him.

Our situation had now become unpleasant in the extreme. The summer was so far advanced, that we nearly despaired of a ship arriving to our relief, and with that expectation, almost relinquished the hope of ever having it in our power to quit this savage land. We were treated too with less indulgence than before, both Thompson and myself being obliged, in addition to our other employments, to perform the laborious task of **1** cutting and collecting fuel, which we had to bring on our shoulders from nearly three miles distant, as it consisted wholly of dry trees, all of which near the village, had been consumed. To add to this, we suffered much abuse from the common people, who, when Maquina or some of the chiefs were not present, would insult us, calling us wretched slaves, asking us where was our Tyee or captain, making gestures signifying that his head had been cut off, and that they would do the like to us; though they generally took good care at such times to keep well out of Thompson's reach, as they had more than once experienced to their cost the strength of his fist. This conduct was not only provoking and grating to our feelings in the highest degree, but it convinced us of the ill disposition of these savages towards us, and rendered us fearful lest they might at some time or other persuade or force Maquina and the chiefs, to put us to death.

1 *cutting and collecting fuel.* Jewitt's journal, 16 August 1804 entry: "Employed to bring firewood; sat down and ate some green pease, which I accidentally found growing wild on the side of the river."

We were also often brought to great distress for the want of provision, so far as to be reduced to collect a scanty supply of muscles and limpets from the rocks, and sometimes even compelled to part with some of our **1** most necessary articles of clothing, in order to purchase food for our subsistence. This was, however, principally owing to the inhabitants themselves experiencing a great scarcity of provisions this season there having been, in the first place, but very few salmon caught at **2** Friendly Cove, a most unusual circumstance, as they generally abound there in the spring, which was by the natives attributed to their having been driven away by the blood of our men, who had been thrown into the sea, which with true savage inconsistency, excited their murmers against Maquina, who had proposed cutting off our ship. Relying on this supply, they had in the most inconsiderate manner squandered away their winter stock of provisions, so that in a few days after their return, it was entirely expended. Nor were the king and **3** chiefs much more fortunate in their whaling, even after I had furnished Maquina with the improved weapon for that purpose; but four whales having been taken during the season, which closes the last of May, including one that had been struck by Maquina and escaped, and was afterwards driven on shore about six miles from Nootka, in almost a state of putridity. These afforded but a short supply, to a population, including all ages and sexes, of no less than fifteen hundred persons, and **4** of a character so very improvident, that after feasting most gluttonously whenever a whale was caught, they were several times for a week together, reduced to the necessity of eating but once a day, and of collecting cockles and muscles from the rocks for their food. And even after the cod and halibut fishing commenced in June, in which they met with tolerable success, such was the savage caprice of Maquina that he would often give us but little to eat, finally ordering us to buy a

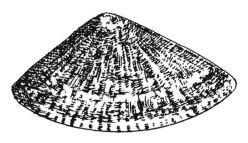

Limpet (Notoacmea scutum), *found on upper intertidal zone. Diameter up to 5 cm (2").* 23

1 *compelled to part with . . .* Jewitt's journal entry for 1 April 1805: "Employed cutting up a new pair of canvas trowsers to unravel out into thread, for the purpose of buying something to eat.

2 *very few salmon.* Although the coast provided an abundance of food much of the time, the reliance on salmon migrations often meant hunger if the run was late or small. And even preserved supplies could spoil in storage through insect infestation.

3 *Nor were the king and chiefs . . .* Jewitt's journal records eight whales struck and lost by Maquinna, with only one taken.

4 *fifteen hundred persons.* Cook estimated an even higher population of 2000. Jewitt observed more than twenty houses in the village, giving an average of seventy-five people in each of the large houses, though many houses would have less.

canoe and fishing implements, and go out ourselves and fish, or we should have nothing. To do this, we were compelled to part with our great coats, which were not only important to us as garments, but of which we made our beds, spreading them under us when we slept. From our want of skill, however, in this new employ, we met with no success, on discovering which, Maquina ordered us to remain at home.

Another thing, which to me in particular, proved an almost constant source of vexation and disgust, and which living among them had not in the least reconciled me to, was their extreme filthiness, not only in eating fish, especially the whale, when in a state of offensive putridity, but while at their meals of making a practice of taking the vermin from their heads or clothes, and eating them, by turns thrusting their fingers into their hair, and into the dish, and spreading their garments over the tubs in which the provision was cooking, in order to set in motion their inhabitants. Fortunately for Thompson, he regarded this much less than myself, and when I used to point out to him any instances of their filthiness in this respect, he would laugh and reply, Never mind John, the more good things the better. I must however do Maquina the justice to state, that he was much neater both in his person and eating than were the others, as was likewise his queen, owing no doubt to his intercouse with foreigners, which had given him ideas of cleanliness, for I never saw either of them eat any of these animals, but on the contrary they appeared not much to relish this taste in others. Their garments, also, were much cleaner, Maquina having been accustomed to give his away when they became soiled, till after he discovered that Thompson and myself kept ours clean by washing them, when he used to make Thompson do the same for him.

Yet amidst this state of endurance and disappointment, in hearing repeatedly of the arrival of ships at the

north and south, most of which proved to be idle re-
ports, while expectation was almost wearied out in
looking for them, we did not wholly despond, relying
on the mercy of the Supreme Being, to offer up to
whom our devotions on the days appointed for his worship, was our chief consolation and support, though we
were sometimes obliged by our task-masters to infringe
upon the Sabbath, which was to me a source of much
regret.

We were nevertheless, treated at times, with much
kindness by Maquina, who would give us a plenty of
the best that he had to eat, and occasionally, some small
present of cloth for a garment, promising me, that if **1**
any ship should arrive within a hundred miles of
Nootka, he would send a canoe with a letter from me to
the captain, so that he might come to our release. These
flattering promises and marks of attention were however, at those times, when he thought himself in personal danger from a mutinous spirit, which the scarcity
of provision had excited among the natives, who, like
true savages, imputed all their public calamities, of
whatever kind, to the misconduct of their chief, or
when he was apprehensive of an attack from some of
the other tribes who were irritated with him for cutting
off the Boston, as it had prevented ships from coming
to trade with them, and who were constantly alarming
him with idle stories of vessels that were preparing to
come against him, and exterminate both him and his
people the Cayuquets. At such times, he made us keep
guard over him both night and day, armed with cutlasses and pistols, being apparently afraid to trust any of
his own men. At one time, it was a general revolt of his
people that he apprehended—then three of his principal
chiefs, among whom was his elder brother, had con-
spired to take away his life, and at length he fancied that
a small party of Klaooquates, between whom and the
Nootkians, little friendship subsisted, had come to

1 *cloth for a garment.* Jewitt's journal entry for 15 July 1803:
"Pleasant weather. Our chief gave us four yards of canvas, of
which Thompson made trowsers."

Nootka, under a pretence of trade, for the sole purpose of murdering him and his family, telling us, probably to sharpen our vigilance, that their intention was to kill us likewise; and so strongly were his fears excited on this occasion, that he not only ordered us to keep near him armed by day, whenever he went out, and to patrole at night before his house while they remained, but to continue the same guard for three days after they were gone, and to fire at one and at four in the morning, one of the great guns, to let them know, if, as he suspected, they were lurking in the neighbourhood, that he was on his guard. While he was thus favourably disposed towards us, I took an opportunity to inform him of the ill treatment that we frequently received from his people, and the insults that were offered us by some of the stranger tribes in calling us white slaves, and loading us with other opprobrious terms. He was much displeased, and said that his subjects should not be allowed to treat us ill, and that if any of the strangers did it, he wished us to punish the offenders with death, at the same time directing us for our security, to go constantly armed. This permission was soon improved by Thompson to the best advantage; for a few days after, having gone to the pond to wash some of our clothes, and blanket for Maquina, several Wickinninish who were then at Nootka, came thither, and seeing him washing the clothes, and the blanket spread upon the grass to dry, they began according to custom to insult him, and one of them bolder than the others, walked over the blanket. Thompson was highly incensed, and threatened the Indian with death if he repeated the offence, but he, in contempt of the threat, trampled upon the blanket, when drawing his cutlass, without farther ceremony, Thompson cut off his head, on seeing which the others ran off at full speed; Thompson then gathering up the clothes and blanket on which were the marks

1

Thompson killing the Indian.

of the Indian's dirty feet, and taking with him the head, returned and informed the king of what had passed, who was much pleased, and highly commended his conduct. This had a favourable effect for us, not only on the stranger tribes, but the inhabitants themselves, who treated us afterwards with less disrespect.

In the latter part of July, Maquina informed me that he was going to war with the *A-y-charts,* a tribe living at about fifty miles to the south, on account of some controversy that had arisen the preceding summer, and that I must make a number of daggers for his men, and cheetoolths for his chiefs, which having completed, he wished me to make for his own use a weapon of quite a different form, in order to dispatch his enemy by one blow on the head, it being the calculation of these nations on going to war, to surprise their adversaries while asleep. This was a steel dagger, or more properly a spike, of about six inches long made very sharp, set at right angles in an iron handle of fifteen inches long, terminating at the lower end in a crook or turn, so as to prevent its being wrenched from the hand, and at the

2

1 Here is another artistic inconsistency—Thompson did not use a musket for the slaying, but a cutlass.

2 *a steel dagger* . . . This weapon has some similarity to one of stone collected from Nootka Sound by Captain Cook in 1778.

upper, in a round knob or head, from whence the spike protruded. This instrument I polished highly, and the more to please Maquina, formed on the back of the knob, the resemblance of a man's head, with the mouth open, substituting for eyes, black beads, which I fastened in with red sealing wax. This pleased him much, and was greatly admired by his chiefs, who wanted me to make similar ones for them, but Maquina would not suffer it, reserving for himself alone this weapon.

When these people have finally determined on war, they make it an invariable practice for three or four weeks prior to the expedition, to go into the water five or six times a day, where they wash and scrub themselves from head to foot with bushes intermixed with briars, so that their bodies and faces will often be entirely covered with blood. During this severe exercise, they are continually exclaiming, *"Wocash Quahootze, Teechamme ah welth, wik-etish tau-ilth—Karsab-matemas—Wik-sish to hauk matemas—I ya-ish kah-shittle—As-smootish warich matemas*—Which signifies, Good, or great God, let me live—Not be sick—Find the enemy—Not fear him—Find him asleep, and kill a great many of him. During the whole of this period they have no intercourse with their women, and for a week, at least, before setting out, abstain from feasting or any kind or merriment, appearing thoughtful, gloomy, and morose, and for the three last days, are almost constantly in the water, both day and night, scrubbing and lacerating themselves in a terrible manner. Maquina having informed Thompson and myself that he should take us with him, was very solicitous that we should bathe and scrub ourselves in the same way with them, telling me that it would harden our skins so that the weapons of the enemy would not pierce them, but as we felt no great inclination to amuse ourselves in this manner, we declined it.

The expedition consisted of forty canoes, carrying **1** from ten to twenty men each. Thompson and myself armed ourselves with cutlasses and pistols, but the natives, although they had a plenty of European arms, took with them only their daggers and cheetoolths, with a few bows and arrows, the latter being about a yard in length, and pointed with copper, muscle shell, or bone: the bows are four feet and a half long, with strings made of whale sinew.

To go to A-y-chart, we ascended from twenty to **2** thirty miles, a river about the size of that of Tashees, the banks of which are high and covered with wood. At midnight, we came in sight of the village, which was situated on the west bank near the shore on a steep hill difficult of access, and well calculated for defence. It consisted of fifteen or sixteen houses, smaller than those at Nootka, and built in the same style, but compactly placed. By Maquina's directions, the attack was deferred until the first appearance of dawn, as he said that was the time when men slept the soundest.

At length all being ready for the attack, we landed with the greatest silence, and going around so as to come upon the foe in the rear, clambered up the hill, and while the natives, as is their custom, entered the several huts, creeping on all fours, my comrade and myself stationed ourselves without, to intercept those who should attempt to escape, or come to the aid of their friends. I wished if possible, not to stain my hands in the blood of any fellow creature, and though Thompson would gladly have put to death all the savages in the country, he was too brave to think of attacking a sleeping enemy. Having entered the houses, on the war-whoop being given by Maquina, as he seized the head of the chief, and gave him the fatal blow, all proceeded to the work of death. The A-y-charts being thus surprised, were unable to make resistance, and with the exception of a very few, who were so fortunate as to make their

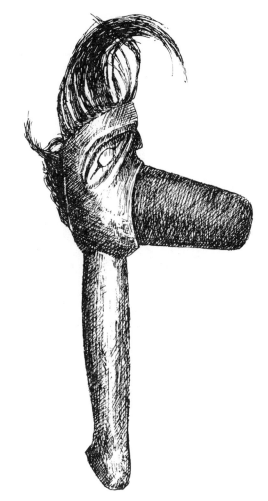

Ceremonial axe, collected by Captain Cook, 1778. HM/13

1 *The expedition* . . . Jewitt makes no mention of a raid in his journal. Most likely he heard about a war between the Clayoquot and the Haachaht, which occurred around his time, and wrote it into the narrative to add interest.

2 *To go to A-y-chart* . . . The A-y-chart were the Haachaht, a group in Barkley Sound who were annihilated by Wickanninish. Jewitt's geographical description is rather inexact.

Stone fighting weapons collected from Nootka Sound by Cook expedition, 1778. BM/5

escape, were all killed or taken prisoners on condition of becoming slaves to their captors. I also had the good fortune to take four captives, whom Maquina, as a favor, permitted me to consider as mine, and occasionally employ them in fishing for me; as for Thompson, who thirsted for revenge, he had no wish to take any prisoners, but with his cutlass, the only weapon he would employ against them, succeeded in killing seven stout fellows who came to attack him, an act which obtained him great credit with Maquina and the chiefs, who after this, held him in much higher estimation, and gave him the appellation of *Chehiel-suma-har,* it being the name of a very celebrated warrior of their nation in ancient times, whose exploits were the constant theme of their praise.

1

Thompson slaying the Natives.

After having put to death all the old and infirm of either sex, as is the barbarous practice of these people, and destroyed the buildings, we re-embarked with our booty in our canoes, for Nootka, where we were received with great demonstrations of joy by the women and children, accompanying our war-song with a most furious drumming on the houses. The next day a great

1 Again, the illustration is not only incompatible with the description of the raid, but it would appear that the artist has added a third seaman.

feast was given by Maquina, in celebration of his victory, which was terminated as usual with a dance by Sat-sat-sak-sis. **1**

Repeated applications had been made to Maquina, by a number of kings or chiefs, to purchase me, especially after he had showed them the harpoon I had made for him, which he took much pride in, but he constantly refused to part with me on any terms.—Among these, the king of the Wickinninish was particularly solicitous to obtain me, having twice applied to Maquina for that purpose, once in a very formal manner, by sending his messenger with four canoes, who, as he approached the shore, decorated in their highest style, with the white down on his head, &c. declared that he came to buy *Tooteyoohannis*, the name by which I was known to them, for his master, and that he had brought for that purpose four young male slaves, two highly ornamented canoes, such a number of skins of the metamelth, and of the *quartlack,* or sea-otter, and so many fathoms of cloth and of I-whaw, while as he mentioned the different articles, they were pointed out or held up by his attendants, but even this tempting offer had no influence on Maquina; who in the latter part of the summer, was again very strongly urged to sell me by Ulatilla, or as he is generally called, Machee Ulatilla, chief of the Klaizzarts, who had come to Nootka on a visit.

This chief, who could speak tolerable English, had much more the appearance of a civilized man, than any of the savages that I saw. He appeared to be about thirty, was rather small in his person, but extremely well formed, with a skin almost as fair as that of an European, good features, and a countenance expressive of candour and amiableness, and which was almost always brightened with a smile. He was much neater both in his dress and person than any of the other chiefs, seldom wearing paint, except upon his eye-brows,

Model of archaic style of Nuu-chah-nulth canoe shows low sloping bow typical of early period. BCPM

*Steersman in stern of canoe, on Tlupana Inlet. *BCPM*

1 *feast.* All spoils of war were turned over to the chief, in this case Maquinna, who later redistributed most of it to his people, according to rank, at a potlatch. This practice upheld a chief's status and reputation while providing for the community at large.

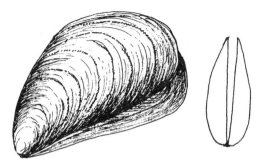

Hinged pair of mussel shells (Mytilus edulus) *used as tweezers for removing facial hair.* 6.4 cm (2½"). 23

which after the custom of his country, were plucked out, and a few strips of the *pelpelth* on the lower part of his face. He always treated me with much kindness, was fond of conversing with me in English and in his own language, asking me many questions relative to my country, its manners, customs, &c. and appeared to take a strong interest in my fate, telling me, that if he could persuade Maquina to part with me, he would put me on board the first ship that came to his country; a promise, which from his subsequent conduct, I have good reason to think he would have performed, as my deliverance, at length, from captivity and suffering was, under the favour of divine providence, wholly owing to him, the only letter that ever reached an European or American vessel, out of sixteen that I wrote at different times, and sent to various parts of the coast, having been delivered by him in person. So much pleased was I with this man's behaviour to me while at Nootka, that I made for him a Cheetoolth, which I burnished highly, and engraved with figures; with this he was greatly delighted; I also should have made for him a harpoon would Maquina have consented.

With hearts full of dejection and almost lost to hope, no ship having appeared off Nootka this season, did my companion and myself accompany the tribe on their removal in September to Tashees, relinquishing in consequence, for six months, even the remotest expectation of relief.

Soon after our establishment there, Maquina informed me, that he and his chiefs had held council both before and after quitting Nootka, in which they had determined that I must marry one of their women, urging as a reason to induce me to consent, that as there was now no probability of a ship coming to Nootka to release me, that I must consider myself as destined to pass the remainder of my life with them, that the sooner I conformed to their customs the better, and that a wife

and family would render me more contented and satisfied with their mode of living. I remonstrated against
this decision, but to no purpose, for he told me that
should I refuse, both Thompson and myself would be
put to death, telling me however, that if there were
none of the women of his tribe that pleased me, he
would go with me to some of the other tribes, where he
would purchase for me such an one as I should select.
Reduced to this sad extremity, with death on the one
side, and matrimony on the other, I thought proper to
choose what appeared to me the least of the two evils,
and consent to be married, on condition, that as I did
not fancy any of the Nootka women, I should be permitted to make choice of one from some other tribe.

This being settled, the next morning by day-light
Maquina with about fifty men in two canoes, set out
with me for A-i-tiz-zart, taking with him a quantity of
cloth, a number of muskets, sea-otter skins, &c. for the
purchase of my bride. With the aid of our paddles and
sails, being favoured with a fair breeze, we arrived some
time before sun set at the village. Our arrival excited a
general alarm, and the men hastened to the shore,
armed with the weapons of their country, making many
warlike demonstrations, and displaying much zeal and
activity. We in the mean time remained quietly seated in
our canoes, where we remained for about half an hour,
when the messenger of the chief, dressed in their best
manner, came to welcome us, and invite us on shore to
eat. We followed him in procession to the chief's house,
Maquina at our head, taking care to leave a sufficient
number in the boats to protect the property. When we
came to the house, we were ushered in with much ceremony, and our respective seats pointed out to us, mine
being next to Maquina by his request.

After have been regaled with a feast of herring spawn **1**
and oil, Maquina asked me if I saw any among the
women who were present that I liked. I immediately

1 *After having been regaled* . . . This account of Jewitt's marriage is
vastly different from the entry in his journal for 10 September 1804:
"This day our chief bought a wife for me, and told me that I must
not refuse her, if I did he would have both Thompson and myself
killed. The custom of the natives on their being married is that the
man and his wife must not sleep together for ten nights
immediately succeeding their marriage. It is very much against my
inclination to take one of these heathens for a partner, but it will be
for my advantage while I am amongst them, for she has a father
who always goes fishing, so that I shall live much better than I have
at any time heretofore."

Jewitt no doubt witnessed an elaborate wedding and used an
account of it, rather than his own ceremony.

pointed out to him a young girl of about seventeen, the
1 daughter of *Upquesta,* the chief, who was sitting near
him by her mother. On this Maquina making a sign to
his men, arose and taking me by the hand, walked into
the middle of the room, and sent off two of his men to
bring the boxes containing the presents from the
canoes. In the mean time Kinneclimmets, the master of
ceremonies, whom I have already spoken of, made himself ready for the part he was to act, by powdering his
hair with the white down.—When the chests were
brought in, specimens of the several articles were taken
out, and showed by our men, one of whom held up a
musket, another a skin, a third a piece of cloth, &c. On
this Kinneclimmets stepped forward, and addressing
the chief, informed him that all these belonged to me,
mentioning the number of each kind, and that they
2 were offered him for the purchase of his daughter *Eu-
stoch-ee-exqua,* as a wife for me. As he said this, the men
who held up the various articles, walked up to the chief,
and with a very stern and morose look, the com-
plimentary one on these occasions, threw them at his
feet. Immediately on which, all the tribe, both men and
women, who were assembled on this occasion, set up a
cry of Klack-ko-Tyee, that is, Thank ye chief. His men,
after this ceremony, having returned to their places,
Maquina rose, and in a speech of more than half an
hour, said much in my praise to the A-i-tiz-zart chief,
telling him that I was as good a man as themselves, dif-
fering from them only in being white, that I was besides
acquainted with many things of which they were ignorant; that I knew how to make daggers, cheetoolths,
and harpoons, and was a very valuable person, whom
he was determined to keep always with him; praising
me at the same time for the goodness of my temper, and
the manner in which I had conducted since I had been
with them, observing that all the people of Nootka, and
even the children loved me.

1 *daughter of Upquesta, the chief.* Normally a slave could never hope
to marry a chief's daughter, since people had to marry within their
own social position. But Jewitt was an unusual case: he had much
appreciated skills and abilities, and Maquinna held him in high
regard—at least some of the time.

2 *Eu-stoch-ee-exqua.* The name means "sunrise."

While Maquina was speaking, his master of ceremonies was continually skipping about, making the most extravagant gestures and exclaiming *Wocash*. When he had ceased, the A-i-tiz-zart chief arose amidst the acclamations of his people, and began with setting forth the many good qualities and accomplishments of his daughter; that he loved her greatly, and as she was his only one, he could not think of parting with her. He spoke in this manner for some time, but finally concluded by consenting to the proposed union, requesting that she might be well used and kindly treated by her husband. At the close of this speech, when the chief began to manifest a disposition to consent to our union, Kinneclimmets again began to call out as loud as he could bawl, Wocash, cutting a thousand capers and spinning himself around on his heel like a top.

When Upquesta had finished his speech, he directed his people to carry back the presents which Maquina had given him, to me, together with two young male slaves to assist me in fishing. These, after having been placed before me, were by Maquina's men taken on board the canoes. This ceremony being over, we were invited by one of the principal chiefs to a feast, at his house, of *Klussamit,* or dried herring, where after the eating was over, Kinneclimmets amused the company very highly with his tricks, and the evening's entertainment was closed by a new war-song from our men, and one in return from the A-i-tiz-zarts, accompanied with expressive gestures, and wielding of their weapons.

After this, our company returned to lodge at Upquesta's, except a few who were left on board the canoes to watch the property. In the morning I received from the chief his daughter, with an earnest request that I would use her well, which I promised him, when taking leave of her parents, she accompanied me with apparent satisfaction on board of the canoe.

The wind being ahead, the natives were obliged to

*Young Nuu-chah-nulth boy. *BCPM*

have recourse to their paddles, accompanying them with their songs, interspersed with the witticisms and buffonry of Kinneclimmets, who, in his capacity of king's steersman, one of his functions which I forgot to enumerate, not only guided the course of the canoe, but regulated the singing of the boatmen. At about five in the morning, we reached Tashees, where we found all the inhabiiants collected on the shore to receive us. We were welcomed with loud shouts of joy, and exclamations of Wocash, and the women taking my bride under their charge, conducted her to Maquina's house, to be kept with them for ten days; it being an universal custom as Maquina informed me, that no intercourse should take place between the new married pair during that period. At night Maquina gave a great feast, which was succeeded by a dance, in which all the women joined, and thus ended the festivities of my marriage.

The term of my restriction over, Maquina assigned me as an apartment, the space in the upper part of his house, between him and his elder brother, whose room was opposite. Here I established myself with my family, consisting of myself and wife, Thompson and the little Sat-sat-sak-sis, who had always been strongly attached to me, and now solicited his father to let him live with me, to which he consented. This boy was handsome, extremely well formed, amiable, and of a pleasant, sprightly disposition. I used to take a pleasure in decorating him with rings, bracelets, ear jewels, &c. which I made for him of copper, and ornamented and polished them in my best manner. I was also very careful to keep him free from vermin of every kind, washing him and combing his hair every day. These marks of attention were not only very pleasing to the child, who delighted in being kept neat and clean, as well as in being dressed off in his finery, but was highly gratifying both to Maquina and his queen, who used to express much satisfaction at my care of him.

In making my domestic establishment, I determined, as far as possible, to live in a more comfortable and cleanly manner than the others. For this purpose, I erected with planks, a partition of about three feet high, between mine and the adjoining rooms, and made three bedsteads of the same, which I covered with boards, for my family to sleep on, which I found much more comfortable than sleeping on the floor amidst the dirt.

Fortunately I found my Indian princess both amiable and intelligent, for one whose limited sphere of observation must necessarily give rise to but a few ideas. She was extremely ready to agree to any thing that I proposed relative to our mode of living, was very attentive in keeping her garments and person neat and clean, and appeared in every respect, solicitous to please me. She was, as I have said, about seventeen; her person was small, but well formed, as were her features, her complexion was, without exception, fairer than any of the women, with considerable colour in her cheeks, her hair long, black, and much softer than is usual with them, and her teeth small, even, and of a dazzling whiteness, while the expression of her countenance, indicated sweetness of temper and modesty. She would, indeed, have been considered as very pretty in any country, and excepting Maquina's queen, was by far the handsomest of any of their women.

With a partner possessing so many attractions, many may be apt to conclude, that I must have found myself happy, at least comparatively so; but far otherwise was it with me, a compulsory marriage with the most beautiful and accomplished person in the world, can never prove a source of real happiness, and in my situation, I could not but view this connection as a chain that was to bind me down to this savage land, and prevent my ever again seeing a civilized country; especially, when in a few days after, Maquina informed me that there had been a meeting of his chiefs in which it was determined,

Bird-form rattle used ceremonially; probably collected from Nootka Sound by Vancouver expedition, 1792. 48.5 cm (19½"). HMG

1 *Their religious celebration . . .* The date for moving to the winter village to start the Winter Ceremonials varied each year, depending on the fishing. When a sufficient supply of salmon had been taken, Maquinna made the decision to move from Tashees to Cooptee.

2 *As I was now considered as one of them . . .* Maquinna probably allowed Jewitt and Thompson to take part in the two-week ceremony because they had both undergone the required seven-day ritual seclusion the previous year. Jewitt does not seem to have understood the significance of the earlier banishment but thought that he was allowed to remain for the ceremony because Maquinna had told him that, having married one of their women, Jewitt "must be considered as one of them, and conform to their customs."

3 *dejection and humiliation . . .* Since people wore red-dyed headbands on many ceremonial occasions, dejection and humiliation would not necessarily have been the symbolism here.

4 *with six bayonets run into his flesh . . .* This may have been a theatrical trick of the type used by Northwest Coast people, and at which they excelled. Gilbert Sproat witnessed a dance performance in the mid-nineteenth century, in which a man appeared to be knifed. He staggered and fell lifeless, blood flowing, only to wash himself after and put on his blanket again. Sproat commented: "I never saw such acting more to the life; the performers would be the making of a minor theatre in London . . . the blood, which by some contrivance flows down the back at the moment the strike is given, is a mixture of a red gum, resin, oil and water—the same as is used in colouring the inside of canoes." On the other hand, the demonstration of bravery Jewitt saw took place much earlier, and may not have been faked.

that as I had married one of their women, I must be considered as one of them, and conform to their customs, and that in future, neither myself nor Thompson should wear our European clothes, but dress in Kutsaks like themselves. This order was to me most painful, but I persuaded Maquina, at length, so far to relax in it as to permit me to wear those I had at present, which were almost worn out, and not to compel Thompson to change his dress, observing, that as he was an old man, such a change would cause his death.

1   Their religious celebration, which the last year took place in December, was in this, commenced on the 15th **2** of November, and continued for fourteen days. As I was now considered as one of them, instead of being ordered to the woods, Maquina directed Thompson and myself to remain, and pray with them to Quahootze to be good to them, and thank him for what he had done. It was opened in much the same manner as the former. After which, all the men and women in the village assembled at Maquina's house, in their plainest dresses, and without any kind of ornaments about them, having their heads bound around with the red fillet, a token of **3** dejection and humiliation, and their countenances expressive of seriousness and melancholy. The performances during the continuance of this celebration, consisted almost wholly in singing a number of songs to mournful airs, the king regulating the time by beating on his hollow plank or drum, accompanied by one of his chiefs, seated near him with the great rattle. In the mean time, they eat but seldom, and then very little, retiring to sleep late, and rising at the first appearance of dawn, and even interrupting this short period of repose, by getting up at midnight and singing. It was terminated by an exhibition of a similar character to the one of the last year, but still more cruel. A boy of twelve **4** years old, with six bayonets run into his flesh, one through each arm and thigh, and through each side close to the ribs, was carried around the room, suspended upon them, without manifesting any symptoms of pain. Maquina, on my enquiring the reason of this display, informed me that it was an ancient custom of his nation, to sacrifice a man at the close of this solemnity in honour of their God, but that his father had abolished it, and substituted this in its place. The whole closed on the evening of the 29th, with a great feast of salmon spawn and oil, at which the natives as usual, made up for their late abstinence.

A few days after a circumstance occurred, which, from its singularity, I cannot forbear mentioning. I was sent for by my neighbour *Yealthlower,* the king's elder brother, to file his teeth, which operation having performed, he informed me that a new wife, whom he had a little time before purchased, having refused to sleep with him, it was his intention, provided she persisted in her refusal, to bite off her nose. I endeavoured to dissuade him from it, but he was determined, and in fact, performed his savage threat that very night, saying that since she would not be his wife, she should not be that of any other, and in the morning sent her back to her father.

This inhuman act did not, however, proceed from any innate cruelty of disposition, or malice, as he was far from being of a barbarous temper; but such is the despotism exercised by these savages over their **1** women, that he no doubt considered it as a just punishment for her offence, in being so obstinate and perverse; as he afterwards told me, that in similar cases, the husband had a right, with them, to disfigure his wife in this way, or some other, to prevent her ever marrying again.

About the middle of December, we left Tashees for Cooptee. As usual at this season, we found the herring in great plenty, and here the same scene of riotous feasting as I witnessed the last year, was renewed by our im-

*Man from Nootka Sound wearing cedar bark headring and cape with shredded cedar bark strands, both ceremonial items. *BCPM*

1 *over their women* . . . Jewitt's journal has an 11 January 1804 entry concerning another problem marriage: "Arrived a canoe from Esquates with our chief's daughter; her husband had been beating her and she came to complain of it to her father. It was thought a war would be the consequence."

Torch made of resinous sticks lashed to shaft; burns for about twenty minutes or longer. 23

1 *the moon.* A total eclipse of the moon occurred at 11:41 P.M. on the fourteenth, not the fifteenth, of January. Jewitt's dates were out by a day because, in keeping his journal, he had forgotten that the previous year, 1804, was a leap year and had omitted February 29.

2 *great cod-fish.* This was the supernatural creature Sky Codfish (a codfish being characterized by its large mouth). Fires, drumming and powerful spirit songs never failed to achieve the desired result of freeing the moon.

3 *her.* Jewitt refers to the moon as "her." Nuu-chah-nulth mythology held that all celestial bodies—sun, moon, stars and even rainbows—were relatives of the Sky Chief, and that the moon was a female.

4 *I suffered more than I can express from the cold.* Jewitt's journal entry for 26 June 1805 notes: "Our situation would not be so bad if it were not for the high prices the natives ask for their skins; for could we purchase four or five skins Thompson could make jacket and trousers of them, he being a good tailor."

provident natives, who, in addition to their usual fare, had a plentiful supply of wild geese, which were brought us in great quantities by the Esquates. These, as Maquina informed me, were caught with nets made from bark, in the fresh waters of that country. Those who take them, make choice for that purpose, of a dark and rainy night, and with their canoes stuck with lighted torches, proceed with as little noise as possible, to the place where the geese are collected, who, dazzled by the light, suffer themselves to be approached very near, when the net is thrown over them, and in this manner, from fifty to sixty, or even more, will sometimes be taken at one cast.

On the 15th of January, 1805, about midnight, I was thrown into considerable alarm, in consequence of an **1** eclipse of the moon, being awakened from my sleep by a great outcry of the inhabitants. On going to discover the cause of this tumult, I found them all out of their houses, bearing lighted torches, singing and beating upon pieces of plank; and when I asked them the reason of this proceeding, they pointed to the moon, and said **2, 3** that a great cod-fish was endeavouring to swallow her, and that they were driving him away. The origin of this superstition I could not discover.

Though in some respects, my situation was rendered more comfortable since my marriage, as I lived in a more cleanly manner, and had my food better and more neatly cooked, of which, besides, I had always a plenty, my slaves generally furnishing me, and Upquesta never failing to send me an ample supply by the canoes that came from A-i-tiz-zart; still, from my being obliged at this season of the year, to change my accustomed clothing, and to dress like the natives, with only a piece of cloth of about two yards long, thrown loosely around me, my European clothes having been for some time **4** entirely worn out, I suffered more than I can express from the cold, especially as I was compelled to perform the laborious task of cutting and bringing the fire wood, which was rendered still more oppressive to me, from my comrade for a considerable part of the winter, not having it in his power to lend me his aid, in consequence of an attack of the rheumatism in one of his knees, with which he suffered for more than four months, two or three weeks of which he was so ill as to be unable to leave the house. This state of suffering, with the little hope I now had of ever escaping from the savages, began to render my life irksome to me, still, however, I lost not my confidence in the aid of the Supreme Being, to whom, whenever the weather and a suspension from the tasks imposed on me, would permit, I never failed regularly, on Sundays, to retire to the woods to worship, taking Thompson with me when he was able to go.

On the 20th of February, we returned to our summer quarters at Nootka, but on my part, with far different sensations than the last spring, being now almost in despair of any vessel arriving to release us, or our being permitted to depart if there should.—Soon after our return, as preparatory to the whaling season, Maquina ordered me to make a good number of harpoons for himself and his chiefs, several of which I had completed with some lances, when on the 16th of March, I was taken very ill with a violent cholic, caused, I presume, from my having suffered so much from the cold in going without proper clothing. For a number of hours I was in great pain, and expected to die, and on its leaving me, I was so weak as scarcely to be able to stand, while I had nothing comforting to take, nor any thing to drink but cold water. On the day following, a slave belonging to Maquina died, and was immediately, as is their custom in such cases, tossed unceremoniously out of doors, from whence he was taken by some others, and thrown into the water. The treatment of this poor creature made a melancholy impression upon my mind, as I

could not but think, that such probably, would be my
fate should I die among these heathen, and so far from
receiving a decent burial, that I should not even be allowed the common privilege of having a little earth
thrown over my remains.

The feebleness in which the violent attack of my disorder had left me, the dejection I felt at the almost hope-
lessness of my situation, and the want of warm clothing
and proper nursing, though my Indian wife, as far as
she knew how, was always ready, and even solicitous,
to do every thing for me she could, still kept me very
much indisposed, which Maquina perceiving, he finally
told me, that if I did not like living with my wife, and
that was the cause of my being so sad, I might part with
her. This proposal I readily accepted, and the next day
Maquina sent her back to her father. On parting with
me, she discovered much emotion, begging me that I
would suffer her to remain till I had recovered, as there
was no one who would take so good care of me as her-
self. But when I told her she must go, for that I did not
think I should ever recover, which in truth I but little
expected, and that her father would take good care of
her, and treat her much more kindly than Maquina, she
took an affectionate leave, telling me that she hoped I
should soon get better, and left her two slaves to take
care of me.

Though I rejoiced at her departure, I was greatly affected with the simple expressions of her regard for me,
and could not but feel strongly interested for this poor
girl, who in all her conduct towards me, had discovered
so much mildness and attention to my wishes; and had
it not been that I considered her as an almost insuperable
obstacle to my being permitted to leave the country, I
should no doubt have felt the deprivation of her society
a real loss. After her departure, I requested Maquina,
that, as I had parted with my wife, he would permit me
to resume my European dress, for, otherwise, from not

having been accustomed to dress like them, I should certainly die. To this he consented, and I once more became comfortably clad.

Change of clothing, but more than all, the hopes which I now began to indulge, that in the course of the summer I should be able to escape, in a short time restored me to health, so far, that I could again to go work in making harpoons for Maquina, who, probably, fearing that he should have to part with me, determined to provide himself with a good stock.

I shall not however, longer detain the reader with a detail of occurrences that intervened between this period, and that of my escape, which, from that dull uniformity that marks the savage life, would be in a measure, but repetitions, nor dwell upon that mental torture I endured, from a constant conflict of hope and fear, when the former, almost wearied out with repeated disappointment, offered to our sinking hearts no prospect of release, but death, to which we were constantly exposed from the brutal ignorance and savage disposition of the common people, who in the various councils that were held this season to determine what to do with us, in case of the arrival of a ship, were almost always for putting us to death, expecting by that means to conceal the murder of our crew, and to throw the blame of it on some other tribe. These barbarous sentiments, were, however, uniformly opposed by Maquina and his chiefs, who would not consent to our being injured. But as some of their customs and traits of national character, which I think deserving of notice, have not been mentioned, I shall proceed to give a brief account of them.

The office of king or chief, is, with those people, hereditary, and descends to the eldest son, or in failure of male issue, to the elder brother, who in the regular line, is considered as the second person in the kingdom. At feasts, as I have observed, the king is always placed

*Part of whaler's shrine, used in whaling ceremonies, located on an island in Jewitt Lake. Note central figure with lines attached to two carved whales; skulls are those of successful whaling ancestors. *AMNH*

in the highest, or seat of honour, and the chiefs according to their respective ranks, which appear, in general, to be determined by their affinity to the royal family; they are also designated by the embellishments of their mantles, or Kutsaks. The king or head Tyee, is their leader in war, in the management of which he is perfectly absolute. He is also president of their councils, which are almost always regulated by his opinion. But he has no kind of power over the property of his subjects, nor can he require them to contribute to his wants, being in this respect, no more privileged than any other person. He has in common with his chiefs, the right of holding slaves, which is not enjoyed by private individuals, a regulation probably arising from their having been originally captives taken in battle, the spoils of war being understood as appertaining to the king, who receives and apportions them among his several chiefs and warriors, according to their rank and deserts. In conformity with this idea, the plunder of the Boston, was all deposited in Maquina's house, who distributed part of it among his chiefs, according to their respective ranks or degree of favour with him, giving to one, three hundred muskets, to another, one hundred and fifty, with other things in like proportion. The king is, however, obliged to support his dignity by making frequent entertainments; and whenever he receives a large supply of provisions, he must invite all the men of his tribe to his house, to eat it up, otherwise, as Maquina told me, he would not be considered as conducting like a Tyee, and would be no more thought of than a common man.

With regard to their religion—They believe in the existence of a Supreme Being, whom they call *Quahootze,* and who, to use Maquina's expression, was one great Tyee in the sky, who gave them their fish, and could take them from them, and was the greatest of all kings. Their usual place of worship, appeared to be the water, for whenever they bathed, they addressed some words in form of prayer to God above, intreating that he would preserve them in health, give them good success in fishing, &c. These prayers were repeated with much more energy, on preparing for whaling or for war, as I have already mentioned. Some of them would sometimes go several miles to bathe, in order to do it in **1** secret; the reason for this I could never learn, though I am induced to think it was in consequence of some family or private quarrel, and that they did not wish what they said to be heard; while at other times, they would repair in the same secret manner to the woods, to pray. **2** This was more particularly the case with the women, who might also have been prompted by a sentiment of decency, to retire for the purpose of bathing, as they are remarkably modest. I once found one of our women more than two miles from the village, on her knees in the woods, with her eyes shut, and her face turned towards heaven, uttering words in a lamentable tone, among which I distinctly heard, *Wocash Ah-welth,* meaning good Lord, and which has nearly the same signification with Quahootze. Though I came very near her, she appeared not to notice me, but continued her devotions; and I have frequently seen the women go alone into the woods, evidently for the purpose of addressing themselves to a superior being, and it was always very perceptible on their return, when they had thus been employed, from their silence and melancholy looks.

They have no belief however, in a state of future exis- **3** tence, as I discovered in conversation with Maquina, at Tootoosch's death, on my attempting to convince him, that he still existed, and that he would again see him after his death: but he could comprehend nothing of it, and pointing to the ground, said that there was the end of him, and that he was like that. Nor do they believe in ghosts, notwithstanding the case of Tootoosch would

1 *in secret*. Ritual bathing was a very sacred act which required secrecy, as did rubbing the body with medicines. They practised ritual bathing to bring about certain weather conditions necessary for seal hunting and netting wildfowl or to bring a dead whale ashore.

2 *secret manner*. A person seeking special powers often went to a particular place that was kept secret.

3 *future existence* . . . Native people did not believe in life after death, as defined by Jewitt's religion, but they had a strong belief in the spirits of the dead and had many rituals to prevent them from returning and possibly causing trouble, the sick being particularly vulnerable.

*Clayoquot shaman, or medicine woman, wearing headdress of cut feathers and cedar bark, sprinkled with eagle down. *23*

1 *a kind of conjuror* . . . The shaman was the equivalent of Jewitt's idea of a priest. Shamans were trained men and women who had supernatural powers and were highly revered. They specialized in such things as healing the sick, foretelling the future, advising chiefs, calling the salmon upriver and other beneficent (and sometimes evil) acts. A shaman who healed the sick very often affected a cure through shaking rattles, incantations, singing and the use of powerful charms. A modern doctor has suggested that by putting patients into a trance state, shamans were able to reach their subconcious and use auto-suggestion to cure maladies.

2 *On the birth of twins* . . . Most peoples of the Northwest Coast believed that twins were salmon people before birth, and that the father of twins had supernatural powers to call the salmon upriver at migration time. The twins, too, had a special rapport with salmon.

appear to contradict this assertion, but that was a remarkable instance, and such a one as had never been known to occur before; yet from the mummeries performed over the sick, it is very apparent that they believe in the agency of spirits, as they attribute disease to some evil one that has entered the body of the patient.

1 Neither have they any priests, unless a kind of conjuror may be so considered, who sings and prays over the sick, to drive away the evil spirit.

2 On the birth of twins, they have a most singular custom, which, I presume, has its origin in some religious opinion, but what it is, I could never satisfactorily learn. The father is prohibited for the space of two years from eating any kind of meat, or fresh fish, during which time, he does no kind of labour whatever, being supplied with what he has occasion for from the tribe. In the mean time he and his wife, who is also obliged to conform to the same abstinence; with their children, live entirely separate from the others, a small hut being built for their accommodation, and he is never invited to any of the feasts, except such as consist wholly of dried provision, where he is treated with great respect, and seated among the chiefs, though no more himself, than a private individual. Such births are very rare among them; an instance of the kind however occurred while I was at Tashees the last time, but it was the only one known since the reign of the former king. The father always appeared very thoughtful and gloomy, never associated with the other inhabitants, and was at none of the feasts but such as were entirely of dried provision, and of this, he eat not to excess, and constantly retired before the amusements commenced. His dress was very plain, and he wore around his head the red fillet of bark, the symbol of mourning and devotion. It was his daily practice to repair to the mountain, with a chief's rattle in his hand, to sing and pray, as Maqaina informed me, for the fish to come into their waters.

When not thus employed, he kept continually at home, except when sent for to sing and perform his ceremonies over the sick, being considered as a sacred character, and one much in favour with their gods.

These people are remarkably healthful, and live to a very advanced age, having quite a youthful appearance for their years. They have scarcely any disease but the **1** cholic, their remedy for which, is friction, a person rubbing the bowels of the sick violently, until the pain has subsided, while the conjuror or holy man, is employed, in the mean time, in making his gestures, singing, and repeating certain words, and blowing off the evil spirit, when the patient is wrapped up in a bear skin in order to produce perspiration. Their cure for the rheumatism, or similar pains, which I saw applied by Maquina, in the case of Thompson, to whom it gave relief, is by cutting or scarifying the part affected. In dressing wounds, they simply wash them with salt water, and bind them up with a strip of cloth, or the bark of a tree. They are, **2** however, very expert and successful in the cure of fractured or dislocated limbs, reducing them very dexterously, and after binding them up with bark, supporting them with blocks of wood, so as to preserve their position. During the whole time I was among them, but five natural deaths occurred, Tootoosch and his two children, an infant son of Maquina, and the slave whom I have mentioned, a cirumstance not a little remarkable in a population of about fifteen hundred; and as respects childbirth, so light do they make of it, that I have seen **3** their women the day after, employed as usual, as if little or nothing had happened.

The Nootkians in their conduct towards each other, are in general pacific and inoffensive, and appear by no means an ill tempered race, for I do not recollect any instance of a violent quarrel between any of the men, or the men and their wives, while I was with them, that of Yealthlower excepted. But when they are in the least of-

1 *They have scarcely any disease* . . . The absence of communicable diseases among peoples of the Northwest Coast meant they had not built up natural immunities, so they were extremely vulnerable to diseases brought by Europeans: smallpox, measles, influenza, tuberculosis and other ills.

2 *a strip of cloth.* Strips of softened cedar bark made ideal bandaging material.

3 *childbirth.* Jewitt's journal entry for 6 January 1804: "Last night a woman was delivered of a child; this morning I saw her sitting by a fire roasting herring and singing a song." Jewitt may have misunderstood just when the event occurred. To give birth, a woman retired to a small hut, made for her from brush or matting, where her mother assisted in the delivery. Four days later the new mother and child returned to the house.

fended, they appear to be in the most violent rage, acting like so many maniacs, foaming at the mouth, kicking and spitting most furiously; but this is rather a fashion with them, than a demonstration of malignity, as in their public speeches, they use the same violence, and he is esteemed the greatest orator, who bawls the loudest, stamps, tosses himself about, foams and spits the most.

In speaking of their regulations, I have omitted mentioning, that on attaining the age of seventeen, the eldest son of a chief, is considered as a chief himself, and that whenever the father makes a present, it is always done in the name of his eldest son, or if he has none, in that of his daughter. The chiefs, frequently purchase their wives at the age of eight or ten, to prevent their being engaged by others, though they do not take them from their parents until they are sixteen.

With regard to climate, the greater part of the spring, summer, and autumn, is very pleasant, the weather being at no time oppressively hot, and the winters uncommonly mild, for so high a latitude, at least as far as my experience went. At Tashees and Cooptee, where we passed the coldest part of the season, the winter did not set in till late in December, nor have I ever known the ice, even on the fresh water ponds, more than two or three inches in thickness, or a snow exceeding four inches in depth; but what is wanting in snow, is amply made up in rain, as I have frequently known it during the winter months, rain almost incessantly for five or six days in succession.

It was now past mid-summer, and the hopes we had indulged of our release, became daily more faint, for though we had heard of no less than seven vessels on the coast, yet none appeared inclined to venture to Nootka. The destruction of the Boston, the largest, strongest, and best equipped ship, with much the most valuable cargo of any that had ever been fitted out for the North-West trade, had inspired the commanders of others with

1 *amply made up in rain . . .* Nearly fifty journal entries begin with "Rainy weather." But wind too, brought hazards, as on 4 March 1804: "Rainy weather. This day one of the natives was drowned while he was fishing, the wind came on to blow so hard that his canoe upset." Also, on 7 January 1804: "A heavy gale of wind which took the planks from the top of the houses. Natives employed in securing them."

a general dread of coming thither; lest they should share the same fate; and though in the letter I wrote (imploring those who should receive them, to come to the relief of two unfortunate Christians who were suffering among heathen), I stated the cause of the Boston's capture, and that there was not the least danger in coming to Nootka, provided they would follow the directions I laid down; still I felt very little encouragement, that any of these letters would come to hand, when on the morning of the nineteenth of July, a day that will be ever held by me in grateful remembrance, of the mercies of God, while I was employed with Thompson in forging daggers for the king, my ears were saluted with the joyful sound of three cannon, and the cries of the inhabitants, exclaiming, Weena, weena—Mamethlee—that is, strangers—white men.

1

Soon after, several of our people came running into the house, to inform me that a vessel under full sail was coming into the harbour. Though my heart bounded with joy, I repressed my feelings, and affecting to pay no attention to what was said, told Thompson to be on his guard, and not betray any joy, as our release, and

2

Arrival of the brig Lydia, at Nootka Sound.

1 *the letter.* Journal entry for 3 July 1805: "This day a canoe set out to the northward with a letter which I hope will fall into some Christian hands." Journal entry for 11 July 1805: "This day returned the natives by whom I sent a letter a week ago. They returned the letter again and told me they were afraid to give it to a ship."

2 *a vessel.* The vessel was another trading ship from Boston, the *Lydia,* commanded by Captain Hill. In a subsequent report from Canton, Hill wrote: "About two months after my arrival on the coast of North America I received a letter (by the hand of an Indian Chief named Ulatilla) the purport of which was, that the ship Boston, commanded by John Salter, was taken by Maquinnah, and his warriors at Nootka Sound. . . . The letter was dated at Nootka Sound and signed by John Rodgers Jewitt and John Thompson; and earnestly entreated whoever received the letter, would come and deliver them from their miserable situation.

"As my business was of commercial nature, I could not, consistant with my duty, persue any measures whereby the success of my voyage might be endangered; yet common humanity demanded that an attempt should be made to relieve these unfortunate men . . . it appeared to me that it could not be thought rash or imprudent to go to Nootka, and take a view of the harbour, and discuss whether the natives were disposed to be friendly or not. With this view I sailed from Newetta [Nawitti, on the northern end of Vancouver Island] on the 11th of July 1805, and arrived at Nootka Sound on the 16th. [Jewitt has it as the nineteenth.] With the help of my glasses I observed six pieces of cannon mounted on a kind of rampart in front of the village, at the head of Friendly Cove. Having ascertained that there were neither men nor guns on Hog Island (which commands the entrance) I stretched into the cove and anchored in a position to command the passage to Hog Island and about two hundred yards [180 m] from the village."

Man from Barkley Sound wearing nose ornament. *BCPM

perhaps our lives, depended on our conducting our-selves so as to induce the natives to suppose we were not very anxious to leave them. We continued our works as if nothing had happened, when in a few minutes after, Maquina came in, and seeing us at work appeared much surprised, and asked me if I did not know that a vessel had come. I answered in a careless manner, that it was nothing to me. How, John, said he, you no glad go board. I replied that I cared very little about it, as I had become reconciled to their manner of living, and had no wish to go away. He then told me, that he had called a council of his people respecting us, and that we must leave off work and be present at it.

The men having assembled at Maquina's house, he asked them what was their opinion should be done with Thompson and myself now a vessel had arrived, and whether he had not better go on board himself, to make a trade, and procure such articles as were wanted. Each one of the tribe who wished, gave his opinion. Some were for putting us to death, and pretending to the strangers, that a different nation had cut off the Boston, while others, less barbarous, were for sending us fifteen or twenty miles back into the country until the depar-ture of the vessel. These, however, were the sentiments of the common people, the chiefs opposing our being put to death, or injured, and several of them, among the most forward of whom were Yealthlower and the young chief, *Toowinnakinnish,* were for immediately releasing us; but this, if he could avoid it, by no means appeared to accord with Maquina's wishes.

Having mentioned Toowinnakinnish, I shall briefly observe, that he was a young man of about twenty-three years old, the only son of Toopeeshottee, the oldest and most respected chief of the tribe. His son had always been remarkably kind and friendly to me, and I had in return frequently made for him daggers, chee-toolths, and other things, in my best manner. He was one of the handsomest men among them, very amiable, and much milder in his manners than any of the others, as well as neater both in his person and house, at least his apartment, without even excepting Maquina.

With regard, however, to Maquina's going on board the vessel, which he discovered a strong inclination to do, there was but one opinion, all remonstrating against it, telling him that the captain would kill him or keep him a prisoner, in consequence of his having destroyed our ship. When Maquina had heard their opinions, he told them that he was not afraid of being hurt from going on board the vessel, but that he would, however, in that respect, be guided by John, whom he had always found true. He then turned to me, and asked me if I thought there would be any danger in his going on board. I answered, that I was not surprised at the advice his people had given him, unacquainted as they were with the manners of the white men, and judging them by their own, but if they had been with them as much as I had, or even himself, they would think very different. That he had almost always experienced good and civil treatment from them, nor had he any reason to fear the contrary now, as they never attempted to harm those who did not injure them, and if he wished to go on board, he might do it, in my opinion, with security.— After reflecting a few moments, he said, with much apparent satisfaction, that if I would write a letter to the captain, telling him good of him that he had treated Thompson and myself kindly since we had been with him, and to use him well, he would go. It may readily be supposed that I felt much joy at this determination; but knowing that the least incaution might annihilate all my hopes of escape, I was careful not to manifest it, and to treat his going or staying as a matter perfectly indifferent to me. I told him that if he wished me to write such a letter, I had no objection, as it was the truth, otherwise I could not have done it.

I then proceeded to write the recommendatory letter, which the reader will naturally imagine was of a somewhat different tenor from the one he had required; for if deception is in any case warrantable, it was certainly so in a situation like ours, where the only chance of regaining that freedom of which we had been so unjustly deprived, depended upon it; and I trust that few, even of the most rigid, will condemn me with severity for making use of it, on an occasion which afforded me the only hope of ever more beholding a Christian country, and preserving myself, if not from death, at least from a life of continued suffering.

The letter which I wrote, was nearly in the following terms:—

> To Captain —————,
> of the Brig —————,
>   *Nootka, July* 19, 1805.

SIR,

THE bearer of this letter is the Indian king by the name of Maquina. He was the instigator of the capture the ship Boston, of Boston in North America, John Salter captain, and of the murder of twenty-five men of her crew, the two only survivors being now on shore—Wherefore I hope you will take care to confine him according to his merits, putting in your dead lights, and keeping so good a watch over him, that he cannot escape from you. By so doing we shall be able to obtain our release in the course of a few hours.

JOHN R. JEWITT, *Armourer*
of the Boston, for himself and
JOHN THOMPSON, *Sail-maker of said ship.*

---

1 *dead lights.* A deadlight was a plate of wood or iron, hinged inboard above a porthole, which was let down and secured to protect the glass in heavy weather. The reference here is to an enclosed space with no portholes or covered ones.

I have been asked how I dared to write in this manner: my answer is, that from my long residence among these people, I knew that I had little to apprehend from their anger on hearing of their king being confined, while they knew his life depended upon my release, and that they would sooner have given up five hundred white men, than have had him injured. This will serve to explain the little apprehension I felt at their menaces afterwards, for otherwise, sweet as liberty was to me, I should hardly have ventured on so hazardous an experiment.

On my giving the letter to Maquina, he asked me to explain it to him. This I did line by line, as he pointed them out with his finger, but in a sense very different from the real, giving him to understand that I had written to the captain, that as he had been kind to me since I had been taken by him, that it was my wish that the captain should treat him accordingly, and give him what molasses, biscuit, and rum he wanted. When I had finished, placing his finger in a significant manner on my name at the bottom, and eyeing me with a look that seemed to read my inmost thoughts, he said to me, "John, you no lie?" Never did I undergo such a scrutiny, or ever experience greater apprehensions than I felt at that moment, when my destiny was suspended on the slightest thread, and the least mark of embarrassment on mine, or suspicion of treachery on his part, would probably have rendered my life the sacrifice. Fortunately I was able to preserve my composure, and my being painted in the Indian manner, which Maquina had since my marriage, required of me, prevented any change in my countenance from being noticed, and I replied with considerable promptitude, looking at him in my turn, with all the confidence I could muster, "Why do you ask me such a question, Tyee? have you ever known me to lie?" "No." "Then how can you suppose I should tell you a lie now, since I have never done it." As I was speaking, he still continued looking at me with the same piercing eye, but observing nothing to excite his suspicion, he told me that he believed what I said was true, and that he would go on board, and gave orders to get ready his canoe. His chiefs again attempted to dissuade him, using every argument for that purpose, while his wives crowded around him, begging him on their knees, not to trust himself with the white men. Fortunately for my companion and myself, so strong was his wish of going on board the vessel, that he was deaf to their solicitations, and making no other reply to them, than, "John no lie," left the house, taking four prime skins with him as a present to the captain.

Scarcely had the canoe put off, when he ordered his men to stop, and calling to me, asked me if I did not want to go on board with him. Suspecting this as a question merely intended to ensnare me, I replied that I had no wish to do it, not having any desire to leave them.

On going on board the brig, Maquina immediately gave his present of skins and my letter to the captain, who on reading it, asked him into the cabin, where he gave him some biscuit and a glass of rum, at the same time, privately directing his mate to go forward, and return with five or six of the men armed. When they appeared, the captain told Maquina that he was his prisoner, and should continue so, until the two men, whom he knew to be on shore, were released, at the same time ordering him to be put in irons, and the windows secured, which was instantly done, and a couple of men placed as a guard over him. Maquina was greatly surprised and terrified at this reception; he however, made no attempt to resist, but requested the captain to permit one of his men to come and see him. One of them was accordingly called, and Maquina said something to him which the captain did not understand, but supposed to be an order to release us, when the man returning to the canoe, it was paddled off with the utmost expedition to the shore. As the canoe approached, the inhabitants, who had all collected upon the beach, manifested some uneasiness at not seeing their king on board, but when on its arrival, they were told that the captain had made him a prisoner, and that John had spoke bad about him in a letter, they all both men and women, set up a loud howl, and ran backwards and forwards upon the shore like so many lunatics, scratching their faces, and tearing the hair in handfuls from their heads.

After they had beat about in this manner for some time, the men ran to their huts for their weapons, as if preparing to attack an invading enemy; while Maquina's wives and the rest of the women, came around me, and throwing themselves on their knees, begged me with tears to spare his life, and Sat-sat-sak-sis, who kept constantly with me, taking me by the hand, wept bitterly, and joined his entreaties to theirs, that I would not let the white men kill his father. I told them not to afflict themselves, that Maquina's life was in no danger, nor would the least harm be done to him.

The men were however, extremely exasperated with me, more particularly the common people, who came running in the most furious manner towards me, brandishing their weapons, and threatening to cut me in pieces no bigger than their thumb nails, while others declared they would burn me alive over a slow fire, suspended by my heels. All this fury, however, caused me but little alarm, as I felt convinced they would not dare to execute their threats while the king was on board the brig. The chiefs took no part in this violent conduct, but came to me and enquired the reason why Maquina had been thus treated, and if the captain intended to kill him. I told them that if they would silence the people, so that I could be heard, I would explain all to them. They immediately put a stop to the noise,

High-ranking Nuu-chah-nulth people, late eighteenth century. BCPM

when I informed them that the captain in confining Maquina, had done it of his own accord, and only in order to make them release Thompson and myself, as he well knew we were with them, and if they would do that, their king would receive no injury, but be well treated, otherwise he would be kept a prisoner. As many of them did not appear to be satisfied with this, and began to repeat their murderous threats—Kill me, said I to them; if it is your wish, throwing open the bear skin which I wore, here is my breast, I am only one among so many, and can make no resistance, but unless you wish to see your king hanging by his neck to that pole, pointing to the yard arm of the brig, and the sailors firing at him with bullets, you will not do it. O no, was the general cry, that must never be; but what must we do? I told them that their best plan would be, to send Thompson on board, to desire the captain to use Maquina well till I was released, which would be soon. This they were perfectly willing to do, and I directed Thompson to go on board. But he objected, saying that he would not leave me alone with the savages. I told him not to be under any fear for me, for that if I could get him off, I could manage well enough for myself, and that I wished him immediately on getting on board the brig, to see the captain, and request him to keep Maquina close till I was released, as I was in no danger while he had him safe.

When I saw Thompson off, I asked the natives what they intended to do with me. They said I must talk to the captain again, in another letter, and tell him to let his boat come on shore with Maquina, and that I should be ready to jump into the boat at the same time Maquina should jump on shore. I told them that the captain, who knew that they had killed my shipmates, would never trust his men so near the shore for fear they would kill them too, as they were so much more numerous; but that if they would select any three of their number to go with me in a canoe, when we came within hail, I could desire the captain to send his boat with Maquina, to receive me in exchange for him.

This appeared to please them, and after some whispering among the chiefs, who from what words I overheard, concluded that if the captain should refuse to send his boat with Maquina, the three men would have no difficulty in bringing me back with them, they agreed to my proposal, and selected three of their stoutest men to convey me. Fortunately having been for some time accustomed to see me armed, and suspecting no design on my part, they paid no attention to the pistols that I had about me.

As I was going into the canoe, little Sat-sat-sak-sis, who could not bear to part with me, asked me, with an affecting simplicity, since I was going away to leave him, if the white men would not let his father come on shore, and not kill him. I told him not to be concerned, for that no one should injure his father, when taking an affectionate leave of me, and again begging me not to let the white men hurt his father, he ran to comfort his mother, who was at a little distance, with the assurances I had given him.

On entering the canoe, I seated myself in the prow facing the three men, having determined if it was practicable, from the moment I found Maquina was secured, to get on board the vessel before he was released, hoping by that means, to be enabled to obtain the restoration of what property belonged to the Boston, still remaining in the possession of the savages, which I thought, if it could be done, a duty that I owed to the owners. With feelings of joy impossible to be described, did I quit this savage shore, confident now that nothing could thwart my escape, or prevent the execution of the plan I had formed, as the men appointed to convey and guard me, were armed with nothing but their paddles. As we came within hail of the brig, they at once ceased

Canoe in Nootka Sound. 23

1 *a sprig of green spruce.* A sprig of spruce fastened to the hair tied in a topknot was a custom used in warfare, and on certain ceremonial occasions; and red and black paint was not an everyday adornment. Jewitt, with his love of theatrics, may have deliberately dressed the part of a long-lost captive for the dramatic moment of rescue to impress the curious audience crowding the rail of the *Lydia*.

paddling, when presenting my pistols at them, I ordered them instantly to go on, or I would shoot the whole of them. A proceeding so wholly unexpected, threw them into great consternation, and resuming their paddles, in a few moments, to my inexpressible delight, I once more found myself along side of a Christian ship, a happiness which I had almost despaired of ever again enjoying. All the crew crowded to the side to see me as the canoe came up, and manifested much joy at my safety. I immediately leaped on board, where I was welcomed by the captain, Samuel Hill, of the brig Lydia of Boston, who congratulated me on my escape, informing me that he had received my letter off Kla-izzart, from the chief Mackee Ulatilla, who came off himself in his canoe, to delivit to him, on which he immediately proceeded hither to aid me. I returned him my thanks in the best manner I could for his humanity, though I hardly knew what I said, such was the agitated state of my feelings at that moment, with joy for my escape, thankfulness to the Supreme Being who had so mercifully preserved me, and gratitude to those whom he had rendered instrumental in my delivery, that I have no doubt, that what with my strange dress, being painted with red and black from head to foot, having a bear skin wrapped around me, and my long hair, which I was not allowed to cut, fastened on the top of my head 1 in a large bunch, with a sprig of green spruce, I must have appeared more like one deranged than a rational creature, as captain Hill afterwards told me, that he never saw any thing in the form of man, look so wild as I did when I first came on board.

The captain then asked me into the cabin, where I found Maquina in irons, with a guard over him. He looked very melancholy, but on seeing me his countenance brightened up, and he expressed his pleasure with the welcome of "Wocash John;" when taking him by the hand, I asked the captain's permission to take off

his irons, assuring him, that as I was with him, there
was no danger of his being in the least troublesome. He
accordingly consented, and I felt a sincere pleasure in
freeing from fetters, a man, who, though he had caused
the death of my poor comrades, had nevertheless, always proved my friend and protector, and whom I had
requested to be thus treated, only with a view of securing my liberty. Maquina smiled and appeared much
pleased at this mark of attention from me. When I had
freed the king from his irons, captain Hill wished to
learn the particulars of our capture, observing that an
account of the destruction of the ship and her crew had
been received at Boston before he sailed, but that nothing more was known, except that two of the men were
living, for whose rescue the owners had offered a liberal
reward, and that he had been able to get nothing out of
the old man, whom the sailors had supplied so plentifully with grog, as to bring him too much by the head
to give any information.

I gave him a correct statement of the whole proceeding, together with the manner in which my life and that
of my comrade had been preserved. On hearing my
story, he was greatly irritated against Maquina, and said
he ought to be killed. I observed that however ill he
might have acted in taking our ship, yet that it would,
perhaps, be wrong to judge an uninformed savage, with
the same severity as a civilized person, who had the
light of religion and the laws of society to guide him. **1**
That Maquina's conduct in taking our ship, arose from
an insult that he thought he had received from captain
Salter, and from the unjustifiable conduct of some
masters of vesssels, who had robbed him, and without
provocation, killed a number of his people. Besides
that, a regard for the safety of others ought to prevent
his being put to death, as I had lived long enough with
these people to know that revenge of an injury, is held
sacred by them, and that they would not fail to retaliate,

1 *the light of religion and the laws of society*. Maquinna's culture
certainly had both religion and a system of laws, but because they
differed considerably from those of England, Jewitt held them in
small regard.

Type of anchor the Boston *would have carried. Courtesy Leonard McCann, curator, Vancouver Museum*

should he kill their king, on the first vessel or boat's crew that should give them an opportunity; and that, though he might consider executing him as but an act of justice, it would probably cost the lives of many Americans.

The captain appeared to be convinced from what I said, of the impolicy of taking Maquina's life, and said that he would leave it wholly with me whether to spare or kill him, as he was resolved to incur no censure in either case. I replied that I most certainly should never take the life of a man who had preserved mine, had I no other reason, but as there was some of the Boston's property still remaining on shore, I considered it a duty that I owed to those who were interested in that ship, to try to save it for them, and with that view I thought it would be well to keep him on board till it was given up. He concurred in this proposal, saying if there was any of the property left, it most certainly ought to be got.

During this conversation Maquina was in great anxiety, as from what English he knew he perfectly comprehended the subject of our deliberation; constantly interrupting me to enquire what we had determined to do with him, what the captain said, if his life would be spared, and if I did not think that Thompson would kill him. I pacified him as well as I was able, by telling him that he had nothing to fear from the captain, that he would not be hurt, and that if Thompson wished to kill him, which was very probable, he would not be allowed to do it. He would then remind me that I was indebted to him for my life, and that I ought to do by him as he had done by me. I assured him that such was my intention, and I requested him to remain quiet, and not alarm himself, as no harm was intended him. But I found it extremely difficult to convince him of this, as it accorded so little with the ideas of revenge entertained by them. I told him however, that he must restore all the property still in his possession, belonging to the ship. This he was perfectly ready to do, happy to escape on such terms. But as it was now past five, and too late for the articles to be collected, and brought off, I told him that he must content himself to remain on board with me that night, and in the morning he should be set on shore as soon as the things were delivered. To this he agreed, on condition that I would remain with him in the cabin. I then went upon deck, and the canoe that brought me having been sent back, I hailed the inhabitants, and told them that their king had agreed to stay on board till the next day, when he would return, but that no canoes must attempt to come near the vessel during the night, as they would be fired upon. They answered, *Woho, woho* — very well, very well. I then returned to Maquina, but so great were his terrors, that he would not allow me to sleep, constantly disturbing me with his questions, and repeating, "John, you know when you was alone, and more than five hundred men were your enemies, I was your friend and prevented them from putting you and Thompson to death, and now I am in the power of your friends, you ought to do the same by me." I assured him that he would be detained on board no longer than the property was released, and that as soon as it was done, he would be set at liberty.

At day break I hailed the natives, and told them that it was Maquina's order that they should bring off the cannon, and anchors, and whatever remained with them of the cargo of the ship. This they set about doing with the utmost expedition, transporting the cannon and anchors by lashing together two of their largest canoes, and covering them with planks, and in the course of two hours, they delivered every thing on board that I could recollect, with Thompson's and my chest, containing the papers of the ship, &c.

When every thing belonging to the ship had been restored, Maquina was permitted to return in his canoe, **2**

Twenty-four-pound cannon. 23

1 *the cannon, and anchors* . . . Captain Hill's report also said: "In the course of twenty four hours after my arrival I recovered the two above mentioned captives, and the guns, anchors, and a few muskets and some other articles of less consideration; these were all they had left in their possession belonging to the Boston." Since ransoming a captured chief was not unknown among the Nuuchah-nulth, the villagers may have viewed the return of the *Boston*'s property as such.

2 *Maquina was permitted to return* . . . Of this matter Captain Hill reported: "I had kept Maquinnah on board, until my business was finished, when I informed him that he was at liberty to go on shore whenever he pleased; this was more than he expected as he had reconciled himself to the idea that he should lose his life; but when he was repeatedly assured to the contrary he thanked me in a very earnest manner, and made promises of good behaviour in future. In what manner he will regard these promises, I cannot pretend to say. I have since visited him at Nootka and he and his people behaved very well."

which had been sent for him, with a present of what skins he had collected, which were about sixty, for the captain in acknowledgment of his having spared his life and allowed him to depart unhurt; such was also, the transport he felt when captain Hill came into the cabin, and told him that he was at liberty to go, that he threw off his mantle, which consisted of four of the very best skins, and gave it to him, as a mark of his gratitude; in return for which, the captain presented him with a new great coat and hat, with which he appeared much delighted. The captain then desired me to inform him that he should return to that part of the coast in November, and that he wished him to keep what skins he should get, which he would buy of him. This Maquina promised, saying to me at the same time, "John, you know I shall be then at Tashees, but when you come make *pow*, which means, fire a gun to let me know, and I will come down." When he came to the side of the brig, he shook me cordially by the hand, and told me that he hoped I would come to see him again in a big ship, and bring much plenty of blankets, biscuit, molasses and rum, for him and his son who loved me a great deal, and that he would keep all the furs he got for me, observing at the same time, that he should never more take a letter of recommendation from any one, or ever trust himself on board a vessel unless I was there. Then grasping both my hands, with much emotion, while the tears trickled down his cheeks, he bade me farewell, and stept into the canoe, which immediately paddled him on shore.

Notwithstanding my joy at my deliverance, and the pleasing anticipation I felt of once more beholding a civilized country, and again being permitted to offer up my devotions in a Christian church, I could not avoid experiencing a painful sensation on parting with this savage chief, who had preserved my life, and in general treated me with kindness, and considering their ideas and manners, much better than could have been expected.

My pleasure was also greatly damped by an unfortunate accident that occurred to Toowinnakinnish.
That interesting young chief had come on board in the
first canoe in the morning, anxious to see and comfort
his king. He was received with much kindness by captain Hill, from the favorable account I gave of him, and
invited to remain on board. As the muskets were delivered, he was in the cabin with Maquina, where was also
the captain, who on receiving them, snapped a number
in order to try the locks; unluckily one of them happened to be loaded with swan shot, and going off, **1**
discharged its contents into the body of poor Toowinnakinnish, who was sitting opposite. On hearing the report, I instantly ran into the cabin, where I found him
weltering in his blood, with the captain who was
greatly shocked at the accident, endeavouring to assist
him. We raised him up, and did every thing in our
power to aid and comfort him, telling him that we felt
much grieved at his misfortune, and that it was wholly
unintentional; this he told me he was perfectly satisfied
of, and while we dressed and bound up his wounds in
the best manner we could, he bore the pain with great
calmness, and bidding me farewell, was put on board
one of the canoes, and taken on shore, where after
languishing a few days, he expired. To me, his misfortune was a source of much affliction, as he had no
share in the massacre of our crew, was of a most amiable character, and had always treated me with the
greatest kindness and hospitality.

The Brig being under weigh, immediately on Maquina's quitting us, we proceeded to the northward,
constantly keeping the shore in sight, and touching at
various places for the purpose of trading.

Having already exceeded the bounds I had prescribed
myself, I shall not attempt any account of our voyage
upon the coast, or a description of the various nations
we met with in the course of it, among whom were a

1 *Swan shot.* A large size of shot used in hunting wildfowl and
other game.

*Haida mask depicts a woman with her face painted wearing a labret.
21.6 cm (8½"). UMP/12*

1 *Wooden-lips.* The nickname refers to the labret, a lip ornament
worn by some groups of native people. It is a disc, often of wood,
sometimes ornamented, inserted into an aperture cut in the lower
lip of a high-ranking woman. If the *Lydia* called at the Queen
Charlotte Islands to trade for furs, then they would have
encountered the Haida who also fit the rest of the description.

2 *Captains Clark and Lewis . . .* The Lewis and Clark Expedition
left St. Louis, Missouri, in 1804, and trekked 12 390 km (7,700 mi.)
overland, arriving at the mouth of the Columbia River in early
November 1805. Jewitt missed meeting them because they had
gone 11 km (7 mi.) to the south to spend the winter at Fort
Clatsop.

people of a very singular appearance, called by the
1 sailors the *Wooden-lips.* They have many skins, and the
trade is principally managed by their women, who are
not only expert in making a bargain, but are as dexterous in the management of their canoes, as the men
are elsewhere.

After a period of nearly four months from our leaving
Nootka, we returned from the northward to Columbia
river, for the purpose of procuring masts, &c. for our
brig, which had suffered considerably in her spars during a gale of wind. We proceeded about ten miles up the
river, to a small Indian village, where we heard from
2 the inhabitants, that Captains Clark and Lewis, from
the United States of America, had been there about a
fortnight before, on their journey over-land, and had
left several medals with them, which they showed us.
The river at this place, is of considerable breadth, and
both sides of it from its entrance, covered with forests
of the very finest pine timber, fir and spruce, interspersed with Indian settlements. Here, after providing
ourselves with spars, we sailed for Nootka, where we
arrived in the latter part of November. The tribe being
absent, the agreed signal was given, by firing a cannon,
and in a few hours after a canoe appeared, which landed
at the village, and putting the king on shore, came off to
the brig.—Enquiry was immediately made by Kinneclimmets, who was one of the three men in the canoe, if
John was there, as the king had some skins to sell them
if he was. I then went forward and invited them on
board, with which they readily complied, telling me
that Maquina had a number of skins with him, but that
he would not come on board unless I would go on shore
for him. This I agreed to, provided they would remain
in the brig in the mean time. To this they consented,
and the captain taking them into the cabin, treated them
with bread and molasses. I then went on shore in the
canoe, notwithstanding the remonstrances of Thomp-

son and the captain, who, though he wanted the skins, advised me by no means to put myself in Maquina's power; but I assured him that I had no fear as long as those men were on board. As I landed Maquina came up and welcomed me with much joy: on enquiring for the men, I told him that they were to remain till my return. "Ah John," said he, I see "you are afraid to trust me, but if they had come with you, I should not have hurt you, though I should have taken good care not to let you go on board of another vessel." He then took his chest of skins, and stepping into the canoe, I paddled him along-side the brig where he was received and treated by Capt. Hill with the greatest cordiality, who bought of him his skins. He left us much pleased with his reception, enquiring of me how many moons it would be before I should come back again to see him and his son, who had begged him hard to let him come with him to see me: saying, that he would keep all his furs for me, and that as soon as my son,[1] who was then about five months old, was of a suitable age to take from his mother, he would send for him, and take care of him as his own.

As soon as Maquina had quitted us, we got under weigh, and stood again to the northward. We continued on the coast until the eleventh of August, 1806, when having completed our trade, we sailed for China, to the great joy of all our crew, and particularly so to me. With a degree of satisfaction that I can ill express, did I quit a coast to which I was resolved nothing should again tempt me to return, and as the tops of the mountains sunk in the blue waves of ocean, I seemed to feel my heart lightened of an oppressive load.

We had a prosperous passage to China, arriving at Macao in December, from whence the brig proceeded to Canton. There I had the good fortune to meet a townsman and an old acquaintance, in the mate of an English East-Indiaman, named John Hill, whose father,

Labret inlaid with abalone shell. 7.6 cm (3″). BM/12

1 *my son.* This is the only reference Jewitt makes to having a child, who would have been about a month old at the time he and Thompson were rescued. His simple statement here gives no hint as to whether or not he had known of the birth before his rescue. The infant was born close to nine months after the marriage, so perhaps Jewitt was not quite as distressed over having a beautiful Indian woman for a wife as he made out to be. At least not to begin with.

a wealthy merchant in Hull, in the Baltic trade, was a next door neighbour to mine. Shortly after our arrival, the captain being on board the English ship, and mentioning his having had the good fortune to liberate two men of the Boston's crew from the savages, and that one of them was named Jewitt, my former acquaintance immediately came on board the brig too see me.

Words can ill express my feelings on seeing him. Circumstanced as I was, among persons who were entire strangers to me to meet thus in a foreign land, with one between whom and myself, a considerable intimacy had subsisted, was a pleasure that those alone who have been in a simular situation can properly estimate. He appeared on his part, no less happy to see me, whom he supposed to be dead, as the account of our capture had been received in England some time before his sailing, and all my friends supposed me to have been murdered. From this young man, I received every attention and aid, that a feeling heart, interested in the fate of another, could confer. He supplied me with a new suit of clothes, and a hat, a small sum of money for my necessary expences, and a number of little articles for sea-stores on my voyage to America. I also gave him a letter for my father, in which I mentioned my wonderful preservation, and escape, through the humanity of captain Hill, with whom I should return to Boston. This letter he enclosed to his father, by a ship that was just sailing, in consequence of which it was received much earlier than it otherwise would have been.

We left China in Februrary, 1807, and after a pleasant voyage of one hundred and fourteen days, arrived at Boston. My feelings on once more finding myself in a Christian country, among a people speaking the same language with myself, may be more readily conceived than expressed. In the Post-Office in that place, I found a letter for me from my mother, acknowledging the

1 *Sea-stores.* A term used in early sailing days to refer to supplies, particularly foodstuffs, laid in by a passenger for a sea voyage.

2 *a letter for me* . . . In an excerpt from that letter (punctuation revised for clarity) dated 16 July 1807, his stepmother says: "I rec'd your letter Dated the 27th of Decr. 1806, the other has not come to hand yet. You will remember how unwilling I was for you to go. The Blessing of God has reached you; you have been considered dead by every person but myself, no pain has been spared to convince me of it being true . . . the trouble I have had on my mind concerning yourself is beyond expression, the Almighty is merciful and delivered you from captivity . . . the fortunate news was almost too much to bear . . . lose no opportunity in writing long letters to me as often as you can, let me know what you received a Blow on the forehead with an axe for, and w[h]ether you are marked with it or no . . . let me know . . . what became of the steam cooking vessel, and Iron Forge, w[h]ether you saved anything valuable or no, I want a full description of everything."

Arrival of the brig Lydia at Boston.

receipt of mine from China, expressing the great joy of my family on hearing of my being alive and well, whom they had for a long time given up for dead, and requesting me to write to them on receiving her letter, which I accordingly did. While in Boston, I was treated with much kindness and hospitality by the owners of the ship Boston, Messrs. Francis and Thomas Amory of that place, to whom I feel myself under great obligations for their goodness to me, and the assistance which they so readily afforded a stranger in distress.

WAR-SONG OF THE NOOTKA TRIBE.

*Commencing with a chorus repeated at the end of
each line.*

Hah-yee hah yar har, he yar hah.
Ie yie ee yah har—ee yie hah.
Ie yar-ee yar hah—ee yar hah.
Ie yar ee I yar yar hah—Ie yar ee yee yah!

I-ye ma hi-chill at-sish Kla-ha—Ha-ye-hah.
Que nok ar parts-arsh waw—Ie yie-yar.
Waw-hoo naks sar hasch—Yar-hah. I-yar hee I-yar.
Waw hoo naks ar hasch yak-queets sish ni-ese,
Waw har. Hie yee ah-hah.

Repeated over and over with gestures and brandishing of weapons.

NOTE.

Ie-yee ma hi-chill, signifies, Ye do not know. It appears to be a poetical mode of expression, the common
one for you do not know, being, *Wik-kum-atash;* from
this, it would seem that they have two languages, one
for their songs and another for common use. The general meaning of this first song appears to be, Ye little
know ye men of Klahar, what valiant warriors we are.
Poorly can our foes contend with us, when we come
with our daggers, &c.

The Nootkians have no songs of a historical nature,
nor do they appear to have any tradition respecting their
origin.

THE END.

PART III
ENDINGS

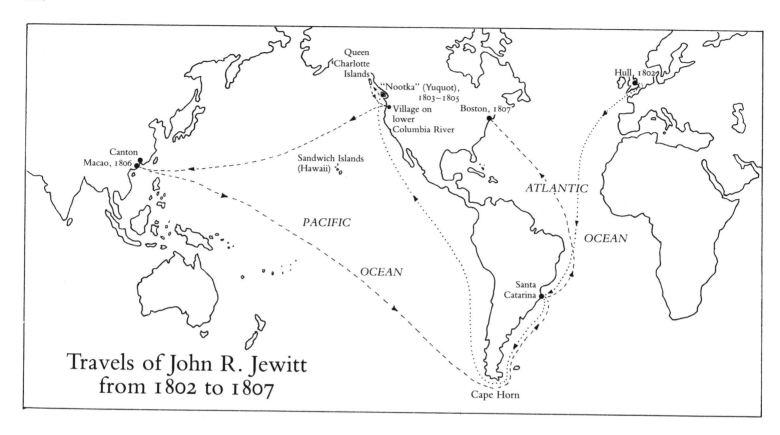

Queen
Charlotte
Islands

"Nootka" (Yuquot),
1803–1805

Village on
lower
Columbia River

Boston, 1807

Hull, 1802

Canton
Macao, 1806

Sandwich Islands
(Hawaii)

ATLANTIC

PACIFIC

OCEAN

OCEAN

Santa
Catarina

Cape Horn

Travels of John R. Jewitt
from 1802 to 1807

ENDINGS

In recounting nearly five years of adventures and sufferings after leaving England on 3 September 1802, John Rodgers Jewitt concludes his narrative with his eventual return to a "civilized country" in the summer of 1807. Yet the remarkable saga of the young seaman does not end there, for continued travels and troubles added a little-known sequel to Jewitt's colourful story.

As for John Thompson, Jewitt's unsavoury companion in captivity, history records two different accounts of his death. One, published in *Analectic Magazine* in 1815, states that he died in Havana, Cuba, not long after the *Lydia*'s arrival there, en route to Boston, Massachusetts. The other is in an 1816 edition of the *Narrative,* published in London, England; a preface "To the English Reader" says that on his arrival in Boston, Thompson went to his native Philadelphia, "where he was soon taken ill and died." As there is no mention of Thompson's death in the *Narrative,* the latter account may be correct.

With the return of the *Lydia* to its home port of Boston, Massachusetts, in the early summer of 1807, Jewitt again found himself in a strange country, but this time he was free to build his own life and be his own master. Before the year was out, with the tale of his captivity still fresh among Bostonians, Jewitt's *A Journal Kept at Nootka Sound* was in print for all to read.

While not much is known of his activities over the next couple of years, Jewitt likely spent time promoting and peddling his little book, as he did with his later publication, and perhaps worked at blacksmithing in the busy port of Boston. In 1809 John R. Jewitt married Hester Jones, daughter of James and Hester Jones. Born in 1787, young Hester had emigrated to America from England with her older brother, Lewis, when she was

Harbour of Boston, Massachusetts, in the eighteenth century. NMM

seventeen years old. The wedding took place on Christmas day—and one cannot help wondering if Jewitt recalled the occasion of his first marriage. One of the wedding gifts, from "a friend, in Boston, in America," was a large leather-bound Bible inscribed to the couple with solicitations for divine guidance in their present and next life.

Not long after their marriage, the Jewitts moved to Middletown, Connecticut, where their first child, Harriet, was born on 2 June the following year—a little over five months after the wedding. The family later moved to the nearby town of Berlin, where two sons, Edward and John, were born. A final move to Hartford, the capital city of Connecticut, was followed by the birth of a second daughter, Mary, with a third and final son, James, arriving in 1820. The latter died of tuberculosis of the hip at the age of twelve.

In March of 1815, between the third and fourth child, Jewitt's *Narrative,* written by Richard Alsop in close co-

Inscriptions on two blank pages at the back of a copy of an 1815 second edition of Jewitt's Narrative. *UBC*

operation with Jewitt and printed in Middletown by Loomis & Richards, was on the market at $1.00 a copy, and meeting with great success. A review of the leather-bound book in *Analectic Magazine* that summer declared: "There is scarce any relation of savage manners which can lay higher claim to authenticity, than this simple narration. The facts are undoubted, and the book was prepared for the press by a literary gentleman of Connecticut, who has scrupulously abstained from all digression or embellishment of style, and restricted himself to a plain relation of the story in simple and correct language."

The same magazine again reviewed the 1816 edition of the *Narrative,* and though criticizing its format and poor illustrations (the latter indeed being amateurish and lacking in research), maintained its stand on the contents. The reviewer believed in the simplicity and good faith of the writing, and could tell from Jewitt's

consistency in repeating the story at different times "that what he has given the world is a faithful record of the facts."

Meanwhile, with a scar across his forehead bearing witness to the truth of his amazing story, Jewitt travelled from town to town by horse and wagon. He went to Maine, Maryland, Rhode Island, New York, Philadelphia and even to Nantucket Island, a long ferry ride from the mainland. In a letter to his wife, from Philadelphia on 7 April 1817, he wrote:

I exerted myself this Cold winter in the public streets when the Snow was verry deep and I was doeing well, but some evil minded disposed person or persons, in the night, when I had just received four Hundred Dollars worth of my Books, went and broke open the barn which was verry secure, and picked the locks of my Boxes and stole all my books did not leave me a Single One.

He asked his wife to assure a Mr. French that Jewitt "would not wrong him out of one cent," and that he would repay him as soon as he could. He also wrote that for the past six weeks he had been troubled with "a violent pain in the head, right in the place where I was wounded."

Not content with literary success, the restless young man, whose life "would never be dull or boring," worked with a noted biographer and playwright, James Nelson Barker, on the dramatization of his "adventures and sufferings." Jewitt's long-time interest in theatre, his ability to sing and his love of performing came together as he took the leading role in a two-act melodrama about his captivity.

At the Philadelphia Theatre ("illuminated with gas," the playbill noted) on the evening of Friday, 21 March 1817, the curtain rose at 6:30 P.M. on a double-bill performance, a popular format in those days. It started with a favourite comedy, *The Busy Body,* followed by *The Armourer's Escape; Or, three years at Nootka Sound.* No less than seven scenes presented such depictions as the *Boston* lying at anchor moored to a tree, the destruction of the crew, the village of Nootka, a wood, the interior of Maquinna's house, the moon in eclipse, the *Boston* on fire and "wholly consumed," an attack by the Aycharts, a procession of several native tribes, a war dance, a dance of young girls and a couple of ceremonies, all with a wide range of accoutrements and props. Jewitt supervised the costumes and choreography and held centre stage much of the time, no doubt revelling in being in the limelight with well-known actors of the day. He sang a war song in the language of his captors and ended the performance with "The Song of the Armourer Boy." The latter, a close imitation of "The Poor Cabin Boy" by Charles Dibdin (a popular song at the time), Jewitt had printed up as a broadside entitled "The Poor Armourer Boy," which he sold. The song's author is not known, but Jewitt held the copyright as the proprietor, as he did for the play.

For this melodramatic extravaganza, the elite in the audience paid $1.00 for a seat in the box, the others 75¢ in the pit and 50¢ in the gallery. The show ran for three nights, with box office receipts totalling $1,362.85; not an outstanding financial success by all records, perhaps due in part to the bad weather on the third night. The only manuscript of the play has not survived.

The same year that Jewitt was enacting his adventures on stage, a French trader named Camille de Roquefeuil sailed into Nootka Sound on the *Borderlais.* Anchoring in the cove, he fired the now customary salute to the chief at Yuquot, and from out of his house, crippled with rheumatism but ever eager to trade, came Maquinna, who, by then, would have been about sixty years old.

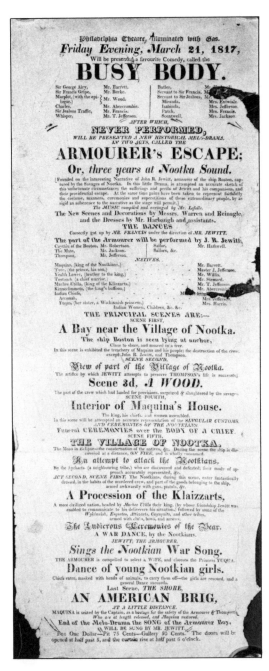

Playbill for the Philadelphia Theatre performance, 21 March 1817, featuring The Armourer's Escape *and starring John Jewitt. HSP*

A page of Jewitt's letter to his wife, from New York in 1817. Courtesy John R. Jewitt VI.

The last known written reference to the legendary chief appeared in 1825, when a Hudson's Bay Company trader referred to Maquinna as "an ageing man."

The keepers of aural history tell of Maquinna's demise. According to Andy Callicum, the indefatigable chief was plotting a raid on his uncle's village at the head of Muchalat Inlet, on what is now the Gold River, intending to kill him and his people (the Muchatlaht) and take over their salmon stream. Two women, originally from that village, overhead the plot and set out in

a canoe to give warning. En route they met two Muchatlaht men to whom they entrusted the news. Forewarned of the raid, the uncle and his warriors hid in the forest and ambushed Maquinna's war party as they paddled upriver. The uncle himself attacked Maquinna's canoe and drowned the renowned chief by holding his head underwater.

Later in 1817, at a summer resort outside Philadephia, Jewitt again appeared in public singing songs while dressed in native costume. His wife Hester was appalled by her husband taking to the stage, for at that time a theatrical career was not considered at all respectable. But no doubt flushed with the success of his theatrical ventures, Jewitt again set off to sell his books from town to town.

Before going to New York City in November, he was quite ill for eight weeks with "a complaint in my head attended by a fever which brought me verry low," but recovered from the malady. When he could, Jewitt sent money to his family with letters full of loving concern and pious wishes for them: "I hope you and the little children are all well . . . I am trying my best for you and my family." Also: "I have enclosed to you fifteen dollars which I hope you will lay out to the best advantage you know Dear Hester what to do best." In one letter, whose ink is smudged, he says tears are running down his cheeks as he writes: "May God almight bless you and all our little family, and preserve you all in peace and Safety is the sincer prayer of your ever loving & dutiful Husband." A letter from New York in November 1817 tells Hester that he has not yet sold out of books but hopes that he soon shall, and comments on the high rents of the city.

Little is known about Jewitt over the next and last four years of his life, though he probably continued his itinerant ways, selling the *Narrative* and the broadside, and sending money home to his family. Perhaps the pain in his head was more serious than he knew. On 7 January 1821, John Rodgers Jewitt died of unstated causes at the age of thirty-seven years, in Hartford. Several newspapers, including the Hartford *Times* and the Hartford *Courant* of 9 January 1821 carried his obituary. Since extensive research has failed to locate his place of burial, it is likely that no grave marker was erected—perhaps his widow Hester could not afford it. She survived him by fifteen years and died at the age of forty-eight in Middletown.

Whether or not Jewitt's original handwritten journal has survived I do not know, but part of a lengthy and sad letter from his stepmother may be significant. In February of 1825 she wrote from London, England, where they had moved early in 1806, pleading with her stepson to answer her "numerous letters." She wrote: "The last letter I received from you, contained your journals, inclosed in a parcell, being out at the time they was delivered, I never saw the person who brought them, I was sorry." It is not clear if she is to referring to Jewitt's original handwritten journal kept at Nootka Sound or copies of the printed ones. Since she received them in 1809, it could be either. Mrs. Jewitt went on to say that a friend went to a sale of books and "discovered a Narrative of your life and purchased one, and Brought it me, and asked if it was not the same person I had for years regretted the loss of." She begged him to tell her

"what business or profession you follow, whether married, or any family or what." Obviously, he had not written for a great many years, and sadly she would never hear from him, for Jewitt had died four years previously.

Jewitt's *Journal* and *Narrative* have intrigued armchair adventurers, historians, ethnologists and archaeologists for nearly two centuries, and his observations continue to be quoted in academic papers, theses and books. As well as the information Jewitt's books provide, the personal saga of this seafarer adds a very warm human dimension to the written archives of the Northwest Coast—about both traders and the aboriginal people.

Jewitt and Maquinna are remembered through geographic features and streets named after them. The armourer is recalled in Jewitt Lake, near Yuquot; his ship is remembered in Boston Point, and the captain of the ill-fated brig in Salter Point, both in Nootka Sound. In the modern town of Tahsis, named after Maquinna's fishing village and situated close to it, roads are named after the *Boston*, Jewitt and Maquinna, as well as Tootoosh, Maquinna's brother-in-law.

The recognition that Jewitt sought ultimately went far beyond any expectations he might have had for himself, for his name is now an indelible part of the Northwest Coast. The name Maquinna, too, lives on, carrying with it the longstanding prestige of an extremely high-ranking family.

REFERENCE KEY

Museums and Archives

AL Archaeology Laboratory, University of British Columbia

AMNH American Museum of Natural History, New York

AVM Alberni Valley Museum, Port Alberni

BCPM British Columbia Provincial Museum, Victoria

BM British Museum, London

CMC Canadian Museum of Civilization, Hull

FMNH Field Museum of Natural History, Chicago

GM Glenbow Museum, Calgary

HM Historical Museum, Berne

HMG Hunterian Museum, Glasgow

HSP Historical Society of Pennsylvania

MCRC Makah Cultural Research Centre, Neah Bay

MNM Museum of New Mexico, Santa Fe

NA National Archives, Washington D.C.

NMI National Museum of Ireland, Dublin

NMM National Maritime Museum, London

OHS Oregon Historical Society, Portland

PAA Provincial Archives of Alberta, Edmonton

PABC Provincial Archives of British Columbia, Victoria

PC Parks Canada, Ottawa

RAM Royal Albert Museum, Exeter

ROM Royal Ontario Museum, Toronto

RSM Rogers Sugar Museum, Vancouver

TBM Thomas Burke Memorial Washington State Museum, Seattle

UM University Museum, Cambridge

UMP University Museum, Philadelphia

VM Vancouver Museum, Vancouver

VPL Vancouver Public Library, Vancouver

WSHS Washington State Historical Society, Tacoma

Other Sources

1. "Artificial Curiosities" of the 18th Century. Exhibition catalogue. Honolulu: Bishop Museum, 1978.

2. Cedar: Tree of Life to the Northwest Coast Indians, Hilary Stewart. Vancouver: Douglas & McIntyre, 1984.

3. Indian Artifacts of the Northwest Coast. Seattle: University of Washington Press, 1973.

4. Indian Fishing: Early Methods on the Northwest Coast, Hilary Stewart. Vancouver: J. J. Douglas, 1977.

5. Indian Life on the Northwest Coast, Erna Gunther. Chicago: University of Chicago Press, 1972.

6. Indians of the Northwest Coast, Philip Drucker. New York: American Museum of Natural History, 1963.

7. Indians of the Pacific Northwest. Ruth Underhill. Washington D.C.: U.S. Department of the Interior, 1945.

8. Indian Primitive. Ralph Andrews. New York: Bonanza Books, 1960.

9. The Northern and Central Nootkan Tribes, Philip Drucker. Washington, D.C.: Smithsonian Institution, 1951.

10. The Nootkan Indian, John Sendy. Port Alberni: Alberni Valley Museum, 1977.

11. Nu·tka· The Survival and History of Nootkan Culture. Sound Heritage, Vol. VII. No. 2. Victoria: Provincial Archives of British Columbia, n.d.

12. Portrait Masks from the Northwest Coast of America, J. C. H. King. London: Thames and Hudson, 1979.

13. The West Coast (Nootka) People, E. Y. Arima. Victoria: British Columbia Provincial Museum, 1983.

14. Yuquot, British Columbia: The Prehistory and History of a Nootkan Village, Part II, John T. Dewhirst. Paper presented at the 22nd Annual Northwest Anthropological Conference, n.d.

15. European American Arms, c. 1810–1850, Claude Blair. New York: Bonanza Books, 1962.

16. A Glossary of the Construction, Decoration and Use of Arms and Armour, George Cameron Stone and Jack Brussel. New York, 1934.

17. Weapons—a Pictorial History, Edward Tukis. New York: World Publishing, 1954.

18. The Mammals of British Columbia. Ian McTaggart and Charles J. Guiget, British Columbia Provincial Museum Handbook No. 11. Victoria: 1965.

19. Fishes of the Pacific Coast of Canada. W. A. Clemons

and G. V. Wilby. Fisheries Research Board of Canada Bulletin No. 68. Ottawa: 1967.

20. Guide to the Marine Life of British Columbia. G. Clifford Carl. Victoria: British Columbia Provincial Museum, 1966.

21. Wild Teas, Coffees, and Cordials. Hilary Stewart. Vancouver: Douglas & McIntyre, 1981.

22. Webster's New International Dictionary, 2nd Edition Unabridged. Springfield, Mass.: C. & G. Merriam Co., 1961.

23. Author's picture file

24. The Arts of the Sailor. Harvey G. Smith. Funk & Wagnalls, 1953.

25. Blacksmith Shop and Iron Forging. Lost Technology Series. Reprinted from 1906 volume, International Correspondence Schools. Bradley, Ill.: Lindsay Publications, 1953.

26. Flickering Flames. Leroy Thwing. Rutland: Charles E. Tuttle & Co., 1958.

READING LIST

HISTORY

Kendrick, John. *The Men with Wooden Feet: The Spanish Exploration of the Pacific Northwest.* Toronto: New Canada Publications, 1985.

Mozino, José Marino. *Noticias de Nutka: An Account of Nootka Sound in 1792.* Trans. and ed. by I. H. Wilson. Toronto: McClelland and Stewart, 1970.

Nu·tka· Captain Cook and the Spanish Explorers on the Coast. Sound Heritage Series, Vol. VII, No. 1. Victoria: Provincial Archives of British Columbia, 1978.

Pethick, Derek. *The Nootka Connection: Europe and the Northwest Coast 1790–1795.* Vancouver: Douglas & McIntyre, 1980.

Walker, Alexander. *An Account of a Voyage to the Northwest Coast of America in 1785 and 1786.* Ed. by Robin Fisher and J. M. Bumstead. Vancouver: Douglas & McIntyre, 1982.

ARCHAEOLOGY AND ETHNOLOGY

Arima, E. Y. *The West Coast (Nootka) People.* British Columbia Provincial Museum Special Publication No. 6. Victoria: 1983.

Drucker, Philip. *The Northern and Central Nootkan Tribes.* Bureau of American Ethnology Bulletin 144. Washington: U.S. Government Printing Office, 1951.

Jones, Chief Charles, with Stephen Bosustow. *Queesto: Pacheenaht Chief by Birth.* Nanaimo: Theytus Books, 1981.

Kirk, Ruth. *Wisdom of the Elders.* Vancouver: Douglas & McIntyre, 1986. In U.S. under title *Tradition and Change on the Northwest Coast.* Washington: University of Washington Press, 1986.

Nu·tka· The History and Survival of Nootkan Culture. Sound Heritage Series, Vol. VII, No. 2. Victoria: Provincial Archives of British Columbia, n.d.

Sendy, John. *The Nootkan Indian: A Pictorial.* Port Alberni, B.C.: Alberni Valley Museum, 1977.

Sproat, Gilbert. *The Nootka: Scenes and Studies of Savage Life.* Ed. and ann. by Charles Lillard. Victoria: Sono Nis Press, 1987.

Stewart, Hilary. *Cedar: Tree of Life to the Northwest Coast Indians.* Vancouver and Seattle: Douglas & McIntyre and University of Washington Press, 1977.

Vaughn, Thomas, and Bill Holm. *Soft Gold.* Portland: Oregon Historical Society, 1982.

FICTION

Houston, James. *Eagle Song: An Indian Saga Based on True Events.* Toronto: McClelland and Stewart, 1983.

INDEX

References to text, *Narrative* and annotations are in roman type. *References to illustrations and captions are in italic type.*